'A fascinating insight into the living legacy of Islam in Europe. Tharik takes us to places where few readers will have ventured and explores the shared heritage of Muslims, Jews and Christians'
Levison Wood

'"How can we care about something we don't even know is there?" asks Tharik Hussain. Europe has long turned a blind eye or, worse, looked askance, at its own Islamic self – the Muslims of the Balkans. Tharik Hussain opens our eyes to this vivid, varied and still vital Muslim presence. His title is romantic, but not his vision: he ignores neither current sectarian tensions, nor histories scarred by violence and hatred. And yet he constantly reminds us of the long periods of tolerance and symbiosis, often forgotten in the din of war. This is a richly detailed travelogue by a humane and passionate pilgrim.'
Tim Mackintosh-Smith

'A scintillating voyage in the footsteps of the Ottoman explorer Evliya Çelebi'
Ziauddin Sardar
author of *Desperately Seeking Paradise*
and *Mecca: The Sacred City*

D1127120

Tharik Hussain is an author, travel writer and journalist specialising in Muslim heritage and culture. Tharik's work often serves to counter popular religious and cultural histories and narratives. He is the creator of Britain's first Muslim heritage trails – The Woking Trail and The Muslim Cemetery Walk – and has produced award-winning radio for the BBC on America's earliest mosques and Muslim communities. Tharik writes about his travels exploring Muslim cultures and heritage across the globe for many of the world's leading media brands and is the author of several travel guidebooks for countries including Saudi Arabia, Bahrain and Thailand. He has been named one of the UK's most inspiring British Bangladeshis and is a Fellow at the University of Groningen's Centre for Religion and Heritage.

MINARETS IN THE
MOUNTAINS
A JOURNEY INTO MUSLIM EUROPE

Tharik Hussain

Reprinted July 2021, September 2021
First published in the UK in July 2021 by
Bradt Guides Ltd
31a High Street, Chesham, HP5 1BW, England
www.bradtguides.com

Print edition published in the USA by The Globe Pequot Press Inc,
PO Box 480, Guilford, Connecticut 06437-0480

Text copyright © 2021 Tharik Hussain
Edited by Ross Dickinson
Photographs copyright © 2021 Tharik Hussain
Cover design and illustrations by Ollie Davis Illustration; www.olliedavisillustration.com
Layout and typesetting by Ian Spick
Production managed by Sue Cooper, Bradt Guides & Zenith Media

ISBN: 9781784778286

British Library Cataloguing in Publication Data
A catalogue record for this book is available from the British Library

Digital conversion by www.dataworks.co.in
Printed in the UK by Zenith Media

*To my parents, my wife, Tamara, and my daughters,
Amani, Anaiya and Maya*

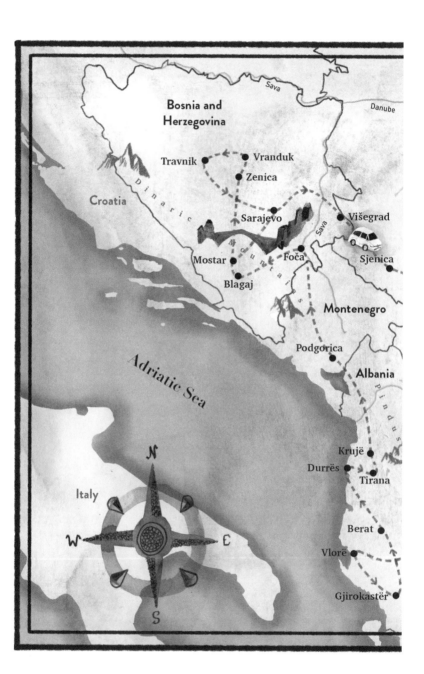

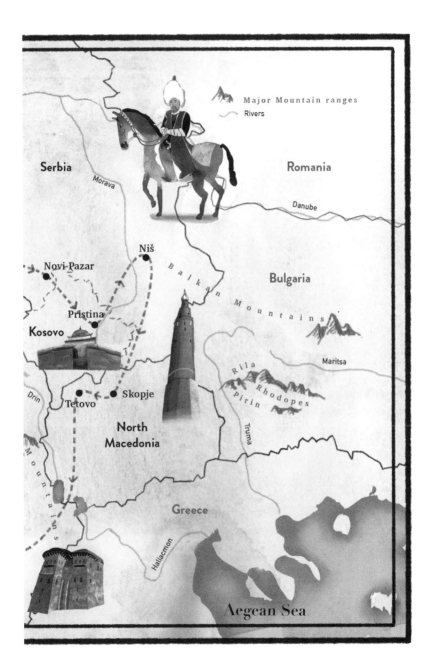

Major Mountain ranges
Rivers

Serbia

Romania

Morava

Danube

Novi Pazar

Niš

Bulgaria

B a l k a n   M o u n t a i n s

Pristina

Kosovo

Maritsa

Rila

Rhodopes

Drin

Pirin

Tetovo

Skopje

North
Macedonia

Struma

M o u n t a i n s

Greece

Haliacmon

Aegean Sea

Notes

Accessing Evliya Çelebi While some attempts have been made historically to translate Evliya Çelebi's *Seyahâtnâme* into English, the scale and nature of the task means that much of it remains inaccessible to English speakers. The author therefore wishes to acknowledge the immense efforts of Robert Dankoff and Sooyong Kim, the foremost translators of the *Seyahâtnâme* into English, whose works were essential in allowing him to access the great Ottoman traveller.

Names in the text The names of some individuals have been changed to respect their privacy.

Spellings In this book, the names Qur'an, Makkah and Madinah are spelt contrary to more common English literary convention. The author feels that the conventional spellings of these names, which are based on historic, inaccurate transliterations from Arabic that lead to them often being mispronounced, do a disservice to Islam's most sacred text and its two most sacred cities. As a Muslim, the author feels it important to rectify this, and wishes to acknowledge and applaud the publisher's willingness to respect his decision.

Contents

INTRODUCTION
An Intimate Tolerance

PALAMARTSA, BULGARIA

Pencil-thin, snow-white minarets topped by sharp pointed cones peered up at us as we wound our way down the sweeping plains of northern Bulgaria, close to the Romanian border. Each one stood beside the unmistakeable outline of a small mosque.

Some lay in ruins. Others were locked up. One or two, though, had tiny cemeteries, where the grass was neatly trimmed around historic, turban-shaped tombstones. When we stopped to peer through the windows, colourful prayer rugs were piled up against walls where worn *tasbihs* (prayer beads) hung from small hooks. It began to dawn on me: these were living ancient Muslim villages. But what on earth were they doing here?

We were on our way to an eco-farm in the remote village of Palamartsa, nestled in Bulgaria's northeastern hills. After a week of chasing Dracula in Transylvania with my two girls, Amani and Anaiya, we had completed our family unit by picking up my wife, their mother Tamara, from Bucharest airport. Now our sole intention was to spend the rest of our summer holiday doing very little.

The farm had featured in a *Guardian* article, describing the owners as advocates of 'slow-living', and that was what we had come to do: live slowly for a while. We were a family of Londoners constantly playing catch-up with time, where every day was an attempt to juggle work with after-school clubs and childminders. Forever spinning several plates at once and trying to kill two birds with one stone, our lives had become all the clichés that make up modern society.

A week on the farm in Palamartsa was meant to be the exact opposite: days on end lying in hammocks, reading books and picking our own veg from an organic garden. The unexpected discovery of 'living' Muslim villages, however, had now presented a plate I longed to spin.

Up until that trip, the only thing I really knew about Bulgaria was that it had given birth to one of the most gifted footballing talents I had ever seen, Hristo Stoichkov. I can still remember watching the USA '94 World Cup as a football-mad teenager and being in complete awe of the left-footed genius with jailhouse looks who seemed to score goals for fun. Stoichkov's Bulgaria knocked out the likes of Argentina and Germany on a fairy-tale run that saw them reach the semi-finals, and Stoichkov ended the games as the tournament's top scorer. Brazil would eventually lift the World Cup, but nobody would forget Stoichkov and his plucky little nation, which turned up and gave the big boys a real scare that year.

So that was the extent of my knowledge of Bulgaria: Stoichkov was born there; it was a former communist country; and their flag looked like Italy's on its side. Needless to say, there was no reason for me to think Bulgarians could be Muslim.

When English writer Patrick Leigh Fermor wandered through central Bulgaria in the 1930s on his coming-of-age journey from the Hook of Holland to Istanbul, he was passing through lands that had been Muslim for almost five hundred years as part of the Ottoman Empire – a legacy that was still highly visible to Fermor. He describes seeing 'Turks in turbans and fez everywhere' and their womenfolk in outfits that left only their eyes visible. He recalls passing numerous mosques, even spending the night in the ruins of an abandoned one. Arriving at another, he found locals sitting cross-legged, either sipping on minute thimbles of coffee or smoking a *nargileh*, whilst others busied themselves at water fountains, making their ritual ablutions ahead of the call to prayer. The scene could easily have been in the heart of Fez, Tunis or Algiers, yet for the young Fermor these Muslims were no different to their fellow countrymen.

It was now almost a century since Fermor had written those words, and in that time the image of eastern Europe as Muslim has been consigned to history. Like the Moorish Muslim presence in Spain, Portugal and Italy, it is almost never mentioned as part of the region's official or popular historical narrative. The long anti-religious period of communism that followed Fermor's now faded footsteps is partly to blame for this. Modern eastern Europe's popular image as a secular, harsh, grey place ravaged by ethnic wars is the one much of the world has come to accept, and it is an image that completely ignores the region's six centuries of Muslim history and its huge native Muslim population. No wonder the Bulgarian Muslim villages and their little white mosques came as such a shock to us.

As a family of Muslims living in Europe at a time when Muslims are made to feel like outsiders, the villages offered a tantalising prospect: the chance to meet indigenous versions of us.

Born in Bangladesh, I moved to London's East End in the early 1980s, when racism in the area was hitting something of a peak. 'Paki-bashing' was a local pastime, gollywogs still appeared on jam jars and the British National Party had an office on Brick Lane – a street in the heart of the newly arrived Bangladeshi migrant community.

Right from the start it was made clear to me that *I* didn't belong here. As a confused and terrified child, I watched a racist thug assault my father on our doorstep; I listened to police lament not being able to catch the skinheads that had split my brother's head open; I heard my mother's terrified shrieks every time a fire 'bomb' was posted through our letter box and I watched in horror as a Nazi-saluting yob sliced open the cheek of my friend before being chased by his fellow fascist.

I grew up feeling like there were huge swathes of society that hated me just for being me and would happily kill me to prove that. Imagine trying to compute that as a child.

So in a strange way, when the racism began to subside – or at least stopped being so blatant – and a new prejudice emerged after the turn of the century, it felt all too familiar. Where before I was told I didn't belong here because I was a 'Paki', now I was told I didn't belong here because I was a Muslim. And it wasn't just Britain telling me this; it seemed as though the entire Western world wanted me and my 'kind' out. From the academic voices of Bernard Lewis and Samuel P Huntington to hate-mongering celebrities like Katie Hopkins and Melanie Phillips, the message was loud and clear: Muslims are not Europeans.

I also had a young family now, after marrying my childhood sweetheart. Our family was a Muslim one of multi-ethnic, multi-cultural and multi-religious heritage – with Christian, Jewish and Muslim roots. Somehow, I would have to start making sense of all this hate and rejection that I knew my children would also encounter.

This was what made the Muslims of the Balkans so important. They were not the result of immigration nor were they converts to Islam or deemed 'foreign' to Europe. They were Muslims whose identity had been forged in and of Europe. It was an identity entrenched fully in local society. They were as European as they were Muslim.

I wanted to know if they suffered any of the internal conflicts we did. Did they worry about belonging? How did they balance being European and being Muslim? Did they feel the rejection many of us do? Were they *anything* like us?

Intrigued, that summer in 2014 we went on several day trips to visit the Muslim villages and towns near Palamartsa. Our favourite was Shumen, a small Bulgarian city like any other – dominated by grey, monolithic housing blocks, and overlooked by a giant, typically macho and garish communist monument. Shumen was also home to the beautiful, Ottoman-era Sherif Halil Pasha Mosque – also known as the Tombul Mosque – on the eastern edge of the city, close to the historic old town and framed by the surrounding lush green hills. Deemed one of the finest examples of the Tulip style, the stunning mosque combines colourful European baroque patterns with classical Ottoman aesthetics, including the multi-dome design and an elegant, slimline minaret. Inside the mosque, beneath a web of scaffolding, we prayed the Friday congregational *Jumua'ah* prayer before making our way to the inner courtyard, where a quaint fountain said to pour out holy water stood beneath a lead dome held aloft by white Corinthian pillars. The August sunshine warming our faces, we sat on a step and watched as the locals embraced each other just as they would've done when Fermor passed through these lands, except they no longer wore turbans or fezzes. The men in their trousers, jeans, shirts and T-shirts looked just like every other Bulgarian we had seen.

Later, some of them proudly showed us their new *madrasa*, a large modern structure opposite the historic mosque built using money from Turkey and Bosnia. Those that could speak a little English shared stories about their lives living with non-Muslim friends and neighbours – again, contradicting our expectations of the Balkan country.

It turned out this was nothing new in Shumen. In a fascinating image of religious pluralism and cross-pollination, a French traveller writing in 1785 described the locals as 'half Turkish, half Bulgarian; Muslims and Christians' who lived side by side, married each other, drank 'bad wine' together and 'violated both the ramazan and the Christian fast'. He claimed there was a mutual respect and reverence for both faiths in a society where children were left to choose, where households were often home to both the cross and the crescent, and where turbans and icons could be found on shelves beside both the Qur'an and the Bible.

There was something familiar about this picture. In the East End of my youth, despite the racists, I grew up surrounded by people of all faiths and none, and my friends and I were equally good at violating the Ramadan fast: sneaking off to smoke an illicit fag or tucking into a clandestine bag of chips. We would return at sunset pretending to be famished, taking extra care not to get too close to parents or more pious siblings, lest they smelt our smoky, vinegary breath. Even on the days of Eid, what the Bulgarians call *Bayram*, after attending the prayer in the morning, we often spent our evenings celebrating with 'bad wine' and strong spirits, merrily getting drunk with our non-Muslim friends. And, of course, some of us also went on to marry each other.

Our delightful hosts at the eco-farm were an expat couple, Claire Coulter, a reiki master originally from Ireland, and Chris Fenton, an English archaeologist. They had bought two cheap farmhouses after falling in love with the Bulgarian countryside while drifting through it in a camper van almost eight years earlier. One of these was now their charming home, and the other they had lovingly turned into a rustic homestay run on sustainable energy, complete with a compost toilet. Claire and Chris kept their own livestock – a goat, several pigs and some chickens – and they grew their own organic fruit and veg, in an idyllic Bulgarian version of *The Good Life*. Intelligent and curious, to my utter delight they also took an interest in the local Muslim heritage.

'Our goatherd is Muslim,' Claire told me one morning, as she brought over our daily supply of fresh goat's milk, cheese, fruit preserve and freshly baked bread. 'The elderly woman who lives across the road is also Muslim.'

I looked over at the stone cottage hidden by a large vine, half expecting to see a woman in a hijab in the front garden, but it didn't work like that. Neither the goatherd nor our neighbour across the road looked any different to the rest of the villagers. The mixing of cultures and heritage was so ancient in these parts that the lines had been blurred centuries ago.

Nowhere was this more apparent than a tomb Chris took me to visit one day, about an hour's drive from the farm, close to the village of Sveshtari. Tamara and the girls don't get as excited about dead people as I do, so I was joined by a young Spanish couple who were also staying at the farm. The three of us were led by Chris down a steep set of winding concrete steps that took us into woodland. Above us, colourful pieces of material tied to branches arched over in a canopy of little rainbows. Halfway down, Chris pointed out a tombstone, set on a flat section of the hillside. Any words had been worn away with age, but the carved headstone – shaped like an Ottoman turban – was clear for us all to see.

The 16th-century Ottoman tomb, known as a *türbe* in Turkish, had been built on an ancient Thracian site dating back to the 4th century BC, explained Chris. In a large clearing in the forest, surrounded by steep hills, the Ottoman tomb is said to have the body of an Alevi Muslim saint called Demir Baba inside. After its construction, the area became a site of religious pilgrimage. Historic prints inside the *türbe's* tiny museum showed the elaborate tomb in its clearing with a mosque beside it, where men in large turbans stood outside. Next to them were two wooden buildings, one a lodging for adherents of the monastic order founded around the saint's teachings, and the other an *imaret* (hospice) that fed and housed the weary pilgrims who could be seen arriving at the site.

'But it's not just Muslims that come down here,' Chris explained as we stood over the 'holy' water source believed to have miraculously appeared to the saint. 'Christians also visit the tomb. They don't believe it contains the body of Demir Baba; they think it is the body of St George.'

The real miracle, said Chris, was that this caused no apparent conflict between the two sets of believers, who had somehow found a way to respect each others' beliefs and share the holy site.

As I stepped into the cool, heptagonal mausoleum, I was greeted by a wonderfully organised scene of religious tolerance. The sacred space had been carefully and respectfully split down the middle. On one side, Shia Muslim icons of Ali, Hasan and Husayn (members of the Prophet's family) hung on the walls, beside Arabic inscriptions praising God, the Prophet and his family. Beneath them in neat little piles were *tasbih* beads, rugs and more of the colourful ties from outside. On the other side of the split, arranged equally neatly, were Christian icons, crucifixes, candles and rosary beads. Both met in the middle where the religious lines became blurred, Muslim and Christian offerings scattered all over the tomb in the centre.

This intimate tolerance of each other's beliefs left me genuinely moved. I had never come across anything like it before in Europe.

So why, I began to wonder, was this not celebrated? Why didn't more of us know about these examples of religious tolerance in the Balkans?

For some reason, the region's Muslim history – like Europe's Muslim history – tends to be remembered negatively, when it is remembered at all. Even Fermor describes the capture of Constantinople by the Ottomans in 1453 as the 'greatest disaster on Europe since the sack of Rome by the Goths'. As if nothing good came of Ottoman Europe.

Part of the answer, I soon discovered, was sitting on Chris and Claire's well-stocked bookshelf. Browsing it one lazy afternoon, I came across two intriguing books: *The Turks of Bulgaria: History, Traditions, Culture* and *A Guide to Ottoman Bulgaria*. Both had been edited by Bulgarian journalist Anthony Georgieff. They were the first books I had come across in English celebrating the Muslim heritage of Bulgaria, or any Balkan nation for that matter. In the preface to the first one, titled *Not in Black-and-White,* Georgieff explains that from the very creation of the modern country known as the People's Republic of Bulgaria in 1945, Bulgarian historians had gone out of their way to represent the five centuries of Ottoman rule as nothing more than a 'series of mass murders, impalings and rivers of blood'. Nothing, claims Georgieff, was written about any of the fabulous architecture, the fascinating culture, tolerant society or liberal Ottoman sultans.

In truth, says Georgieff, apart from the very beginning and the very end of Ottoman rule, 'Bulgar and Turk lived side by side in relative harmony', just as it had been described by the French traveller in 1785.

Those five centuries of Muslim rule had shaped Bulgaria irreversibly. Many aspects of 'Bulgarian' culture are in fact Ottoman in origin. This includes numerous Bulgarian words, local cuisine, proverbs and tales. Even the habit of snacking on sunflower seeds can be traced back to the Muslims.

Georgieff also highlighted how tolerant the Ottomans were for their time. In fact, were it not for the empire's practice of religious plurality – inspired by Islam – there might not have been many medieval European Jews. When the Catholic Monarchs of Spain, Ferdinand and Isabella, were killing and exiling the Sephardic Jews of the Iberian peninsula during the 15th and 16th centuries, the Ottomans welcomed the refugees into their territories. Sultan Bayezid II actually sent ships to collect them, along with Spanish Muslims, who were all being kicked out for refusing to convert to Catholicism. Like other non-Muslims, all the Jews had to do to guarantee their safety in the Ottoman territories was pay their taxes. It's true that some rulers abused this and enforced higher taxes on non-Muslims – it wasn't a perfect system – but it was far better than most other non-Muslim systems in Europe prior to the Enlightenment. Before the Ottomans, the last time Europe's Jews had felt so safe was probably under the Muslim Umayyad rulers of Spain, having been consistently persecuted or expelled by numerous European nations. England expelled them in 1290, Germany in the 1380s and France in 1394. Many Jewish massacres took place across Europe often inspired by Christian religious leaders. The early 13th century Pope Innocent III forbade Christians from living, working or trading with Jews and even the 16th century Protestant reformer Martin Luther famously said 'we are at fault for not slaying them [Jews]'. Europe's religious intolerance wasn't just reserved for the Jews either; in the 13th century France began extinguishing the Christian

Cathars and later did the same with the Protestant Huguenots as part of the European wars of religion. These took place during the 16th and 17th centuries between Christians of different denominations and claimed an estimated fifteen million lives across Europe.

The sheer variety of different religious refugees that voluntarily entered Ottoman territories speaks for itself. Like any imperial movement, the Ottomans were far from perfect but, as Georgieff says, their reign shouldn't be remembered as purely black or white.

Today, Bulgarian Turks make up a mere eight per cent of the country's population. The ethnic cleansing by insurgent Balkan Christian nationalism in the late 19th century, combined with horrific anti-Muslim pogroms throughout the 20th century as part of the nation's infamous 'Revival Process', is the reason the numbers are so low. The whitewashing of the nation's cultural heritage saw 'Muslim' clothing and the Turkish language banned, place names changed, and mosques and Ottoman monuments, including cemeteries, defaced or destroyed. Thousands of ethnic Bulgarian Muslims – Pomaks – and Gypsies were forcibly converted to Christianity and ethnic Turks forced to change their Muslim names to Slavic ones. Anyone who tried to resist was beaten, killed or imprisoned. This terrifying assault on Bulgarian Muslims forced many to abandon their homes, leave their country and head mainly for Turkey. There were at least three major mass emigrations in the 1950s, '70s and '80s. The last wave of nearly 360,000 came after the forced name changing of around 800,000 Muslims between 1984 and 1985. Known as the 'Big Excursion', it was the largest forced migration in Europe since World War II. The national census the following year had no question on ethnicity. As far as Bulgaria was concerned, everyone was now 'Bulgarian'.

Spending that summer in Bulgaria had opened our eyes to the tantalising possibility that there was still a living indigenous 'Muslim Europe' out there. It had also opened my eyes to just how precarious its existence was and the efforts being made to eradicate and deny it, and this left me overcome with a sudden and urgent desire to see what was still left before it was too late, and not just by myself, but with my family. As far as I was concerned, this was their heritage too, both as Europeans and as Muslims: a heritage and history I knew they wouldn't learn any other way. Plus, travelling with them would also enhance the journey, opening doors to spaces I couldn't enter alone and offering important and different perspectives. My family were mixed-race British Muslims. They would see the places we would visit through a lens very different to my own. They *had* to come. So as I sat in that delightful farmhouse in the middle of a Bulgarian nowhere that summer, a plan began to formulate.

Scanning the map of Europe, it became obvious to me that the place to go looking for this heritage was the one corner of the continent we might still rightfully call 'Muslim Europe': the western Balkans. A collection of six countries with centuries of Islamic history and three still boasting Muslim-majority populations: Bosnia and Herzegovina, Kosovo and Albania are effectively Europe's only 'Muslim' countries. Meanwhile, their neighbours – Serbia, North Macedonia and Montenegro – also had long-established Muslim communities. Not only was this area rich in European Muslim culture and heritage, but its modest size meant we could visit all six countries on one fascinating summer road trip.

As Tamara and I began planning our route I quickly realised there was very little to guide me through the area's Muslim heritage. Nothing comprehensive had been written about its Muslim towns, people, customs, mosques and monuments, past or present. Even when celebrated British traveller Michael Palin came through these countries a mere decade ago, he was more interested in the recent communist history and paid scant attention to its centuries of Muslim heritage. It seemed, besides my own nose, I would be relying on the glimpses offered by travellers like Fermor, who were non-Muslim and from the western half of Europe, which came with its own problems.

To counteract these voices, I needed someone who *really* knew Muslim Europe, someone who was also Muslim, someone from the east. In truth, there was only one candidate: the great medieval Ottoman traveller, Evliya Çelebi. Not only had Evliya visited many of the towns and cities on the itinerary we were putting together, but he had done so in the middle of the 17th century, when the Ottoman Empire had reached the absolute limit of its expansion into Europe. Evliya's Europe was the most 'Muslim' it would ever be, and he was travelling through it as a member of the most cultured society in the world. Evliya's father had served under the legendary Sultan Suleiman the Magnificent, whose rule is seen as the cultural zenith of Ottoman civilisation: a time when the Muslim empire was the world's great patron of the arts, music, literature and all things *haute culture*, stretching from the edge of Austria in the west to the Persian Gulf in the east, and home to a vast range of ethnicities, religions and people.

Renowned for his wit, knowledge and oratory skills, Evliya, who claimed to be descended from poets and even the Prophet Muhammad, carved out a career spanning over forty years on the road alongside some of the great pashas (Ottoman governors) of the day, mainly it seems because he was great fun to be with. Ten of these years were spent in the Balkans (between 1660 and 1670), which is why Evliya's accounts of his travels offer a tantalising and unique window into Muslim Europe.

Evliya's *Book of Travels* or *Seyahâtnâme*, where he recorded his epic journeys across the former Ottoman territories, has made him one of the first great European Muslim travel writers and amongst the most widely quoted authors on the Balkans. Walking in the footsteps of such a cultured expert of historic Muslim Europe as we went in search of its modern equivalent meant that, even if the history and heritage we were looking for were no longer there, Evliya might still be able to offer us a glimpse – and in doing so, remind us just how 'Muslim' Europe once was.

PART ONE

BOSNIA AND HERZEGOVINA

An Ottoman City

SARAJEVO

It was the melodious cry of the *muezzin* that hastened me towards my first destination in Sarajevo. The sacred words inviting Muslims to prayer cascaded through the valley where Bosnia and Herzegovina's capital city nestles. Squeezed along a narrow east–west corridor on the banks of the Miljacka River as it emerges serpentine from the surrounding mountains, old Sarajevo still resembles a bustling medieval city.

All around me were narrow alleyways leading to historic quarters once the exclusive domain of metalworkers, leather markets, gold dealers and coffee sellers. Some were still home to their modern incarnations, jostling for room with the new al fresco restaurants, cafés and boutique tourist shops.

The late evening *adhan* (call to prayer) is always quite enchanting. An inky darkness enveloped the green hills as the serene Arabic words rippled through the valley; one by one the mosques came alive. Every time a new one joined the growing chorus, I turned my head to notice another tall, historic minaret I hadn't seen before. They seemed to be everywhere, each an ancient testimony that Sarajevo has always been a Muslim city.

Founded in 1461, just two years before Bosnia officially became an Ottoman *sanjak* (district), Sarajevo's establishment effectively confirmed Bosnia as a Muslim land, and it has remained proudly so ever since.

Growing up, I didn't know there were cities in Europe where the *adhan* could be such a normal part of the landscape. I certainly wouldn't have imagined that such a city lay just a thousand miles to the east, and wasn't called Cairo or Istanbul.

Like most children in the 1990s, the first time I heard the name Sarajevo it was from the mouth of a middle-aged white man with a received-pronunciation accent, sitting behind a news desk on the TV. Whenever he mentioned Sarajevo, the TV would cut to grainy images of men, women and children running for cover amid flashes of bright light and the most awfully violent noises. These scenes of utter terror and destruction were no different to the ones I saw every time the same man said 'Baghdad' or 'Mogadishu'.

Sarajevo then, was a place of war, somewhere far, far away – maybe even near Baghdad and Mogadishu? No. That much I did know. I was distinctly aware that both Iraq and Somalia were 'Muslim' countries and the people there looked like me. Furthermore, my parents and the mosque elders regularly expressed their sadness for the suffering Iraqi and Somali Muslims. They even dedicated prayers to them, but I don't recall any prayers ever being dedicated to the Bosnians in Sarajevo.

I entered the large stone courtyard of the Gazi Husrev-beg Mosque and headed straight for the entrance to the main hall. I could hear verses of the Qur'an being recited over the tannoy system. This told me I was late for the congregational session. Rushing past the ornate outdoor fountain, I kicked off my shoes, threw them on to the wooden shoe rack and burst through the large doors, expecting to be greeted by a neat row of worshippers. But there was no row. In fact, everyone in the half-empty hall looked very relaxed: a few were finishing off *Sunnah* (bonus) prayers alone; others were still reading the Qur'ans in their hands; one or two elders were trying not to doze off.

Did I really hear verses from the Qur'an?

The voice started up again; I immediately recognised *surah al-Ikhlas*. It was a deep, elderly voice, but I couldn't see where it was coming from. There was no imam at the front, only the colourful and elaborate marble *mihrab*. I was momentarily confused. This was not how prayer normally started.

But it did, here in Bosnia.

Like the stunning mosque I stood in, Bosnia's Islamic practice is also inspired by Turkey, where it is common to recite certain important chapters of the Qur'an ahead of the congregational prayer. As this all began to dawn on me, I realised, much to my relief, I hadn't missed the prayer after all. I would get to start my search for Muslim Europe just as I had envisioned it: bowing down to God beside Europe's indigenous Muslims.

Once the old man had recited *al-Ikhlas* three times, he made a *dua* with the *fātiḥah* before giving the *Iqama* (the shorter call to announce the start of the congregational prayer), prompting everyone to slowly get to their feet. The men lined up in neat rows in front of the *mihrab*, and the women made straight lines beneath a section of the *mahvil* (wooden balcony at the back). There was no physical barrier between the genders.

I found myself in the front row close to a huge marble *mimbar*, from where the imam gave his Friday sermons. Either side of me were two elderly gentlemen, one of whom I was certain had been dozing only minutes earlier.

After a few seconds, a rustling of the curtains beneath the *mimbar* announced the arrival of the imam in full-length robe and a red hat that resembled a fez. He was young, around thirty, but his congregation – four rows deep, filling a quarter of the mosque – were mostly those entering the golden years of their lives. When the imam began his recitation of the *fātiḥah,* it was in a higher-pitched, more melodious style. He paused in all the right places and elongated the correct words in a manner that told me his recitation was the result of years of practice, most likely at the feet of a classical teacher. This was no surprise; the Gazi Husrev-beg Mosque is Sarajevo's largest, built by one of its most famous governors in the 16th century. Naturally, the man chosen to lead the prayer here would have to be someone truly accomplished.

The imam's beautiful words travelled through the main hall, bouncing off the tall ceiling and decorated central dome in an acoustic style that sounded like it belonged in a cathedral.

Standing there, arms clasped across my midriff, shoulders and feet inches from the old boys either side of me, I was for a moment transported to the huge cathedral-like mosques of Istanbul in Turkey, the Gazi Husrev's architectural and spiritual home.

The mosque was built during the Golden Age of the Ottoman Empire in 1531, when Sultan Suleiman the Magnificent sat on the throne. It was part of a huge complex of buildings, funded by the *waqf* (charitable endowment) of one of the great sultan's most trusted advisors, Gazi Huzrev-beg, the then-governor of Bosnia and a grandson of Sultan Bayezid II. As well as the mosque, the *waqf* also paid for the construction of several schools, libraries, public baths, travel inns (*han*), charitable hospices (*imaret*) and clock towers in Sarajevo, helping elevate it into one of the most important cities in the region. Some of the buildings still survive, as does the tomb of Gazi Husrev-beg, but it is the mosque, one of the finest examples of classical Ottoman architecture in Bosnia, that is the main attraction.

Built during the auspicious era of the great architect Mimar Sinan, like every major Ottoman mosque from this period – as I was to discover on this journey – there was an attempt to link the Gazi Husrev-beg to the great man no matter how tenuous, and this was tenuous. Sarajevo's Muslims were keen to prove that Sinan had 'inspected' the Gazi Husrev-beg Mosque. Such was the greatness of the empire's chief architect that even a possible inspection by him was worthy of mention.

As the imam finished the final *salaam* over his left shoulder to signal the end of the prayer, I looked up at the floral patterns that framed the windows, and the red and green honeycombed squinches holding aloft the huge central dome with its ring of delicate calligraphy. Like many Ottoman mosques from this period, the Gazi Husrev had several other smaller domes integrated in its design. They all lined up over the large outdoor portico at the entrance, which was built to ensure travellers had somewhere clean and dry to perform their worship outside of the five daily prayer times, when many mosques were locked up. A Muslim traveller is not obliged to pray at the designated times and can offer them when it is more practical.

The patterns I was admiring inside the Gazi Husrev were not original though. Those were sadly lost during a 'renovation' in the Austro-Hungarian period. The current interior – inspired by contemporary Ottoman mosques – dates from the rebuild after the 1990s Bosnian War, when it was devastated by Serb bombings. Targeting the mosque had been deliberate. In any war, bombing monuments of heritage and culture tells your enemy you are going for their identity – by destroying the very things that make them who they were. The Germans and the Brits did this to each other in World War II, the most famous example being the Baedeker Raids carried out by the Luftwaffe. Using the popular *Baedeker's Guide to Great Britain*, the Germans identified 'every building in Britain with three-stars' – the top sites of British heritage and culture – and then bombed the hell out of them. This was why the Serbs went for the Gazi Husrev-beg Mosque. Attacks of this nature, labelled 'cultural genocide' by one Harvard observer, became a Serb hallmark during the war that devastated the country between April 1992 and December 1995.

The Bosnian War was one of several fought as Yugoslavia began to fall apart in 1991, and stemmed from historic nationalisms developed along ethno-religious lines. So when Muslim-majority Bosnia and Herzegovina declared its independence in March 1992, preaching an idealised multi-ethnic future built on its tradition of *komšiluk* or 'good neighbourliness', the country's Orthodox Bosnian Serbs refused to accept this, and eventually neither did the country's Catholic Bosnian Croats. Both groups declared their own autonomous states and went to war with the country's majority Bosnian Muslims (Bosniaks). The Bosnian Serb and Bosnian Croat factions were supported by Serbia and Croatia who were accused of trying to carve up the newly independent Republic of Bosnia and Herzegovina to expand their own territories. It was religious terrorism, before it became popular to call it that.

The bitter conflict saw former neighbours, friends and even family members fighting against each other. Its legacy is one of indiscriminate shelling of towns and cities, ethnic cleansing, genocide and systematic rape, with the Serb forces seen as the main perpetrators, though Bosnian and Croat forces were also guilty of war crimes. The war claimed the lives of 100,000 people, displaced a further two million, and remains one of the largest ethnic cleansing exercises since World War II.

When it eventually came to an end with a peace agreement signed in Paris on 14th December 1995, an unusual new country emerged: one where two borderless 'nations' with their own laws, parliaments and capital cities, exist within a larger nation. The country of Bosnia and Herzegovina is therefore home to both Bosnia and Herzegovina, where the majority population is Bosniak and Muslim, and the Republic of Sprska, where the majority population is ethnic Serb and Orthodox Christian.

My route from the mosque led me to tiny Baščaršija Square, close to where the town's ageing blue and yellow trams trundle to a noisy halt at one of the more popular stops. The square is home to the iconic Sebilj, an ornate wood structure that resembles a small kiosk with an Ottoman-style domed top – a popular place to sit and watch children chase the local pigeons and tourists pose by what has become the symbol of Sarajevo.

I decided to stop for a bite to eat and pulled up a chair outside one of the local restaurants overlooking the Sebilj. The structure was originally built in 1752 for the purpose of quenching the thirst of weary travellers. The reason it looks like a kiosk is because once upon a time a man called the 'Sebilja' – from the Arabic for 'road' – sat inside to draw water for thirsty wayfarers. Sadly, the original Sebilj burned down in 1852 and when it was replaced by the late-19th-century rulers of Bosnia, the Austro-Hungarians, they rigged up a small fountain to one side so that visitors could drink refreshingly cool water any time of the day or night.

The ready availability of fresh water was one of the things that impressed Ottoman traveller Evliya Çelebi when he was sent to Sarajevo in 1660 with a victory announcement (possibly about the Transylvanian campaign) for his maternal uncle, Melek Ahmed Pasha, the governor of the Eyalet of Bosnia. Melek, who was married to Sultan Murad IV's daughter and briefly the Empire's grand vizier, would become Evliya's main patron and facilitate most of his travels. Melek was one of several esteemed connections Evliya had to the imperial court. His father, Dervish Mehmed Aga Zilli, had been the chief goldsmith to several sultans and was given the lofty honour of making the holy Kaaba's golden waterspout known as the 'Waterspout of Mercy' – a feature still seen protruding from the revered building's roof in Makkah today.

Evliya was born in the great imperial capital of Istanbul. The highly cosmopolitan and fashionable city was arguably the grandest metropolis of its day with Evliya dedicating an entire volume of his epic ten-volume book to his beloved city. So it was high praise indeed when Evliya turned up in Sarajevo for the first time and referred to it as a 'progressive, beautiful, and lively' city. The Ottoman traveller put the beauty down to Sarajevo's abundance of water, which flowed fresh from the surrounding mountains, allowing the locals to nurture stunning gardens and grow plenty of fruit and vegetables. Meanwhile, the reason Sarajevo appeared lively and progressive to him was because of the city's diverse religious and ethnic make-up and seemingly peaceful coexistence of its inhabitants – a historic version of the Bosnian tradition of *komšiluk,* if you will. As well as Muslims from all over the region, Evliya came across different European Christians and huge numbers of Sephardic Jews all living in Sarajevo, the latter rehomed here by the Ottomans following their exile from Catholic Spain. He wrote that all of them were free to build and worship in their respective churches and synagogues on two conditions: none of their buildings were to exceed the city's tallest mosque in height; and churches could not have bells.

Despite these restrictions, this was remarkably tolerant for its time and is the reason Sarajevo would later be dubbed the 'Jerusalem of Europe'. Elsewhere on the continent, barring the odd exception in areas like the recently independent Dutch provinces, Jews were either being exiled, having their books banned or being accused of witchcraft, whilst Catholic priests were being executed in England, and Huguenots massacred in France.

In Sarajevo, according to Evliya, Jews and Christians went about their business like any other Ottoman citizens, and, most interestingly, Evliya wrote about this in an unremarkable fashion, as though it were nothing unusual at all.

There is just no getting away from the Ottomans in Sarajevo. As well as the fact that the city was built and shaped by the great Muslim empire and therefore home to hundreds of years of Ottoman heritage, unlike other major Balkan cities, here in Sarajevo this association is celebrated.

The sign above the entrance of the restaurant I sat outside read: 'Osmanli Pide Döner'. This was no ordinary doner-kebab shop; it was an Ottoman doner-kebab shop – never mind the fact that doner kebabs were invented several decades after the collapse of the Ottomans.

'Osmanli' was the eastern variant of the anglicised 'Ottoman'. In it is the name of the empire's founder Osman, who in the year 1300, as the leader of a small Turkoman tribe – one of many vying for power in Anatolia – reportedly had a dream that would inspire the greatest and longest Muslim dynasty the world has ever seen. The Ottoman Empire lasted more than 600 years and every single sultan that sat on the imperial throne could trace his lineage back to Osman, the very first Ottoman.

The front window of the shop displayed a large Turkish flag, which blocked from view the Arab families who sat inside. The scene I looked out on was also a Middle Eastern one: Arab fathers following their toddlers around, camera phone in hand, as they chased the Sebilj pigeons. On the fringes, beside vacated pushchairs, were their wives in black head-to-toe burkas and niqabs. Occasionally I spotted an uncovered face, but these were not Arab. Their features were southeast Asian; they were the Filipino and Malaysian nannies who accompanied their wealthy employers on their summer holidays. When the fathers got bored filming, it was usually these women who swept up young Abdullah and placed him back in his pushchair.

Sarajevo and Bosnia's willingness to retain its Muslim roots and embrace its Islamic heritage has made it one of the Gulf's hottest new European destinations. Many Bosnians speak fluent Arabic, having been taught it as part of their Islamic education; all the food here is halal; and the prices are much lower than western Europe, where 'visible' Muslims are increasingly made to feel unwanted. Such is the success of Bosnia in attracting Gulf tourists that you can fly direct to Sarajevo from Dubai, but you can't do the same from London.

The juxtaposition of the new tourists and the locals represented the difference between the Gulf Muslims and their indigenous European counterparts. For every *niqabi* in a burka, there were ten local women wandering around in jeans, short skirts and dresses, sometimes with a headscarf, though this was rare amongst the younger women.

The meal I ordered was also Turkish in origin, and may even have been Ottoman, a Turkish pizza called a *pide*. A good *pide*, like the ones baked in the wood-fired ovens of Samsun, on Turkey's northern Black Sea coast – the *pide's* spiritual home – will have a generous amount of gently spiced minced lamb running through the centre of the boat-shaped pizza. The dough will be light and crispy, and the meat might be topped with that salty ewe's cheese so favoured by Anatolians.

Mine arrived perfectly cooked but lacking in meat, which was rather disappointing. The dough, however, was excellent, and the waiter, a wide Bosnian with a soiled apron, looked so rushed off his feet I didn't have the heart to bother him. Instead, I tore off a large chunk of cheesy, meatless 'meat' *pide* and popped it into my mouth. Much to my delight, it actually tasted rather good. I washed this down with a bitter lemon drink I had ordered by accident – my Bosnian wasn't quite up to scratch (it was non-existent), nor was my Arabic, and the waiter spoke very little English.

The tourists had now filtered to a trickle, and overtired toddlers in the square were playing up. I reflected on a brief and delightful first evening in Sarajevo, albeit alone – Tamara and our daughters, Amani and Anaiya, were resting back at our apartment, the 18-hour journey having taken its toll.

I was glad I had made the effort. Tomorrow we would begin the road trip proper by heading southwest to Mostar, the famous bridge-city near the Croatian border, which meant this was our only evening in Sarajevo for now – we had set aside five days in the city towards the end of our trip. We figured that would be a nice way to recover from what was set to be a whirlwind tour. Five whole days in the 'Ottoman Jerusalem' would also allow us to really get beneath the skin of this fascinatingly proud Muslim city. I had lined up a city tour and interviews with a host of interesting people, including a curator at the Gazi Husrev-beg Mosque, to try and understand why Sarajevo wore its Muslim and Ottoman heritage so proudly on its sleeve. A return to Sarajevo felt right. It would mean starting and ending a journey through former Ottoman lands in a city proud of its Ottoman roots.

By then, I would be able to compare notes with all the other amazing sites and places we were due to visit. What would the contrast be like? Were there other smaller, hidden Sarajevos out there, I wondered. And, more importantly, would I find a decent meat *pide* anywhere?

The Bridge Built by Barbarians

MOSTAR

I first saw the destruction of Mostar's Stari Most on an old, grainy video online. It shows a battered, pockmarked, old stone bridge with a perfect rainbow arch being bombarded with missiles and mortar bombs. The crude tin shelter, built along the top so locals could be hidden from snipers as they walked across it, is a crumbling mess, especially in the middle where the HVO (Hrvatsko Vijeće Obrane) – Croatian Council of Defence – have been aiming most of their rockets. The time on the screen is 15:52, an hour before the mid-afternoon call to prayer would have been heard on the eastern bank, had the ancient mosques and their minarets not been bombed to oblivion. The footage is set to the melancholic score of *Sarabande* from Stanley Kubrick's Oscar-winning 1975 movie *Barry Lyndon*.

An authoritative voice shouts a command and a missile hits the bridge right of centre; debris falls to the water below and a huge dust cloud rises from the bridge. The makeshift shelter along the top completely collapses and the camera struggles to steady itself as it films what now looks like a bunch of trampled matchsticks.

The slow, anguished score adds to the very real sense that we are witnessing a death.

Seconds later, another smaller missile hits the same spot. The lingering carcass of the 427-year-old architectural marvel is momentarily framed by greenery in the foreground and the few remaining red tiles on the roofs of bombed houses in the background, before the music's pace picks up, anticipating the inevitable. The bridge takes one last hit and suddenly the entire structure comes crashing down into the waters below in a series of almighty splashes causing an enormous wave – tsunami-like – to race towards the camera. And just like that, the bridge said to have defied the laws of physics for five centuries is destroyed forever.

The targeted destruction of Mostar's Stari Most (or 'Old Bridge') was probably one of the most successful examples of the cultural genocide inflicted on Bosnia's Muslim heritage during the Bosnian War. It took more than sixty missiles and three days of concentrated, targeted shooting and bombing to bring down this great relic once said to be so marvellous, that it outshone the sky itself.

Eyewitnesses claim that, when it finally collapsed into the waters of the Neretva, the Croat soldiers celebrated by shooting bullets into the air. On Tuesday 9th November 1993, the bridge commissioned by the Ottoman Sultan Suleiman the Magnificent, overseen by the architect Mimar Sinan, and built by his student Mimar Hayreddin, was no more.

The drive out of Sarajevo southwest towards Mostar took us through countryside with an alpine feel. The road snaked past a number of vast lakes and rivers, their aqua-blue waters shimmering in the stunning summer sun. Above them loomed mountains covered in green slopes and dense woodland, where you could spot clusters of white houses with red-tiled roofs; one or two had stone wells at the front – like villages from a fairy tale.

When Evliya visited Mostar's famous Old Bridge it was called the 'Bridge of Sultan Suleiman' and its beauty was such that it left the widely travelled Ottoman genuinely stupefied. He compared the engineering of the bridge's rainbow arch to the ancient Sassanid Iwan of Chosroes near Baghdad in Iraq – the world's largest unreinforced vault of brickwork, considered an architectural marvel. Evliya had been travelling non stop for twenty-seven years at this point and listed all the bridges he had seen in the sixteen kingdoms he'd traversed, including the Mehmed Paša Sokolović Bridge in Višegrad – our next stop. However, he claimed none was worth seeing as much as the Mostar bridge. It is 'peerless', he wrote, describing the elegance and refinement of the Stari Most as incomparable.

Evliya was not the only one enamoured by the stunning bridge. The Mostar-born Turkish poet, Dervish-Pasha Bajezidagić, claimed the bridge's arch was so great it overshadowed the sky above it. Arguably, he was biased, unlike the early 20th-century Austro-Hungarian writer, Robert Michel, who spent several years resident in Mostar and claimed he had 'never been so impressed by another building'.

Everything about Bosnia's fifth-largest city centres on its iconic bridge. Even the name comes from the Slavic term for bridge: *most*. The bridge then is essential to the very identity of the city, which is why, five years after its destruction by the Croat army work began – with the help of UNESCO and the international community – to faithfully reconstruct and resurrect it.

We were staying in Mostar for just the one night in a modern apartment building surrounded by run-down communist-era tower blocks in Mostar's northwestern suburb of Zgoni. Our new build was home to several apartments and built in a wide horseshoe, beneath which smart-looking coffee shops with stylish tables and chairs poured out on to a landscaped patio. Locals sat in the shade of newly planted palms beside manicured lawns. The block was the nouveau riche flexing their muscles, and felt in stark contrast to its surroundings. Our apartment was owned by a Croatian woman called Slavica who lived across the border in Croatia.

I parked the white Renault Megane we had rented for the trip beneath a beige concrete housing block, being sure to leave nothing on display as we each grabbed the small overnight bags we had packed for the short stay. Close to the car, painted on to a concrete bus stop in large black font were the words 'Zapamtite Vukovar', above it the stencilled outline of what looked to be an air-control tower with a Dutch flag hanging from it. I could make no sense of it. The mural was 'signed' by the 'Ultras Mostar' – the hardcore fan base for local side HŠK Zrinjski Mostar, one of the country's oldest and most successful football teams, with Catholic Croatian roots. After being banned for playing in a league in the wartime Independent State of Croatia, a Nazi puppet state, the club was reformed in 1992, again as a Catholic Croatian team. Unsurprisingly, their main city rivals, FK Velež Mostar, is a club of mainly Muslim Bosniak players. In the western Balkans, even the football teams have ethno-religious loyalties.

This was the reason the Ultras had painted the mural: it translated to 'Remember Vukovar', a city in eastern Croatia where a pivotal eighty-seven-day battle against the Serb army in 1991 turned the Croatian War of Independence – at some cost – in Croatia's favour; Vukovar was almost entirely destroyed. The 'air-control tower' was in fact the city's heavily damaged water tower, which still stands as a reminder of the battle, a Croatian flag proudly flying from the top. The mural artist had forgotten – or run out of time – to paint the red and white check crest on the flag, which was why I had mistaken it for the Dutch one.

The reason our stay in Mostar would be so brief was because it was actually in the opposite direction to that in which we wanted to go. The circular route we had mapped out started east of Sarajevo and headed into southern Serbia before looping clockwise through Kosovo, North Macedonia, Albania, Montenegro and back into southern Bosnia and Herzegovina. Mostar was in fact perfectly located to be one of our last destinations on the trip, but we had decided to go there first so Tamara could fulfil one of her major Balkan travel goals by visiting a little town just south of Mostar called Blagaj, where she had discovered the presence of a beautiful historic Sufi lodge. She was yet to secure the time off work for the whole of the road trip and there was a good chance she would have to return to London a week or so before the rest of us. To leave Blagaj to the end risked Tamara missing it altogether.

However, despite our best-laid plans, Tamara was now harbouring a niggling cough and sore throat. As her priority was Blagaj, we decided it was best she rested tonight in the hope of recovering ahead of a trip there tomorrow. I, on the other hand, had to see Mostar's famous bridge. So after grabbing some cough and flu remedies from the pharmacy beneath our apartment, I left my three ladies watching the *Gilmore Girls* and headed out in search of Evliya's 'peerless' bridge.

The long, dark, winding stairwell was making me feel claustrophobic and a little light-headed as I huffed and puffed my way up the narrow minaret of the early 17th-century Koski Mehmed Pasha Mosque. Historic minarets by design were meant to be traversed by a sole *muezzin* each day with no other human traffic whatsoever. In other words, they were only ever built wide enough for one person. The architect of the Koski had taken this very literally and this was easily the narrowest minaret I had ever climbed. I found myself praying the whole way up that no-one would walk down in the opposite direction, especially as I could hear voices coming up behind me; the thought of a claustrophobia-inducing traffic jam had me genuinely sweating. The Koski's architect had clearly not anticipated that one day his minaret would become the most coveted spot in Mostar to gaze upon the city's fabled bridge.

I reached the top to find I wasn't the only visitor from England desperate to appreciate the Koski's views. Saleh was from Manchester and on a one-day excursion from Dubrovnik in Croatia, which lies about a hundred kilometres southeast of Mostar.

'I saw how close it is on the map and thought I just have to come and see it. Who knows when I'll next be in this part of the world? So I popped over for the day with my wife and two children,' Saleh said in his broad Mancunian accent.

'All for a bridge, huh?'

We both laughed at this. Then Saleh, a large guy with thick black glasses and a warm smile, also of south Asian descent, explained why he wanted to see the bridge so badly.

'I remember seeing it collapse on the news as a kid and wondering what all the fuss was about. It was only when I got older and began looking into Islamic history in the Balkans that I realised what it meant and who built it. It's just a shame that we're looking at a reconstruction.'

I nodded slowly but said nothing.

The top of the minaret barely had enough room for the two of us to stand side by side. The wall around the edge was made from individual stone pieces linked together with thick iron rivets visible along the top. It was a tiny spot but one that really did offer the finest of vistas. Everything that had made travellers of the past wax lyrical about the bridge could be fully appreciated from up here. The two towers, one on each bank – the traditionally Muslim east where we stood and the Catholic west – rose up above the surrounding stone buildings. They once housed a garrison of 160 men that protected the bridge. Later, during the 19th century, one of the towers served as a powder store and the other as the city's dungeon. The towers are part of the bridge's magical symmetry, at the centre of which is a steep apex held aloft by the most perfect rainbow arch. The bridge emerges almost organically from the rocks of each bank. This is its greatest aesthetic quality: appearing to seamlessly connect both banks as if it has always been there.

Completed in 1566 in the final year of the reign of Ottoman Sultan Suleiman the Magnificent, Mostar's bridge, like the Gazi Husrev in Sarajevo, is a monument from the Muslim empire's Golden Age, and upon completion was deemed an architectural masterpiece. It has therefore been inevitably linked to Sinan, the great architect of that period. In fact, Evliya believed the bridge *was* built by him, but it is now widely accepted that, although Sinan would have overseen the plans as the empire's chief architect, the actual builder was Mimar Hayreddin.

The reason every town and city wants their Ottoman monument to be attributed to Sinan is because, along with Sultan Suleiman, he is one of *the* Ottoman stars, often transcending even the Islamophobia of the West, which dubbed Sinan the 'Turkish Michelangelo'. During his lifetime, he was nicknamed *Koca Mi'mâr*, the 'Great Old Architect', and his autobiographers compared him to the mystical saintly figure of Khidr – a kind of time-travelling guide in Islamic tradition. Sinan was the greatest of all Ottoman architects, and his work is seen as the pinnacle of the empire's architectural expression. Sinan became the chief architect in the second half of the 16th century, serving three sultans and living until the ripe old age of one hundred, which might explain why there are so many possible 'Sinans' – monuments attributed to Sinan – still out there.

'Did you know that Western "experts" of Bosnia for years couldn't get themselves to admit that the Ottomans had built the bridge?' I did the bunny ears with my two hands as I said the word 'experts'.

'Hmph,' Saleh laughed, his whole body shaking as he did. 'You're kidding, right?'

'No, I kid you not, bro. They claimed such a perfect bridge – so tall, so solid, built as one single, magnificent arch made using such big blocks – had to be the work of Romans.'

'Romans?' Saleh turned to look at me with incredulity.

The voices I had heard coming up the stairs were now jostling for space on the south-facing edge of the tiny balcony. The two new visitors looked Arab.

'They believed it was built by either Emperor Trajan or Hadrian.'

'As in Hadrian's Wall?'

'Yes, I think so.'

'Wow...' Saleh's voice trailed off in disbelief. 'And just how long did they keep up this merry charade of denial?' he finally asked.

'I'm not sure, bro, but even when they found dates that linked the building of the bridge to Sultan Suleiman, they were not having it. Instead, they tried to say that this was when the bridge was repaired or built over. I remember reading somewhere that they accused the Turks of erasing Roman inscriptions and covering over the "original" Roman bridge.' I again did the bunny ears, this time for the word 'original'. One of the new visitors looked across at us. He was a skinny boy with thick, black, curly locks and a pair of black-rimmed glasses.

'Damn, the Islamophobia was deep,' said Saleh, no longer sounding surprised.

He was right.

Often dismissed as 'Asiatic barbarians in Europe', for many arrogant post-Enlightenment writers, the Ottomans quite simply could not have possessed the skills or technology to produce a bridge as magnificent as the Stari Most. The famous English archaeologist, Sir Arthur Evans, in his 1897 book *Through Bosnia and the Herzegovina,* was still attributing the bridge to Emperor Trajan. He claimed the bridge's 'grandeur' and the form of the arch was so great it simply had to be Roman. This attitude about the bridge's origins and the widespread anti-Turkish Islamophobia it is rooted in is best summed up in the frankness of 19th-century painter Charlotte de Lazen, who fell in love with Mostar's bridge but simply could not accept its Turkish Muslim origins. She described the Stari Most as a 'marvellous remnant of Latin civilisation' in the midst of 'Turkish barbarity'.

What makes the insolence of these western Europeans all the more fascinating is that they were all aware of the inscriptions on the original bridge attributing the date of its construction to the reign of Sultan Suleiman but, as one observer put it, the prejudice was just 'too strong'.

'It's not bad for a recreation though, hey?' Saleh said, pulling up his camera phone to snap the bridge again.

'They've done a good job, there's no denying that. I can't tell the difference when I compare it to old pictures of the original.'

'It was UNESCO, right?'

'Yes. But they were convinced by a local architect called Amir Pašić. From the moment he learned of its destruction he started campaigning for it to be rebuilt exactly as it was before they blew it up.'

Pašić was a visiting scholar at Harvard University in the USA when he first heard about the bridge's destruction. He was so convinced that the bridge would be rebuilt that, as he toured America and Europe raising awareness, he handed out flyers inviting people to the 'Inauguration Ceremony for the Restoration of Mostar' on 5th September 2004 at 5pm. The flyer even had a bird's-eye-view sketch of his beloved city complete with the Stari Most intact. At the time, the date he had set was eleven years into the future, but the leaflet was a powerful symbol. As Pašić continued to campaign, his plight caught the attention of UNESCO, who along with the World Bank pledged their support. Soon the European Bank, the Aga Khan Trust and the World Monuments Fund joined them, along with several countries including Turkey, Bosnia and Croatia. The bridge we were now staring at was unveiled on 23rd July 2004, a little over a month earlier than Pašić had prophesised.

It took scientists, heritage experts and Ottoman specialists four years to recreate the bridge exactly as it was – Pašić insisted on this – by painstakingly going over ancient documents, sourcing and recovering many of the original stones and using building methods not seen in Mostar since the Ottomans. The work also included repairing Mostar's old town.

Standing on the reconstructed bridge later that day, I thought about Pašić's defiance; I had nothing but admiration for the way he simply refused to let the Croats take his heritage away from him. They blew it up and he just said, 'We'll rebuild it, exactly as it was.' The construction I stood on might not have been built by Hayreddin, and Sinan did not inspect these plans, but in his determined single-mindedness to faithfully recreate one of Europe's great Muslim monuments, I sensed hope in the story of Amir Pašić.

At a mere four metres wide and thirty metres long, the Stari Most is essentially a footbridge. No car or even handcart can pass over it. The elderly women holding the thick iron railing, as they nervously negotiate raised stone lines on the slippery incline, will testify to that. The lines are an original feature to help horses keep their footing, but it also means anything with wheels has to be lifted over the bridge. I watched as a young woman in a hijab tried to coax her toddler to get out of his pushchair so she could do just that. The tired little tot in a navy pair of dungaree shorts simply stared blankly at his mother. In the end she and her husband picked the buggy up with him still sat inside, and carried him across like a mini maharaja in a palanquin.

I stood on Stari Most for a while, watching the tourists from different religious and ethnic backgrounds making their way tentatively over the new Old Bridge. Amongst them were a large number of Gulf Arabs who had come from Sarajevo on the increasingly well-trodden itinerary that took in the two battle-scarred cities. As they negotiated the treacherous steps, I could hear them calling out to each other with that ubiquitous Arab phrase, 'Yallah, Yallah!', and was reminded of Evliya's entry for Mostar, which included a description of the local daredevil tradition of diving off the famous Stari Most eighty feet into the waters of the Neretva. Evliya describes how the young boys would also shout 'Ya Allah!' as they threw themselves off the bridge, sometimes in twos or threes, somersaulting and even 'embracing each other'.

The boys did this to entertain visitors to Mostar who rewarded them with money, just like tourists do today every time a local stands atop the apex of the Stari Most and throws themselves off it – except they no longer shout 'Ya Allah!'

Before the war, Mostar's population had numbered around 130,000, with Croats and Muslims in the majority, followed by Serbs – there had also been Jews right up until World War II – all living in relative harmony, something Evliya had noted as well, in what might again be described as an example of *komšiluk*. However, after the Bosnian War the population dwindled to a mere thirty thousand living in a much-divided city.

Mostaris like Pašić have always seen their bridge as a unifying force. In their eyes it embodied the multi-ethnic, multi-religious and multi-confessional place Mostar and Bosnia aspired to be, and when it was gone, so too it seems was that aspiration. After the war, each side of the Neretva had its own currency, police, licence plates and school system. On 10th February 1997, Bosnian Croats and police opened fire on a group of unarmed Muslim mourners, killing one and injuring several. Their crime: coming over to the west bank to visit graves at the cemetery of a destroyed mosque.

It was getting late by the time I began heading towards Mostar's most impressive domed mosque, the Karađoz Bey Mosque, my last stop for the day. Built at the same time as the city's famous bridge, it too has long been falsely attributed to Sinan.

I walked down the newly cobbled, pedestrianised road towards the Karađoz. As the temperature began to drop with the setting sun, small lights appeared inside the tourist shops lining the route. Outside one hung colourful mosaic lanterns, beneath which stood its elderly shopkeeper who I *salaamed*. She smiled and replied, '*Walaikum as salaam.*' I did the same with others who had stepped out to enjoy the cool of the encroaching evening. It felt mildly exhilarating to be walking down a European street and be able to greet complete strangers in this way. I had never done that before, not even in Sarajevo where I hadn't been able to pluck up the courage. Here, wandering through the historic Muslim side of Mostar, it felt natural and rather liberating.

The Karađoz can easily be missed: firstly, because nobody seems to come looking for it, but mostly because it isn't that impressive. In fact, staring at its modestly sized central dome, above a three-domed portico with a tiny courtyard, it is easy to see why experts had dismissed any direct links to Sinan. But then it wasn't Sinan that had brought me here. I wanted to visit the Karađoz because it was built by the same masons as those who had constructed the original Stari Most. I might not have been able to see the original bridge, but in visiting the Karađoz, I could at least see something moulded by the hands of those great medieval artists, who in all likelihood were Catholic masons brought from Dubrovnik – at the time, part of the small Republic of Ragusa. The clue is in the fact that the mosque's domes are made of cut stone just like the segments of the bridge. It is therefore very likely that the mosque was also designed by Hayreddin and the plans overseen by Sinan. The name is believed to be the nickname of the founder, a certain al-Hajj Mehmed Beg al-Za'im, a large-scale fief holder about whom little is known, except that he was charged with overseeing the construction of the city's bridge and, as his title suggests, performed the Hajj pilgrimage to Makkah.

Mehmed's mosque is surrounded by a low stone wall and has a façade dominated by the lead covering the mosque's double portico, which underneath is plain in design except for a few painted, but now faded, potted fir trees and the stylised *muqarnas* that top its columns.

A small fountain beneath a pointed roof, also on slender pillars, sits in the mosque's untidy courtyard overlooked by an L-shaped building that was once a *madrasa*. The original complex had an *imaret* too. Around the back is an overgrown cemetery of ancient tombstones topped with small, round turbans. Many of these lie on their side, or at angles they were blown into during the war. Old pictures of the Karađoz show the mosque was another monument heavily targeted by Serb and Croat forces. Missiles created huge gaping holes in the portico and main dome, and its slender minaret was completely toppled over.

I entered the well-lit central hall to find I was alone except for an old man in a blazer examining the names inscribed on the squinches of the dome. 'Allah' and 'Muhammad' took pride of place at the front, whilst the others – names of the four most-famous early caliphs – were spread out through the rest of the room. I sat down to pray the two customary *rakats* I always offered upon entering a mosque. In front of me was the *mihrab*, a plain white niche crowned with a stuccoed *muqarnas* pattern and a colourful floral design. Above this were Arabic inscriptions: the Islamic declaration of faith, 'There is no god but God and Muhammad is His Messenger'; and two stylised *tugrahs* – imperial signatures – one of which I imagined to be Sultan Suleiman's. The interior of the Karađoz lacked any vibrancy, except for a series of flags decorating the large stone *mimbar.* These were green with a white crescent and star, and resembled the flag of Pakistan minus the white column.

I sat there wondering what flag it was and where I had seen it before, but I simply couldn't remember. It was clearly important as I counted at least six adorning the *mimbar. Maybe it's a historic flag of Bosnia?* I thought, but there was no-one around to ask. Even the man in the blazer had got bored and disappeared.

Mystics and Mountains

BLAGAJ

We left Mostar shortly after breakfast and drove south through the city following the winding river Neretva until the valley broadened and the road split near the small settlement of Gnojnice. From there the vast mountains of the Bišće plain began to edge closer as we neared the town of Blagaj.

Blagaj is a lovely green and fertile place, filled with terracotta-tiled houses mostly painted white or a mellow yellow. The older properties are of stone; several on the outskirts have been abandoned and reclaimed by the local flora.

After passing a small white Orthodox Church, the road arced left and a vast Muslim cemetery opened up before us. Behind a thin green gate, there were a series of tombstones just like the ones I had seen at the Karađoz's cemetery in Mostar. Some were topped with stone turbans and the odd red-painted fez, whilst others were smooth and rounded like the end of a lollipop stick. Most of them looked very old, but a few close to the road were recent burials, judging by the fresh inscriptions.

'Looks like a lot of Muslims live here,' Amani said, as we neared a fork in the road and turned right. Anaiya wasn't so sure.

'I don't know, most of the graves look old,' she observed.

'I think you're right. Maybe Blagaj used to have a lot of Muslims, but it doesn't look like there are that many Muslim burials nowadays,' I said.

'Yeah, that church we passed did look quite new, maybe more Christians have moved into the town since all the fighting and war.' Anaiya was reading *Zlata's Diary,* an account of the Bosnian War through the eyes of 11-year-old Zlata Filipović, which had made her quite aware of the impact the '90s conflict had on locals.

The flowing blue waters of the River Buna soon appeared on our right as the road began to descend towards the bank. We parked up close to a small stone bridge and walked against the river's flow. We passed a small wooden hut selling homemade jam and local honey, and several white signs with *Huwa* written in Arabic in green and black – the first real clue this was a spiritual Muslim space. *Huwa* or *Hu* refers to God and is the sound heard at the end of the Arabic *Allahu* when repeated over and over again by Sufis as part of their meditative 'remembrance' known as *dhikr* – sometimes shortened to just *Hu.* As a result, the phrase has taken on mystical interpretations.

A stone path led down into the main complex and then finally we saw what Tamara had come all this way for. It was so beautiful it stopped us dead in our tracks. Tamara was beaming.

'I can't believe a few months ago I was looking at this on the computer screen, thinking how amazing it would be to visit it one day. And now here I am.' She rested her head affectionately on my shoulder. 'Thank you,' she said.

I squeezed her hand, relieved she had recovered in time.

'I'd like to go here when we visit Bosnia,' she'd said as we had sat planning the trip in our home in northeast London. Smiling, she manoeuvred her laptop screen so I could see what was on it.

A quaint Ottoman lodge sat nestled in the bosom of a dramatic rock precipice, from the foot of which emerged bubbling crystal-blue waters. The fairy-tale house was framed by greenery and the photographer had used a long exposure to blur the cascading water in the foreground as it fell over smooth boulders. It was quite the magical scene.

'What is it?' I had asked.

'A Sufi lodge, called the Blagaj Tekke,' replied Tamara with a smile. She was brilliant like that.

Once we'd decided on a destination, Tamara would spend hours each day looking up all the cool places we could end up visiting. What she found she'd put into little mind maps, tables or mood boards. There would be fun things for the girls to do; stuff we'd all enjoy as a family; nice eateries she'd read about; places to immerse us in the local culture; and, always, she'd indulge me by finding some intriguing piece of Muslim heritage to check out.

I kept staring at it on her laptop, stunned by the Blagaj Tekke's beauty. When I looked up its history, I got even more excited. It was definitely going on our itinerary, as it had also been on Evliya's.

Adnan didn't strike me as a mystic, unless you consider the hairy, gap-year-student look to be that of a modern ascetic's. Marrying a dishevelled beard with handsome young looks, he had the kind of jawline that belonged in a Calvin Klein photo shoot. Not his clothes, mind. Loose, baggy trousers and a top with patterns found in 'boho ethnic' shops across the West, they looked more adept for sleeping rough and travelling cheap. But he wasn't a traveller – well, not in the modern sense, anyway. Adnan was a mystical wayfarer: a Sufi of the Order of Naqshbandis, the current custodians of the Blagaj Tekke.

'I am a dervish,' Adnan explained during a momentary pause in the stream of tourists wanting to get inside the quaint lodge. Our family was amongst them. Tamara and the girls were busy putting on the colourful scarves and loose-fitting skirts made available to ensure all visitors entered the sacred space dressed modestly. 'I wish it served the original purpose but it is not possible. If you come here as *musafir* (traveller), we cannot accommodate you any more.'

'So this is no longer an active *musafirhan* (travel lodge)?' I asked.

'No, it is no longer a *musafirhan*, but it is still active. We still have *dhikr* taking place here in the way of the Naqshbandi Order on Tuesdays and Sundays after *Maghrib salah* (sunset prayer) and anybody is welcome to come along and join in.'

Dhikr literally means 'remembrance', but within Sufi practices this is a meditative form of remembrance often conducted in a group setting led by a learned teacher or sheikh. Sufis are Muslims that focus on the 'inner', mystical dimensions of Islam, which encourage a more ascetic way of life. Historically, they could be either Sunni or Shia and also followed orthodox Islamic law, as they believed that, to reach the 'inner' spiritual Islam, one had to observe the 'outer' external practices, such as performing daily prayers, fasting and giving to charity. Like Adnan, a Sufi normally belonged to an Order, which has its own defined ritual practices, including how to perform *dhikr*, as well as its own doctrines and values inspired by a sheikh. Within these Orders the Sufi or *murīd* (student/wayfarer) is led by a sheikh as they develop and progress spiritually along the Order's defined *tariqa* or 'pathway'. The ultimate aim for all Sufis is nearness to God through a spiritual and mystical 'union'.

The first written record of the tekke is actually made by Evliya, who came here on the same trip that brought him to Mostar. Evliya, whose father was a famous dervish, also saw himself as a dervish and a Sufi.

In fact, Evliya's name is derived from the Arabic word *Awliya*, which in Sufism means 'friends of God', a term normally reserved for saintly figures. Evliya, like many Sufis, would also often refer to himself as *bu hakir*, which means 'poor' or 'humble one'. Even many of the literary references Evliya makes in his book are of revered Sufi figures, like the mystical Khidr and the early female Sufi Rabia. So it is no real surprise that, when the great Ottoman came to Mostar, he decided to make the short trip down to Blagaj.

Evliya came to the tekke in 1664, two years after losing his great patron and uncle, Melek Pasha, having earlier lost his father. These two men were the biggest influences in the great traveller's life. It was his father who urged him to keep a journal of his travels and suggested the name *Seyahâtnâme,* and Melek was his biggest patron, taking Evliya all over the empire with him.

I looked up at the large sand-coloured rock that hung over the beautiful lodge. Nesting swallows danced around it, their cries drowned out by the aqua-green waters of the Buna as it emerged from a spring somewhere deep beneath us. The lodge's gallery hung over the waters like a balcony from a Shakespearean love story, and I imagined Evliya had sat there, pausing and reflecting, maybe even praying on it. It felt thrilling to finally be in a place I knew Evliya had also been – he'd visited the bridge in Mostar of course, but not the bridge *I* saw. This was somewhere I could truly connect with the great Ottoman.

Evliya came as a wayfarer when the tekke was probably home to a mystical Sufi sect known as the Bektashis, the founders of the tekke. The Bektashi Order is named after a 13th-century saint, Haji Bektash Veli, from Khorasan in modern-day Iran. The order favours an unorthodox and mystical interpretation of the Qur'an, which can sometimes lead to practices frowned upon by more conservative

Sunni Muslims. Bektashis also observe many of the traits commonly associated with Shia Islam, like revering Ali, the Prophet's cousin, son-in-law and the fourth caliph; observing Ashura; and commemorating the Battle of Karbala. The Order is led by an experienced spiritual guide known as a 'baba' and, as a sect, Bektashism began to really take shape in the early 16th century, around the same time the Ottoman Empire was expanding and, most importantly, tolerating heterodox forms of Islam. Bektashism was adopted en masse by the empire's janissary corps. These were elite soldiers made up of the sons of Christian subjects – often forcibly through a system known as the *devshirme*. As a result, the Bektashi sect spread far and wide, all over Anatolia and the southern Balkan countries, especially in Bulgaria, Albania and Greece.

Following the abolition of the janissary corps in 1826, Bektashism was banned as the Ottomans began to increasingly favour more orthodox interpretations of Islam. Soon tekkes were closed or destroyed, and the babas and dervishes sent into exile.

'There are two mystics buried here,' Adnan said, pointing towards a smaller building attached to the tekke's northwestern edge. 'One of them, Sarı Saltık, is loved very much by the Bektashis who built this *tekke*.'

'I see, but this is not a Bektashi tekke now?'

'No, Bektashism is no longer popular in Bosnia. It is very popular in Albania, but of course Bektashis still sometimes come here to pay their respects to the babas.'

I later found the tombs Adnan was talking about. Inside a plain white building two graves sat side by side surrounded by a series of colourful rugs with Turkic patterns. Both were shaped like huge Toblerone bars, covered in green velvet with turbaned headstones.

Several giant ornamental *tasbihs* were draped over them, as well as coloured cloth with invocations and prayers written in Arabic. The room was locked so I had to peer through a wooden window, above which, in green, was painted the word 'huwa' again.

A stone tablet outside the mausoleum said the tekke had been built in the 15th century by dervishes who wanted to 'love creatures for the sake of the Creator'. It also said that other Sufi Orders – including the Qadiri, Rifa'I and Halveti – had used the tekke in the past. Finally, the tablet confirmed that one of the graves was indeed Sarı Saltık's, and the other belonged to Acik-Pasha Sheikh. I was the only one reading the tablet, which was inscribed in four different languages. Nobody else seemed interested in the tombs at all.

Very little is known about Acik-Pasha (possibly an early teacher at the tekke), and it is unlikely *the* Sarı Saltık is actually buried here. Sarı was a 13th-century disciple of Haji Bektash Veli, credited with bringing Bektashism to the Balkans, which is why he is venerated as a saint by followers of the order. The great Moroccan Muslim traveller Ibn Battuta claimed to have met Sari during his visit to the northern Balkans, describing him as an 'ecstatic devotee' about whom Battuta had heard things 'reproved by the Divine Law'. It sounds like Sarı was a bit of a maverick and, as with many of these maverick-cum-saints, over time various legends developed about him. He is said to have performed numerous miracles, the most apt of which was his ability to be in a number of places at the same time, which is just as well as there are Sarı Saltık tombs also in Albania, Romania and Turkey.

Sufism has always been a big part of my identity. The northeast of Bangladesh where I was born is home to the tomb of another mystic Ibn Battuta met, Hazrat (the Holy) Shah Jalal, though he left a much better impression on the wandering Moroccan, who considered him a remarkable man and one of the great saints. Like Sarı in the Balkans, Shah Jalal is credited with bringing Islam to the region. As a result, there are roads, schools, airports, hotels and hundreds of mosques named after him in Bangladesh; with the growing size of the Bangladeshi diaspora in the West, this is now also the case in places like the US and the UK.

As children, whenever we visited 'home' – the term used to describe Bangladesh by our parents – a trip to the tomb in the centre of Sylhet town was compulsory. There we would be slowly led around the various sites and relics, which included huge 'miraculous' cooking pots and magical catfish, as we listened to the amazing story of how the saint and his band of loyal followers defeated the local Hindu king in the most fantastical ways. There were flying carpets, magical beasts and miracles aplenty. I loved the stories; it was like having our very own Bangladeshi series of the *Arabian Nights*.

The tour always ended at the tomb of the saint, where we were asked to seek Shah Jalal's blessings and intercession – something that changed over time as our family adopted what they believed to be 'correct' Islam. I still recall the last time I visited the tomb with my parents; my father expressly made the point that I should only pay my respects to Shah Jalal and not direct any prayers or requests to him. Those, he explained, physically positioning us so we were facing Makkah, should be exclusively reserved for God. It was one of the first times I became aware of my family's shifting religious position, but at the time I was too young to appreciate why or towards what.

'I could actually live here,' Tamara whispered, as we entered one of the tekke's large rooms with divan-like seating all the way around.

The cushions had deep-red Turkic patterns, and on the windowsill sat two books on wooden stands: one was the Qur'an and the other a Bosnian translation, on top of which was a *tasbih* – like those used in *dhikr*. We both leaned forward to look out on to the blue waters of the Buna as it rushed forth from a deep cavern.

'It's just so magical, isn't it?' Tamara was looking up at the rock that loomed over us, watching the birds dancing in its shade. I didn't answer, I didn't have to. She wasn't *really* asking at all.

I sat down beside her, overcome by a wonderful sense of contentedness. Because of Tamara, we were now in a room where just a few centuries ago Evliya would have been too. Maybe he prayed or lost himself in ecstatic *dhikr* within the confines of these very four walls. It felt amazing to connect with Evliya in a place as special as this. It was my turn to thank Tamara.

Outside, we could see people had hired canoes and were slowly drifting down the Buna, away from the lodge towards the stone bridge; others were sipping thick Bosnian coffee in the shaded seating of the tekke's café. On the opposite bank, large restaurants overlooking the waters were preparing for the lunchtime rush. It was the very picture of a tourist trap, and yet everyone seemed respectfully restrained. Even the small Arab children who had accompanied their parents from Mostar were sitting seemingly in a trance, licking their ice creams.

Everyone walking around the interior of the lodge was dressed modestly. Nobody wore shoes. People hardly spoke, and if they did it was brief and whispered. Despite the obvious photogenic nature of the space, few people were obsessing over taking any. When they did, it was done respecting the fact that this was an active place of worship, where prayer mats were left out facing Makkah for those that wanted to pause, reflect and remember.

This was a special space.

The spectacular coming together of so many stunning natural elements had created something magical, maybe even mystical. And it was this energy the dervishes of antiquity had sensed when they made it their place of *dhikr*. And it was this energy that no doubt brought Evliya here.

'I think this might be one of the most spiritual places I have been to. It's even more magical than I dreamt it was,' said Tamara, leaning back on one of the divans, her eyes fixed on the blue serenity outside the window.

I smiled and made my way into a smaller room where a man in jeans and a blue stripy polo shirt was kneeling; his cupped hands in front of his closed eyes. Nobody else was in the room, which faced towards the Buna and Makkah. A wooden incense burner sat on the windowsill, where net curtains fluttered in the faintest of breezes. The room was filled with the soothing sound of rushing water. I put down my camera and rucksack and went to assume the position for prayer. As I turned, I noticed Amani and Anaiya walking through. They mouthed that they were going to head downstairs and I gave them a thumbs up, before raising my hands to either side of my head and quietly declaring that God was indeed great.

The Bloody Bridge
on the Drina

VIŠEGRAD

After Mostar and Blagaj, we headed towards Bosnia's border with Serbia to begin our circular route clockwise around the western Balkans. We had booked a few days in a rural getaway in the tiny Serbian village of Rudine, and from there we would move down to the southwest of the country.

I had chosen a route into Serbia that would take us through the town of Višegrad, where I wanted to stop briefly before crossing the border. The main reason for this was to see the UNESCO World Heritage Mehmed Paša Sokolović Bridge near the entrance to Višegrad. This had been commissioned by the grandest of grand viziers, Sokollu Mehmed Pasha and built by the 'Turkish Michelangelo'. A stopover in Višegrad meant finally seeing a genuine Bosnian Sinan.

Our first glimpse of the bridge came as the white Megane rounded one of the last mountains and the road descended into the Drina valley. It was a gloriously sunny afternoon and we had the perfect vista of all eleven solid-masonry arches spanning the beautiful blue river. Each one was perfectly reflected in the jade-coloured waters, creating eleven circles that looked like they could be magical portals to another world.

For Tamara and the girls, the stopover was an opportunity to stretch their legs, have some lunch and maybe sneak in an ice cream. Tamara had humoured me on the bridge's monumental significance, but the girls – at twelve and fourteen – could only get so excited about something that crossed water and looked quite old.

So whilst the three of them explored the banks and cooled off by dipping their toes in the blue waters, I headed to the middle of the bridge to find the centre pile that bore the name of the fascinating grand vizier.

Sokollu Mehmed Pasha's story reads like a Disney movie script: a poor Christian boy snatched by imperialists and thrown into a world of all-powerful sultans, brooding princesses, conspiring sultanas and scheming viziers, before rising up to rule the world. Sokollu's life really was a marvellous tale and the bridge an apt metaphor of that life.

Sokollu began the bridge in 1571 at the height of his powers, having become the de facto ruler of the Ottoman Empire as grand vizier to Sultan Selim II, known as 'The Drunk', who was so uninterested in ruling he effectively left Sokollu in charge. The bridge therefore represented the pinnacle of his life, as did the fact Sinan built it, guaranteeing its status as one of the great Ottoman monuments.

This coming together of the two great Ottomans gave the story another fascinating dimension as both Sokollu and Sinan were *devshirme*: Sinan, like Sokollu, had been taken from his Christian family as a boy and put into the Ottoman ranks. The bridge then was also the story of two Christian victims of this cruel and evil Ottoman practice standing together: one as ruler of the Muslim world and the other as the greatest architect in Muslim history. The bridge was an ode to *devshirme*.

Devshirme was first imposed by the 15th-century Sultan Murad II, who wanted to create an army exclusively loyal to him. The members of this army could not have Muslim ancestry – that way they could make no claims to the throne. The new army he created was called the janissary corps, made up of captured and converted Christian boys who were trained and educated by the Ottomans. It was a practice adopted by all consecutive sultans right up until the early 19th century when Sultan Mahmud II dissolved the janissaries. This meant for four centuries the Ottomans continued the un-Islamic practice of periodically 'harvesting' the most able and talented sons as a 'levy' from their Christian subjects; two of these were named Bajica (Sokollu) and Joseph (Sinan), and both were taken between the ages of sixteen and twenty.

Their childhood stories are not well documented, because *devshirme* boys were expected to leave their Christian identity behind, something Sokollu's bridge has also come to represent. This latter dimension is entirely down to 20th-century Bosnian Croat author, Ivo Andrić, who powerfully evokes the separation of captured young Christian boys from their mothers in his historic novel, *The Bridge on the Drina*. Andrić describes the mothers following their sons wailing, reminding them not to forget who they are, before describing one of the boys as a dark-skinned ten-year-old from Sokolović. Andrić imagines the boy watching his mother get as far as the banks of the Drina, where he is taken across by the ferryboat and she is left helplessly behind. This trauma is what Andrić, in his book, says motivates Sokollu to construct the famous bridge: it is done to 'free himself from this discomfort'.

Andrić went on to win a Nobel Prize for his work of fiction, but he was writing in the early part of the 20th century when anti-

Ottoman sentiments were at their peak in the Balkans. Toeing the same line as the Bulgarian revivalist historians, in his PhD he describes Turkish-Muslim rule as entirely negative and almost every depiction of a Muslim in his novel is derogatory or monodimensional. As a result, most Bosniaks view his work as Islamophobic. In Serbia, where Andrić lived out his days, he is viewed as a national hero.

Nevertheless, Andrić is certainly a convincing orator and his fictionalised imagining of the pain and plight of young *devshirme* moved me in the same way British-Turkish author Elif Shafak said it 'shifted forever' something within her. Andrić's novel made Shafak consider the lives of the 'Other' in the *devshirme* narrative for the very first time.

I felt the same as I stood in the middle of the beautiful stone bridge looking up at the centre pile featuring Sokollu's name. The pile resembles a huge sand-coloured doorway with a pointed arabesque frame in the middle, like a prayer niche only not as deep. Looking beyond the centrepiece to the mountains that wrap themselves around the town of Višegrad, I wondered how far away the grand vizier's village of birth was, and how far his mother might have walked in pursuit of her stolen son. Did she walk at all? After all, Sokollu was probably seventeen years old at this point, a man rather than a boy. Sokollu's story is also intriguing because all the evidence suggests he actually retained a strong connection to his family, helping many of them take up prominent roles within the empire and even carving out a kind of Ottoman Sokolović dynasty.

A small boat of tourists on a river cruise floated towards the bridge, passing through one of its impressive masonry arches. Two men stood knee-deep in the water close to the west bank, patiently holding their fishing rods. One wore a white baseball cap and the other a blue vest.

On the Višegrad side of the bridge, I could see Tamara and the girls had found a small café overlooking the river. The riverbank continued on that side for a short while until it was broken by the Rzav, one of the Drina's tributaries. Here the small black dome of the Orthodox church in the peculiar 'town' of Andrićgrad could be seen. Originally a film set sponsored by the Republic of Sprska for a movie based on Andrić's novel, the town is now a tourist attraction.

I stared out over the terracotta-tiled rooftops of Višegrad's houses, most of them three or four storeys in a style reminiscent of ski chalets. On the river bank there were a few high-rise blocks of apartments with views over the Drina. The town is on a slope and so everything is built in a terraced style, climbing up towards the hills that back on to it. Višegrad looks very green because of large trees that dominate the skyline, except in one area where the beautiful, black, onion-domed Crkva Rodjenja Presvete Bogorodice is, its brilliant-white bell tower reaching for the sky the way minarets once did here in Višegrad.

Our drive to Višegrad had followed the Drina valley for much of the route and the ubiquitous minarets had gradually disappeared the closer we got to the Serbian border. The last major mosque had been in the city of Goražde, just before we entered the Republic of Sprska. The town's multi-domed Džamija Kaserija sat gleaming on the bank of the shimmering Drina. When we stopped to take pictures of it, we noticed local shops with mannequins in the windows wearing hijabs. After Goražde, the mosques were replaced by Orthodox churches.

Looking at Višegrad's skyline today, you could be mistaken for thinking there are no Muslims here, yet before the war Višegrad was a multi-ethnic, multi-religious town, with Muslims making up more than half its population.

That all changed in May 1992, when one of the war's most brutal campaigns of genocide was carried out against the area's Muslims by the Bosnian Serb Army and the local Serb-controlled police, who also created torture camps and brothels where local Muslim women were detained and raped. One of the women, Jasmina Ahmetspahic, was seen throwing herself to her death from the window of one such brothel after being raped for four continuous days.

In total, around three thousand Muslims were murdered in Višegrad, including more than seven hundred women and children. They were killed by being burned alive in locked buildings or lined up and executed on the historic bridge, before being thrown into the Drina. During this period the river Drina is said to have turned crimson with the blood of the victims and became so filled with bloated and mangled bodies that the manager of the Bajina Bašta hydro-electric plant, downstream and across the border in Serbia, complained that the corpses were clogging up his dam.

In 2010, when it was drained for repairs, the remains of the 390 individuals that had 'clogged' it up were discovered in the lake's bed. DNA results identified several of the victims. The oldest was aged ninety-two and the youngest was just three years old. One of those identified was Jasmina Ahmetspahic.

The Višegrad genocide ensured no semblance of Islam was left in the town, except the bridge, where now every May the families of the victims gather to throw three thousand roses into the Drina, and once again turn its waters crimson. They then make their way up to the Straziste cemetery on the northern bank of the Rzav, where many of the victims have since been buried. The cemetery is a ten-minute walk from Višegrad's only mosque, the resurrected Careva Džamija, rebuilt from scratch after the 16th-century mosque was burnt and bulldozed by Bosnian Serbs.

This was paid for by Višegrad's Muslim diaspora now living across the globe, in a similarly defiant act to Mostar's Amir Pašić. The Muslims of Višegrad also refused to have their heritage completely wiped away, but what they couldn't do was bring back the mosque's imam; Safet Effendi Karaman refused to leave Višegrad without his 'flock' when the killings began and paid for this with his own life. At the time of our visit, his remains still had not been found. It is believed he was brought to the bridge on the Drina and had his throat slit before being thrown off it.

PART TWO

SERBIA
AND KOSOVO

Serbia's Dirty Little Secret

RUDINE AND SJENICA

It took us an hour to get to the quaint little village of Rudine from Višegrad. Nestled deep in rural Serbia, our accommodation sat on a gentle slope in a collection of small houses surrounded by farmland. None of our neighbours spoke English, yet every morning the friendly middle-aged woman next door supplied us with fresh yoghurt, milk and cheese, even when we insisted we had enough.

Our house had no Wi-Fi or mod cons, just a huge Soviet-era radio, so for the next few days we unplugged, spent more time cooking, reading, playing games and enjoying the Serbian countryside, which was home to a set of stunning waterfalls. Tamara's health continued to improve and Anaiya adopted a local cat she fed every morning. It was the perfect remedy to a busy first week criss-crossing Bosnia and Herzegovina.

The Serbia we experienced around Rudine was the Serbia we had expected to find: there was no semblance of Muslim culture anywhere; no halal food, no-one in hijab, and certainly no 'Muslim buildings'. The only religious buildings we came across in towns or villages were Orthodox churches. This was the Orthodox Christian Serbia I had read about. Not that the Serbians were any less friendly or hospitable then the Bosnians; as the nature of our neighbours illustrates, everywhere we went we were greeted with warmth and friendliness and we had a thoroughly enjoyable time.

However, we were now heading to the country's southwest which, according to our guidebook, was so Muslim it resembled a little 'slice of Turkey'. I read the descriptions, which sounded like the Serbia of Evliya's day, four centuries ago, and wondered why I hadn't heard about this before.

Prior to the Ottoman arrival in the 15th century, the Serbs had created the last great empire of the Balkans under Tsar Dušan. However, following the pivotal Battle of Kosovo in 1389 when the Serbs suffered defeat to an Ottoman army led by Sultan Murad I, the Serbian state became a vassal of the Ottoman Empire. Serbian nobility were allowed to keep their lands and privileges in return for swearing allegiance to the sultan. In order to 'seal the deal', Sultan Bayezid I married Tsar Lazar's daughter, Maria Despina.

By the end of the 15th century though, any semblance of Serbian autonomy had diminished. Caught between the rising power of the Ottomans and the powerful Kingdom of Hungary, the Serbian nobility often sided with the Turks, but also took up allegiances with the Magyars, Skanderbeg – more on him later – and medieval Hungarian warlord, John Hunyadi. Once the Hungarian Empire fell, most Serbs became Ottoman subjects, though a few nobles did continue to offer their allegiance to the Habsburg Holy Roman Emperor in Vienna.

The Serbs paid their taxes and fulfilled their state obligations through a village headman. They were not allowed to bear arms and had to pay an additional tax if they didn't want to fight for the sultan. In some parts, the Serbs were victims of *devshirme*, and this led many to convert to Islam and rise in rank within the empire, such as the aforementioned Sokollu Mehmed Pasha. Apart from the cruelties of *devshirme*, history suggests the lot of the Serbian peasant under Ottoman rule was actually better than most other peasants across Europe, at least until the 17th century. One of the main reasons for this was the Ottoman millet system, which allowed existing social, religious and political institutes to flourish. Some communities were given further autonomy because of their livelihoods, locations or military service. Many non-Muslim Serbs even fought in the Ottoman army, which liked to employ Christian feudal cavalrymen. The Serbs did this because it meant they were exempt from certain taxes and were also allowed to keep their landholdings. Many Serbs fought at Rovine, Ankara, Varna and Constantinople for the Ottomans, and provided 'security' across their territories.

Meanwhile, the millet system, by accommodating the Serbian Orthodox Church's own legal system, allowed the Serbs to retain their religious and cultural identity. The Serbs kept up their epic poetry and folk customs and were able to develop unique traditions to preserve the memory of great medieval Serbian rulers and holy men. Saints like St Sava, Stefan Nemanja, Dušan the Mighty and Lazar the Martyr remained in popular tradition, and epic poetry like the Kosovo Cycle played a significant role in preserving Serbian identity. During this time, the Serbian church also developed the relatively unique concept of a family patron saint through the practice of Krsna Slava.

This Ottoman tolerance for other faiths was highly unusual in pre-Enlightenment Europe, but quite normal in Muslim Europe, as Evliya had already shown us through his matter-of-fact observations in Ottoman towns. In fact, some historians have even suggested Serbian national identity may well have been preserved because of the autonomy the Serbian church enjoyed under the millet system.

Ottoman power in Serbia began to wane after the first Serbian uprising in 1804, as ethno-religious nationalism took hold across the Balkans in what was an increasingly weak Ottoman Empire. By the middle of the century, Serbia was organising for self-rule.

I had never met a Muslim Serb before; did they even exist? I wondered as we drove through spectacular mountain countryside close to the Uvac Special Nature Reserve. The thought of meeting one filled me with excitement.

'Has anyone ever met a Serbian Muslim?' I asked my family. I could see everyone thinking.

'Erm…' Tamara began. 'No, I don't think I have.'

'I didn't even know there were Serbian Muslims until this trip,' I said.

'Hmm, neither did I. Are there?' Amani asked.

'Well, according to the guidebook, the part of Serbia we're headed to is so Muslim, it's like Turkey.'

'I'm trying to think if I even know any famous Serbians,' said Tamara.

'I only know the odd footballer and the famous tennis player, what's his name? Djok… Djokov…'

'Do you mean Djokovic?' Anaiya interjected.

'Yes. How do you know that?' I asked, as we all looked at her in astonishment. Anaiya just did her trademark cheeky grin.

'Oh look, there's a minaret!' Tam exclaimed, pointing to the thin white outline of a classical Ottoman minaret as we entered the outskirts of the town of Sjenica, where we planned to stop for refreshments.

'Look! There's another one in the distance,' Amani added, pointing to a slightly wider one on the horizon ahead of us.

The minarets were back. I headed for the nearest one, turning on to a bumpy road in front of a small white hotel. The girls spotted an ice-cream sign at a grocery store and Tamara noticed the hotel had a coffee shop with Wi-Fi. It was settled. I had an hour to explore.

The mosque the minaret belonged to was much larger than I expected. It had a classic design; there was a wooden *mahvil* at the back and a large central dome in the middle. The walls were plain white with no decorative features and the floor was carpeted red.

As I walked into the main hall, I passed a baseball cap with the American flag hanging on a nail. The mosque's windowsills had children's drawings sitting on them, like entries for an art competition. I wondered which one had taken first prize. Some of them were Arabic calligraphy and others were drawings of different mosques. It was clear the hall doubled as a *madrasa;* a white board on the back wall still had faded Arabic letters on it from a recent class.

After praying my traveller's prayer in front of the dull-pink *mihrab,* I sat thumbing a green *tasbih.* The whole time I was there nobody else came in, but soon I heard a muted commotion outside the mosque's front door.

I stepped out to be greeted by a large group of locals crowding around an old woman in a black scarf. She was grieving. Hearing the mosque door open, some of the faces looked up at me. I had walked out to a funeral.

The elderly woman was being consoled by her daughter and behind her lay a wooden casket with the body of the deceased. The whole thing was happening outside a small white building attached to the mosque. Like many congregational mosques, this one had a special space for local Muslims to wash and prepare their dead ahead of burial. The crowd were mainly middle-aged men waiting their turn to pay their respects, and the queue led all the way back to the gate. My only exit was blocked.

I sat down under the mosque's portico and waited for the crowds to subside so I could leave without intruding, but it soon became apparent that the deceased was very popular, as more and more locals were turning up to pay their respects. I realised I would have to just walk through the gathered crowd or risk spending my whole hour here. Picking up my rucksack and lowering my gaze, I gently pushed through the men, being sure to *salaam* anyone that made eye contact. This had the desired effect, instantly softening the solemn faces as they reciprocated the greeting. Feeling much more confident, when I got to the back of the crowd I decided to stay and watch for a while. That was how I met Suaid.

'It is *janazah* of one woman,' he whispered.

I nodded in acknowledgement.

Suaid and I stood for a little longer watching the proceedings before deciding to break away. I then introduced myself properly, explaining why I had come to visit the mosque. Suaid asked if I knew anything about it and I shook my head. He then led me towards a sign near the edge of the mosque's cemetery.

The mosque was called the Sultana Valide Mosque and had been built by the mother of the last Ottoman sultan, Caliph Abdul Hamid II, in the 19th century. I explained to Suaid that I had lived in Saudi Arabia where part of Abdul Hamid's ill-fated Hejaz railway was built – the Ottoman Empire's last great engineering project. It had been designed to help pilgrims get quickly and safely to the holy cities of Makkah and Madinah, but almost as soon as it was completed war broke out between the Ottomans and the

British-backed local Saudis, and the railway was destroyed. Suaid's English wasn't great, so as I told him this, I had to make 'choo-choo' train noises, which made us both laugh when he realised what I was talking about.

The mosque had been built when Sjenica was the capital of an Ottoman administrative region and at the time it had the largest dome in the Balkans. The Sultana was one of the most important Ottoman mosques in Serbia and the first one I had come across built by the mother of a caliph. This was highly unusual, and yet when I tried to find it in my guidebook, there was no mention of it. I explained this to Suaid and he shrugged his shoulders before suggesting I visit Sjenica's tourist information office to learn more about the town.

As we headed there, Suaid explained that Sjenica was home to six mosques and a large Muslim population. To make the point he showed me the sign above a bookshop called 'Gradska Biblioteka'.

'Look, name,' he said.

Underneath the shop name it read 'Muhamed Abdagic'. We passed several other shops with similar Muslim names.

'It is good place for Muslims now but not in war,' he said, before suddenly stopping to roll up his trouser leg. A large scar ran down the side of his calf. 'From war.'

Suaid was much taller than me and had a thin, wiry frame. His dark, beady eyes were very alert, and he had a tendency to keep glancing at his small black mobile phone. This made him appear nervous and I wasn't sure if I could ask him more about his scar.

We stopped outside a dingy stairwell attached to an ugly communist-era block.

'Tourist information,' said Suaid, pointing up the stairs.

I looked up to a set of iron gates that appeared firmly locked as Suaid jogged towards them and gave them a push, before glancing at his phone again.

'Closed,' he shouted down.

There was a puddle near the bottom of the stairs with a distinct smell of urine. Suaid glanced at it before tutting in disgust.

'Come, I show map,' he said, and began walking with purpose towards the town centre. I wanted to tell him it was OK, and that I could look for it myself, but he was already several steps ahead of me.

We walked beneath some unfinished buildings with exposed red bricks, and on to a small wooden bridge to cross the city's tiny river. This had manmade concrete banks and looked more like a canal. To our right, tall silver birch trees overlooked a large green area with a children's play park.

We stopped in front of a map showing the entire region but with a focus on the nearby Gostilje National Park, for which Sjenica was clearly a gateway. Suaid began reeling off some of the attractions.

'Good for animal, mountains, water...'

'Are there more *masjids*?' I asked.

'Here... and here, also here,' Suaid pointed to invisible places on the map that were not marked up. As he did this, I heard the faint ring of my phone alarm. My time was up, but Suaid insisted on showing me one more thing.

'Same way to Sultana Valide Mosque,' he reassured me as we headed into the heart of the town.

Along the way Suaid *salaamed* several people; some stayed seated at coffee shops, others came up to him to shake his hand. I also shook their hands after Suaid introduced me using the word *musafir* to mean 'traveller'.

The last thing Suaid wanted to show me was still being built. We could hear the electric machinery and drilling long before we saw it. Two men in work overalls were cutting wood and making holes in what would eventually be Sjenica's very own Sebilj, identical to the one in Sarajevo. I asked Suaid why it was being built.

'Gift.' he said. The Sebilj was a gift from Sarajevo to the people of Sjenica, sent as a reminder of the historic link between them.

The population of Sjenica numbers around fourteen thousand, the majority of whom are Muslims that identify as ethnic Bosniaks. The main reason for this is because historically this part of Serbia fell inside Ottoman administrative regions attached to either Muslim Bosnia or Muslim Kosovo. However, following the Ottoman defeat in the First Balkan War, the region became first a part of the Austro-Hungarian Empire and then the Kingdom of Serbia. When Yugoslavia collapsed, it was again a part of Serbia

Having shown me the Sebilj, Suaid explained he had to return to the funeral. I thanked him for his time and also began making my way back.

On our way out of town, Amani and Anaiya spotted several women in hijabs and Tamara noticed signs on shops that read 'helel'. We passed a few more minarets, and near the edge of Sjenica came across a small building called the 'Skola Kur'ana Casnog'; a sign outside read 'the Islamic Community of Serbia'.

Officially, Muslims make up three per cent of Serbia's population. Yet as we headed to the most 'Turkish' town of all – according to our guidebook – I couldn't help but wonder how true that figure really was, and whether we had somehow stumbled upon Serbia's 'dirty little secret': a Muslim Serbia.

'A Muslim Town'

NOVI PAZAR

Like a procession of janissaries performing a guard of honour, vast, shiny domed structures in a neo-Ottoman style – all shimmering glass façades and tall metallic minarets – lined the main road into the centre.

'Whoa,' Anaiya exclaimed, 'there are a lot of mosques here.'

Arriving in Novi Pazar, I had to check we hadn't accidentally crossed a border somewhere and entered Turkey. When the guidebook had said that this was *the* most 'Turkish' town of all, it was not joking. Could this really be Serbia?

'My goodness, Dad, look, there's one… There's another… and another…' Amani was counting minarets.

Tamara pointed to a cemetery with a sprawling collection of slender white tombstones that stretched for almost a kilometre on raised land either side of the road, guarded by a white metal railing. The tombstones looked exactly like the ones we had seen in the cemeteries for Bosnian War martyrs, cascading down the hills overlooking Sarajevo.

This was easily the most Muslim-looking town we had come upon since leaving Bosnia's capital.

'Pork? Hmph. No, no pork. Novi Pazar Muslim town!' The pizza maker laughed and snorted at the same time with a familiar look of disgust. It was a Saturday evening and, after checking into our hotel, we had decided to head straight into town, where one of the girls had spotted the tiny hole in the wall with the word 'pizza' beside it. The roaring clay oven and our rumbling stomachs told us this was the place to refuel. The earlier mosque parade had suggested halal food wouldn't be hard to come by in Novi Pazar, but we still asked the sausage question because we are Muslims from western Europe: when we read 'sausage and mushroom pizza' on a menu, we hear 'pork sausage and mushroom pizza'. And this was Serbia after all: a proud Orthodox Christian country.

Central Novi Pazar was alive with activity. Cafés and restaurants spilled out on to the paved town centre, overlooked by a hodgepodge of Ottoman, Austro-Hungarian and communist-era buildings. Like Sarajevo and Sjenica, there was a Sebilj in the middle, around which sat families and friends eating al fresco and drinking 'Serbian coffee', which looked and tasted suspiciously like Bosnian and Turkish coffee.

We also wanted to enjoy the cool of the late summer evening and began looking for a spot to sit and enjoy our food. Spying a large white stage in front of which locals had gathered, we pulled up some chairs beside an empty table and sat down in hope as much as expectation. The stage certainly looked set for a performance: the lights were on, there was an audio system in the corner, and a host of people milling around near the back. Maybe, we thought, we might be treated to some authentic Novi Pazar entertainment.

Like Sarajevo, Novi Pazar sits in a valley, encased by the beautiful, biodiverse Dinaric mountain range. From the town's historic centre, a mass of red-tiled roofs, needle-like minarets and ugly tower blocks sprawl outwards, seeping into the surrounding green slopes.

And, like Sarajevo, it is an Ottoman town built in the 15th century – in the very same year, by the very same person: the governor of Bosnia, Isa-Beg Ishaković.

Sitting close to an important historic market, along ancient routes where travellers from Dubrovnik, Sofia, Belgrade and Constantinople passed through, Isa-Beg called his new settlement the 'New Market' – 'Novi' comes from the Serbian word for new (*novo*) and 'Pazar' from the Turkish for market (*bazaar*). As with Sarajevo, he established the town by building a mosque, fort, hammam, *han* and an *imaret*. Over time it too became home to a thriving multi-ethnic, multi-faith population that included Jews and Orthodox Christians. By the time Evliya wandered through with Melek Pasha in 1660, on their way to Melek's new post in the Eyalet of Rumelia, Novi Pazar had become the regional capital and one of the most populated towns in the Balkans.

Novi Pazar's prominence began to dissipate after the 18th century, and when the Ottomans were pushed out of the region in the First Balkan War, the town became a part of the Austro-Hungarian Empire and then the Kingdom of Serbia. Despite Novi Pazar's large majority-Bosniak population and its historic location in the Eyalet of Bosnia, it again became a part of Serbia after the collapse of Yugoslavia in the 1990s. However, like Bosnia's capital city, Novi Pazar is very much a Muslim town with over eighty per cent of the urban population professing the faith, making the Serbian town more Muslim than some 'Muslim' countries. We were into only the second week of our journey and not only had we found a 'hidden' Sarajevo in Novi Pazar, but one that could legitimately claim to be its twin.

For a while nothing happened, and so we hungrily tucked into the delicious, crisp halal-sausage pizza. Then Amani and Anaiya spotted an excited horde of elegantly dressed teenage girls, all in identical outfits, heading to the back of the stage.

'Are they bridesmaids?'

'But where's the bride?'

The girls congregated near the back and appeared to be listening to instructions from someone. Their flowing dresses covered them from head to toe; each one exactly the same, virgin white with a gold trim and a matching hijab. Their white Slavic features made them look like a gang of medieval European princesses. As they disappeared out of sight, it was clear they were the ones who would be taking the stage. But still nothing happened.

Suddenly the air was filled with the *Maghrib adhan*. After several days in the Serbian countryside, it caught me off guard. Not the locals though. Many of them, including children, respectfully stopped talking as the call was made, and one or two men got up and began walking with purpose towards some hidden mosque nearby.

Despite passing all those mosques earlier, it was now impossible to see where the *adhan* was coming from. Shops and restaurants blocked our view at the back and the large, intriguing façade of the Hotel Vrbak – a mass of hexagonal glass panels – obstructed our view at the front.

The *adhan* also seemed to signal that the performance was imminent, as many of the empty seats around us began to quickly fill up. The new arrivals were all clearly related to the 'medieval princesses' who appeared from the side of the stage to greet them, affectionately kissing the cheeks of parents, grandparents, aunts, uncles, and little cousins.

We still had no idea what was about to happen but it was clear the organisers had been waiting for the *adhan* to pass. This was also a practice we had seen across the Muslim world, where everything from a game of football to a live performance would be respectfully worked around prayer times, so that no-one was immersed in a menial worldly pursuit when the *muezzin* was calling the faithful to worship. I remember it well from our time living in Saudi Arabia, when my football matches in the evenings would always start just after the sunset prayer – the timing was also about the coolness of the day – and if they went on for too long, the referee always paused the game, just before the *Isha adhan*. Not just out of respect, but also to allow observant players to attend the prayer.

A good few minutes after the *adhan*, the 'medieval princesses' took to the stage. Standing in two rows, with the back one elevated so all faces were on show, the girls now resembled a Muslim choir. A rhythmic drumbeat and tambourine began and the choir started singing in perfect harmony the Arabic verses to a popular recital praising the Prophet Muhammad. We all looked at each other in disbelief, recognising the words. Their next performance was to a Turkish backing track and this time three of the girls stepped forward to lead a beautiful Arabic *nasheed* (Muslim song) about peace and faith.

Soon toddlers were bouncing their jelly legs in tune with the music, making us all laugh, and the audience joined in with familiar verses.

As I held aloft my camera phone to film a short clip, Tamara and I kept throwing glances at each other. We couldn't quite fathom what was happening. Somehow, in Orthodox Christian Serbia we had stumbled upon a Muslim concert.

When the unexpected concert ended, our bellies full of sausage and mushroom pizza, we headed over to the open square in front of the Hotel Vrbak.

Decorative stone bridges criss-crossed the river Ljudska as it backed on to the paved square where locals came to relax for the evening. Old men chewed the fat on benches beside pretty flower beds and shrieking toddlers zoomed around on rented motorised 4X4 toy cars, their parents nattering away with one eye on the pint-sized racing drivers. Some wandered off to grab a snack from the street vendors lining the edges.

'Dad, can we please get some candyfloss?' Anaiya pleaded, pointing to a man pulling out pink swirls from a spinning metal drum.

'Yes! Please, can we have some?' chimed in Amani.

The vendor didn't speak English and so I signalled we wanted two using my fingers. He pointed to some coloured tubs, which were the flavours. Both the girls chose red and we watched as he did his thing. Tamara asked if we could film, by pointing at her camera phone, and he nodded.

The heavyset man, whose work was clearly exhausting judging by the sweat beads gathered on his forehead, began spinning his drum. He then took out a thin wooden stick, and poured red sugary powder into a tube in the centre, beneath which a flame flickered infrequently. Waiting a few seconds, he held the stick close to the edge of the central tube. We watched, mesmerised. At first, we couldn't see anything, and then slowly, very faint, thin, web-like strands of red began to attach themselves to the stick. We collectively cooed.

As soon as the sweaty vendor finished making our second red candyfloss and handed it to Amani, I tried to thrust a 1000-dinar note into his hand (about eight British pounds). But the vendor moved his hand away and shook his head, before starting his drum up again for the next customers, a small boy and his mother. I was confused. Was the note too large or too small? Surely he wasn't expecting to charge more than £4 each for candyfloss?

Begrudgingly, I added another 1000-dinar note, hoping he had made some mistake and wasn't just trying to rip me off. But again, he refused to take my money, and this time he didn't even look at the notes. Could he even see what I was offering? My confusion increased. Surely this was more than enough for two candyflosses. Our dinner for four had cost less.

I decided to try one last time, stretching out the crisp notes to make it clear what I was giving him. But again he refused without looking at the money, or even me, for that matter. He simply shook his head and turned away. It began to dawn on me he wasn't asking for more money at all, he was flat refusing to take any payment, and I suddenly remembered why.

Now overcome with guilt, I tried putting the money directly into his breast pocket. But he saw it coming and moved away, his face breaking into a warm smile.

'Tourist…' he said, shaking his head again.

'Tamara,' I said, turning to my family, who had been watching the children play and missed the entire exchange. 'He won't take my money.'

'Why, Dad, what's wrong?' Anaiya asked, looking a tad alarmed.

'He won't take your money?' Amani repeated.

'Don't you have enough?'

'No, it's not that, I have more than enough. He just won't take my money.'

'Tourist…' said the vendor again, this time addressing my whole family with a smile.

Tamara and I looked at each other. We both knew what he was doing. It melted our hearts, Tamara was almost tearful.

I had forgotten what she had read to me the night before, which is why I was so confused to begin with. As we had sat in our little cottage in the Serbian countryside, getting excited about visiting a 'Muslim town' in Serbia, Tamara had read aloud a section in our guidebook about a strange tradition amongst the vendors of Novi Pazar, where they refused payment for small items from travellers, instead offering it as a gift. It was their way of honouring the traveller, an ancient tradition in this historic market town, where travellers from the great cities of antiquity used to pass through regularly. Now a forgotten backwater in southern Serbia, it was also a way for the vendors of Novi Pazar to show their appreciation to anyone willing to visit their town. When we had read it, we had not taken too much notice, assuming it was unlikely to happen to us.

I asked the man his name and thanked him in English and Arabic. 'Mehrat,' he replied with a smile, bowing his head slightly and putting his hand on his heart. We were genuinely moved, and as we walked away, I mentally reprimanded myself for being suspicious. We then turned to our two girls, who remained confused, to explain the beautiful tradition of hospitality.

Anaiya ripped a tuft of pink candyfloss from her stick and handed it to me. I could see her mulling over what we had just said, as she chewed away.

'So he just gave this to us free, because we are tourists?' she finally asked.

'Yep.'

She paused. 'Can we get more free stuff then?'

'That's not the point, Anaiya!' Amani snapped, stepping into her role as conscientious older sister.

I took Anaiya by the hand and turned her to face the vendor, just as he wiped the sweat from his brow for the umpteenth time. From where we were sat, we could see the amateur construction of his homemade candyfloss machine. Wires ran from the half-drum, which had been sawn from a whole one, and connected to a car battery near his foot. The drum wobbled ever so slightly every time it did a full orbit on its axis, with the vendor having to regularly readjust it to stop it toppling over completely.

'Look at him, Po.' I used the shortened version of her nickname 'Posie' whenever I spoke to her as if she were my little baby girl again. She was twelve now, and in her mind, a fully grown 'big' girl. 'Look at his machine. He made that himself. Can you see how it runs off a car battery? Does he look like he can afford to give anything away for free?'

Anaiya shook her head.

'So why does he?' she asked.

'Because he knows what he loses in money tonight doesn't come close to what he stands to gain with his little act of kindness.'

We had brought our girls up to understand that charity was an important duty for us as people and as Muslims – it was one of the Five Pillars of our faith. They had joined us in volunteering at soup kitchens, handed out parcels from Ramadan food stalls, and made it a tradition to take food, hygiene items and warm bedding every winter to London's homeless. So Anaiya fully understood charity. But this wasn't quite charity. It came from a similar place, but it wasn't the same, and that's why it was probably a bit more difficult for her to grasp. In a way it was for all of us; we had never experienced anything like it on the road before. We had experienced the kindness of strangers for sure, but not working vendors refusing our money because we were travellers. Our experiences had always been quite the opposite; the vendors always wanted our money because we *were* travellers.

The tradition of looking after travellers has always historically been a strong one in Muslim lands, and is still observed by many Muslims today. For three days, any traveller that comes to stay with you should be treated entirely as your guest. To the best of your ability, you should house and feed them so they do not have to spend their own money. It is one of my favourite Muslim traditions, and I have enjoyed the benefits of it many times when visiting friends and family. I have also tried to observe the tradition when my own friends have come to visit, even with my non-Muslim ones.

One of the first buildings Isa-beg built in Novi Pazar was a *han* – a caravanserai. These huge traveller inns were built at the sultan's expense along key trading routes roughly every thirty to forty kilometres (the distance a traveller covered on foot in a day). Any traveller, pilgrim or trader who turned up would receive free lodging and food for themselves and their 'beasts' for three days, at the expense of the sultan.

Whilst a stick or two of candyfloss was not quite the same, it was a glimpse of the spirit of that beautiful ancient tradition, and it warmed me to see it here in a tiny forgotten town in Serbia.

That evening, as we sat in our hotel room after dinner reading the latest news from England on our phones, Tamara suddenly stopped.

'I'm so glad we got to do this. So much of what we read in the news every day seems to be designed to make us feel terrified of the "Other".'

We had been trying to ignore what was happening in Britain since the start of the trip; 2016 had been a difficult year to be 'different' in Britain. The vitriolic outpouring of xenophobia and Islamophobia induced by the Brexit campaign had left us shell-shocked; groups like the English Defence League (a modern BNP) were growing in popularity off the back of it, and at times it felt like a return to the racist Britain of my childhood. This was not helped by an openly

Islamophobic candidate running for president across the pond – Donald Trump. Leaving England behind for the summer had been a welcome break for us all.

'I hope our girls learn from these experiences that the world isn't a scary place and that there's really nothing to be scared of except our own prejudices,' she continued.

I didn't say anything, I wanted to listen.

As parents, we did our best to protect the girls from the 'hate' that had again become socially acceptable. We knew the immunity afforded by the innocence of childhood was disappearing. Tamara and I had often spoken about how to help them navigate it all, and agreed that seeing the world in an informed way certainly helped.

'I feel so lucky we are able to bring them here to these places so they can see how wonderful Europe's Muslims are, and the culture they have in places like this…'

'Places we didn't even think existed', I interjected.

She nodded.

We both knew it was an important point. One of the key undercurrents of the Brexit campaign was 'selling' Britain the idea that Muslim refugees were swarming Europe – as if Muslims in Europe were something new – and that if we didn't leave Europe, they would soon swarm Britain too. Sadly, many Brits bought this hook, line and sinker.

'I am so glad we're able to broaden their horizons by showing them the richness and diversity of *their* Muslim heritage.'

'Yes, especially now,' I added.

Novi Pazar had really affected Tamara. The Muslim 'choir' girls, not much older than our own girls, singing with confidence about their faith and heritage, as their families proudly watched; the man with the candyfloss refusing our money because we were *musafir* in his town – it had all been a wonderful glimpse into the beauty of Europe's Muslim heritage through its people.

The historic mosques, monuments and the mausoleums might have got me excited about Europe's Muslim heritage, but it was the human 'heritage' that touched Tamara, and she knew it was also bound to touch our girls.

Tamara then said something that filled me with sadness.

'But we're privileged. Not everyone has this privilege.'

Pokémon in Hammams

NOVI PAZAR

The next morning, having risen at the crack of dawn and left Tamara and the girls at our hotel, I went for a walk through Novi Pazar's coffee sellers' quarter, on my way to explore its ancient Ottoman sites.

The glass panes of the stores had their owner's names painted on them. Inside, mounds of ground coffee sat behind the counters next to large, old-fashioned metal scales. The shops seemed to belong to a bygone era. I stopped in front of one displaying an old black-and-white photo of Novi Pazar. It showed a wide street with few cars but lots of people. Some were hunched over, carrying goods as they walked past low-rise houses and shopfronts with unevenly tiled roofs. In the background was the faint silhouette of a thick, wide minaret.

Inside, the store was filled with the aroma of freshly ground coffee, some of which still sat beneath two heavy, iron grinding machines in that fine powder-like consistency needed to make Serbian, Bosnian and Turkish coffee. On the floor beside them were jute sacks filled with the dark beans originally brought here by the Ottomans. Now they came from Brasil, according to the writing on the side of the sacks. The shop sold the freshly ground coffee in quaint, little brown-paper packs with the words 'Brasil Caffe' on them. I asked for two.

As with the candyfloss seller the night before, when I went to pay for my purchase, the young vendor refused my money. Again feeling guilty, I pretended not to understand and took out more notes.

The bearded man pushed them back, smiled and pointed at me before using the Arabic word for traveller: *musafir*.

I felt even more emotional this time, standing in that modest coffee store belonging to a different era – an era maybe when such gestures of kindness were the norm. I thanked him in Arabic and indicated that I would pray for him. He suggested that was what he really wanted in return, not money, and his face broke into a large smile. I had instinctively wanted to give him something material, that's just what I was used to doing, growing up in a consumerist society where 'nothing is for free'. But as a Muslim, I also knew he meant it when he said he was happy with just my prayers. He would see them as more valuable because it was the prayer of a traveller – all Muslims know the famous prophetic tradition that says, 'Three supplications are answered without doubt (by God); the supplication of the oppressed, the supplication of the traveller and the supplication of the parent for their child.'

Hamza and Amre were on their school summer holidays and doing what children all over the world were doing that summer – looking for hidden Pokémon in their home town using their phones. Their search had taken them to Gradski Park, which just happened to be the site of the old Ottoman fort – and that's how they came across me, inspecting the large polygonal bastion in the park's northern corner. I had already been around and seen the other two bastions and remnants of the original 15th century wall.

I saw the boys coming towards me, phones aloft in front of them, moving the screens about as they scanned the locality for their next Pokémon. They had just finished searching near one of the park's octagonal towers, built much later in the 19th century by Sultan Abdulaziz during the Russo-Turkish War. When the boys noticed I too seemed to be looking for something, they asked me who I was and what I was doing here. I told them.

'I love London,' beamed little Hamza.

He was small, had brown eyes and hair, and was full of energy. Amre was taller and more laid-back. At fifteen, they both spoke good English. The friendly pair reminded me of the students I taught back in London, and I immediately warmed to them. Hamza told me all about their Pokémon hunt. It became apparent the boys knew their town well, and so I decided to pick their brains.

'Do you know where the old hammam is?'

'We can take you there, if you want,' said Hamza.

Pushed for time, I took the boys up on the offer.

The walk through the old town took us past ramshackle houses identical to those in the photo from the coffee store, and in between checking their phones for Pokémon lurking nearby, the boys asked me a host of questions. What did I do in London? Was it fun? Did I like being a writer and a teacher? Why was I here? Would I write about them and how did I even find Novi Pazar?

'Nobody knows this place!' Amre shrieked.

Both boys seemed to have a low opinion of their home town, feeling it was obscure and insignificant. They both dreamed of being elsewhere; Hamza wanted to go to London and Amre to America.

We soon entered an area where several homes faced in on each other, like a rural homestead. The houses looked Ottoman, with red tiled roofs and exposed wooden beams. This was where Hamza lived, and around the corner was a collapsed building with grass and weeds growing out of it.

'This is the old hammam!' Amre announced.

Cars were parked in front of the ancient ruins that had once had two floors. A pair of locked wooden doors indicated the original entrance; behind these were a number of ceiling-less rooms filled in with mounds of earth. The building's window frames were just empty holes now and the upper floor's wall had mostly collapsed. Two small raised *tambours* held aloft small pockmarked domes, confirming this had indeed been Isa-beg's bathhouse. I looked at the sad mess and sighed, before pulling up my camera.

'Come, come round here, you can look inside!' Hamza exclaimed.

It turns out the hammam had two sections: the collapsed part and another relatively well-preserved section now reappropriated as a coffee spot for locals. We entered through a low medieval doorway, down a pair of makeshift stairs made from scaffold and painted red, into a sunken courtyard that had once been a large room. Several men sat drinking coffee on plastic patio furniture. Thick green ivy grew up the side of the walls, and small potted flowers decorated the edges. Seeing our little band walk in, a few men looked up, nodded at the boys, and carried on sipping their coffee.

Hamza and Amre led me through the complex like it was their own house, showing me all the different rooms. I noticed drainage grooves running along the ground that once washed away bathing water and on the walls hung rusty lanterns wired up crudely. We entered the rooms through narrow arches; one or two still had original concrete baths in them complete with stone steps. Two of the smaller rooms had the same feature we had seen in the collapsed part; narrow squinches atop tall brick arches held aloft pockmarked domes that allowed light to stream in.

The rooms were mostly empty, except for one with spare chairs and someone's mountain bike, where the faint remnants of a red and white arabesque arch could be made out on the back wall. In a larger room, possibly where the locals sat for coffee in the winter, small discoveries had been propped up and arranged around the edges: patterned ceramic bowls, parts of decorative ancient vessels and pieces of marble with Arabic and Persian script. I was lost photographing these when Amre burst in to announce Hamza's father was looking for him and they both had to go.

'We could come back and show you more things?' they offered, as we said our goodbyes.

'No, it's OK, I'll be all right. Thanks for all your help, boys, you've been great,' I replied, relieving them of the obligation to follow around a boring, middle-aged writer interested in old stuff and collapsed buildings.

Both threw me a beaming smile and promised to follow me on social media before heading off to Hamza's dad, or, as I suspected, to grab that Pokémon Amre had just located before one of their rivals did.

I emerged from the dark rooms to find two fat old men sat outside. They looked me up and down with interest. One of them was wearing a rather smart shirt and hat and spoke a little English. He told me that the completely dilapidated section was where the men used to bathe and this, he said with a salacious grin, was where the 'beautiful girls' used to bathe.

I smiled.

'I see. That's why you have looked after this part and not the other one, huh?'

The two men broke into a hearty laugh.

It was no coincidence that in both Sarajevo and Novi Pazar, hammams were amongst the first public buildings Isa-beg built. The tradition of bathing regularly, almost daily, was a common Muslim trait. Washing is a prerequisite for all Muslims before they stand to pray five times a day. In the 15th century, when there would have been no mains water systems in towns and cities, providing large public baths was essential. Isa-beg and the Ottomans were building these baths at a time when many in Christian Europe believed it was purer not to bathe at all, which meant medieval European Muslims were probably the cleanest people on the continent.

The hammam in Novi Pazar was a rare design, where the same building housed separate sections for men and women. When it was functioning, there was a fountain at the northern end and a heating system in the south. Inside there would've been rooms for bathing, scrubbing and steaming, as well as a large swimming pool.

Ottoman hammams were not simply somewhere you went to wash yourself. These were highly civilised social spaces where men and women came to relax, seal business deals and gossip, safe in the knowledge they could do so away from prying eyes. The better ones were fabulously indulgent spaces, as British aristocrat Lady Mary Wortley Montagu discovered in 1763, when she entered a public female-only hammam in Sofia. She describes an opulent space with sofas, cushions and rich carpets, where women of high rank and their slaves sat around drinking coffee, braiding each other's hair, gossiping, bathing or simply relaxing, sometimes for up to four or five hours. Coming from the more reserved West, Lady Montagu was taken aback by the ease with which these Ottoman women lounged around 'stark naked', unconcerned about each other's bodies.

Leaving the hammam, I walked the short distance to the Arap Mosque at the corner of a busy junction. The tiny mosque has no dome but is easily identified by its distinctive, thick, squat white minaret – the same one from the picture in the coffee house. Reportedly built in 1528, the Arap Mosque is one of Novi Pazar's oldest. The size and location gives it the feel of a local mosque, probably used mostly by those working in the nearby rows of shops.

I entered to find several young men sitting on chairs and talking at the back of the main hall. I walked past, laid my bag down where I could see it and prayed. When I finished, I quickly snapped the plain and uninspiring interior, and went to leave.

'Where are you from?' Hamza asked in perfect English, leaping from his chair as I walked past.

Having listened to my introduction, Hamza then introduced his four friends whose names I instantly forgot, except for Darjan, a tall, fair-skinned boy with Nordic features, broad shoulders and a messy ginger beard. The other friends also had beards; only Hamza was clean shaven and had a Turkish look about him.

'Your names sound Turkish,' I said.

'No, they are Arab,' Darjan replied.

'Hamza means "Lion",' Hamza explained.

'Yes, I know, and of course it was the name of the Prophet's uncle.'

'*Sallallahu alayhi wa sallam*,' they all said in unison upon hearing 'Prophet'. The Arabic phrase means 'peace and blessings of God be upon him' and is something many Muslims believe should be said whenever the Prophet is mentioned.

After the small talk, Hamza and his friends wanted to know if I had seen the main Islamic sites in town. I explained that because of my limited time, I was focusing only on the earliest ones.

'I recognised this mosque's minaret from an old photo I had seen. Why is it called Arap?' I asked.

The mosque was also known as the Hasan Çelebi mosque, explained the boys, and according to historians is mentioned in the Ottoman census for 1528. That much they knew to be true. The rest of the details about the mosque were a mix of legend and hearsay. Some say it is called Arap because Hasan, who is credited with building it, was supposed to have been an Arab, though there is no evidence of this. Others believe it is because when the mosque burned down in the late 17th century, it was rebuilt by an Arab. One of the boys reminded the rest that there's also a legend claiming the 'Arab' in question is buried in the town's largest cemetery and was an Ottoman officer. In truth though, admitted the boys, no-one actually knew why the mosque was called the Arap Mosque.

Thanking them for their time, I explained I had to now leave as I wanted to visit Novi Pazar's oldest mosque, the Altun-Alem. Hamza and Darjan asked if they could accompany me as they were at a loose end and I agreed, excited to have a pair of knowledgeable young locals show me around.

The Altun-Alem Mosque was built in the early part of the 16th century and sat in a complex with one of the region's oldest functioning *maktabs*, housed in a beautiful two-storey classical Ottoman building with a large hanging wooden balcony. The *maktab* had arched windows with painted blue patterns and was still attended by many of the town's children.

Both the mosque and the *maktab* had been constructed using the cloisonné masonry technique borrowed from ancient Byzantine churches. The system, which used small, square stones and thin red bricks, had a distinct look and was very popular with early Ottoman architects. The mosque also had a tall, twelve-sided minaret and elegant, slender pillars made from sandstone, as well as three large lead domes. Two of these sat over a breezy portico.

'This is the most famous mosque in our town,' Hamza beamed as I began to snap away. He noticed me pointing the camera at some tombstones next to the mosque. 'Oh, that's a problem in all Turkish mosques. Our forefathers didn't know the *Sunnah* very well,' he explained.

The *Sunnah* is a term used to refer to what the Prophet Muhammad and his companions reportedly did and said. Following it correctly is what makes you a good Muslim, according to many Muslims around the world. This is where the word 'Sunni' comes from, and it is how most Muslims across the globe would describe themselves. Of course, to follow the *Sunnah*, you have to know it, and Hamza was referring to the conservative Muslim position that says it is not *Sunnah* to bury the dead close to the place of worship. Yet this had been a common practice amongst the Ottomans, who sometimes built ornate tombs of the founders of mosques right next to the mosques themselves – something also frowned upon by the orthodoxy.

The most extreme example of this can be seen in the holy cities of Makkah and Madinah, and the historic pilgrim port town of Jeddah in Saudi Arabia, where we lived briefly. Early black-and-white photos show many of the famous cemeteries in these cities were home to ornate tombs of various celebrated companions of the Prophet. In Jeddah, one of the most decorated was said to be that of Eve, the mother of humanity – this is reportedly why the town was called Jeddah, which means 'grandmother' in Arabic. Many of these sites were popular with pilgrims during the Ottoman period, when they ruled the Hejaz region of Arabia where the three cities are located. Travel writers like Evliya, Ibn Battuta and Ibn Jubayr reported witnessing elaborate ceremonies at some of these graves and tombs, something conservative Muslims believe is heretical. The Saudi authorities are amongst these, which is why after the formation of Saudi Arabia all the cemeteries in the country had their tombstones removed and the graves made to look uniform. That way no-one could identify where the famous personalities of Islam were buried any more.

'Do you think we can go inside?' I asked.

'Yes, of course,' Darjan said, leading the way.

As we entered through a set of thick brown wooden doors, I noticed two individuals sitting on the portico outside. One leant casually against the wall. He was dressed in a long Middle Eastern *thobe* and had a dark, unkempt beard and a kindly face. He didn't look much older than Hamza and Darjan. Beside him, with his back to us, knelt a young boy.

'That was the youngest *hafez* in our town,' Hamza explained, as we entered the cool main hall of the mosque. A *hafez* is someone who has memorised the entire Qur'an.

'Really? How old is he?' I asked.

'He is eleven or... wait...'

Hamza disappeared, leaving me with Darjan to photograph the interior, which had undergone recent renovation work. The Altun-Alem Mosque is believed to have been built between 1516 and 1528 by the Ottoman architect Muslihudin Abdulgani. Like most early Ottoman builders, very little is known about Abdulgani, except his other works: a mosque and *han* in Skopje, North Macedonia; and several other buildings in Novi Pazar, including the mosque's *maktab* and a number of commercial buildings.

Altun-Alem means 'Golden Scholar' and remains Muslihudin's most famous work, mainly because it is one of the only examples of an

Ottoman mosque built using the cloisonné masonry technique left in the Balkans. The only other places where this type of mosque is still found are in the early Ottoman cities of Bursa, Edirne and Istanbul. Evliya mentions the Altun-Alem on his visit to Novi Pazar, describing it as an old place of worship and the most interesting mosque in town. I had found another place the great Ottoman had definitely been to and almost certainly prayed in.

The Altun's interior is illuminated by four windows on the walls and three in the dome's *tambour*. There is a simple white *mihrab* with *muqarnas*-style decoration for the imam to stand in and a wooden *mahvil* at the back for female worshippers.

'This is Abdullah,' Hamza said, bringing in a very shy-looking, bespectacled young boy, who resembled an extra from Harry Potter. 'He completed his memorisation of the entire Qur'an at the age of ten. He is eleven now.'

This was a remarkable achievement, but not unusual in traditional Muslim communities, where young boys were trained to be a *hafez* very early on. They were needed to carry out the prayers in the mosques and have historically been seen as guardians of the faith, because they preserved the Qur'an – the literal word of God – for the rest of the community in their memories.

Evliya was one such guardian, having been trained as a *hafez* by the sultan's imam, Evliya Mehmed Effendi, who Evliya may even have been named after. In fact, Evliya was so proficient in his recitation that he was asked to do so at the Empire's imperial mosque, the Haghia Sophia in Istanbul, and this is how he came to the attention of Sultan Murad IV. After hearing the young Evliya's beautiful recitation, Murad made him a royal entertainer and boon companion. It was in this capacity that Evliya came upon the numerous opportunities to travel, for which he would become so famous. Evliya claimed he knew the sacred text off by heart so well he could recite the entire Qur'an in eight hours, and apparently did this once a week throughout his life.

To be a *hafez* was a great honour, and often led to holding an elevated position in one's community. I wondered if Abdullah wanted that.

'So will he continue into a career of religious instruction now?' I asked Hamza.

Young Abdullah looked like any other teenage boy. Dressed in a striped T-shirt and combat shorts, he could just as easily be looking for Pokémon with Amre and the Hamza I had met earlier.

'He says he doesn't want to go into religious instruction, and instead wants to be a doctor,' Hamza translated, before telling me why he felt this was a good career choice. A medicine student himself, Hamza believed it was important to have god-fearing doctors so they would treat their patients with honesty and integrity.

'Many of them here cheat the people. They ask for big "tips" for surgery,' Hamza explained. 'Someone I know went to a doctor that wanted several hundred euros on top of the insurance fee for a procedure and this made them very sad as they couldn't afford that.'

I asked Hamza what doctors earned in Serbia. He said around one thousand euros a month, before admitting that was probably one of the main reasons many of them did what they did, though it was still very wrong.

We left the Altun-Alem after snapping a picture of Abdullah in front of the mosque's *mihrab*. I thanked him and wished him all the best in his career as a doctor.

It was now getting close to the time I had promised Tamara I would return. I would've loved hanging out with the boys for longer, but my family and I were due to head across the border into Kosovo to visit the tomb of the sultan responsible for bringing Islam to the Balkans, and so we headed back to the coffee sellers' quarter.

The route took us down First of May Street towards the Arap Mosque again, past low, uneven medieval shopfronts, some with hanging balconies like the office for 'Islamska zajednica Srbije' – the Islamic Community of Serbia, the sister branch of the one we had seen in Sjenica. It had blue posters advertising the 'Hadz' (Hajj) in the windows and a large green flag with a white crescent and star, which I had first noticed decorating the *mimbar* of the Karađoz Beg Mosque in Mostar and again hanging off the Altun-Alem's minaret. I asked the boys about the flag and they said it was the flag of the Muslim community of the Balkans, but when I asked about the institute, they were dismissive, instead changing the subject.

'Many of these shopfronts are still the same size and design as they were during Ottoman times,' Darjan said.

Back then, explained the boys, the area was the town's 'old bazaar' and the rows would've been filled with trades now long gone, like blacksmiths, metalworkers and leather tanners.

Evliya would've noted every single one of those trades as he walked down this very street all those years ago. He kept a detailed inventory of all the trades, buildings, monuments and shrines in any place he visited – to the point of tedium. Back then, it would've been called Stamboli Road, as it was the main route leading out of town towards the great capital of the empire and, of course, Evliya's home. Did he ever look down it and ask himself when he might return, I wondered.

It felt amazing to be literally walking in the great Ottoman's footsteps along a road that had probably changed very little since his time. I imagined him examining the different stores and workshops, noting them down just as I was doing now with Hamza and Darjan.

Occasionally, we were stopped by their friends, who would shake hands with us all and embrace them warmly. I couldn't help but notice just how many were bearded like Darjan.

'You all have such beautiful, large beards,' I said, after a friend on a bike had greeted them. He shared something else with Darjan: they both wore trousers that did not extend beyond their ankles – another trait popular with conservative Muslims.

'Yes, it is a *Sunnah* to have a long beard,' Darjan said, shooting Hamza a smirk.

I knew exactly the reason he had done that and didn't embarrass Hamza by asking why he didn't have a beard. This was something I had experienced myself, when conservative Islam came into vogue in the East End of London. Suddenly, a lot of the clean-shaven young men I had grown up with started to cultivate large beards that would have given Hagrid a run for his money. They would tell us it was to emulate the Prophet and his companions, just like Darjan was telling me now; that it was *Sunnah*. But what I didn't like was the way those of us who weren't so convinced by this position were made to feel like somehow we were inferior for not having a beard, like we were less 'Muslim' than them. This derision wasn't just limited to a lack of facial hair, it seeped into other things too. The clothes we wore, the way we prayed, who we hung out with and the scholars we listened to, or not. In time it also extended to our opinions of non-believers – thus sowing the seeds of intolerance.

I hadn't known Hamza and Darjan very long, but I liked them. They seemed like two decent kids with integrity, both studying at university and trying to do what's right. I hoped their obsession with keeping to the *Sunnah* didn't blind them to what the purpose of the actual *Sunnah* was. I hoped it didn't narrow their view of the world or make them more susceptible to intolerant viewpoints. They were part of a large population of young people in a town with really high unemployment where, according to recent government data, several young people had headed off to Syria in search of a 'higher purpose' and to join what they believed to be a *jihad*. Prior to their departure, these boys were supposedly recruited by conservative groups that have emerged in the region, groups that were increasingly isolating themselves from their traditional Muslim communities.

When we approached the Hotel Vrbak, Hamza pointed to it proudly and told me his father worked there. I told them about our experience with the candyfloss man in the square the night before, and the impression it had left on us. This pleased the boys.

'It's a shame you don't have more time, otherwise we would have shown you the Amir-Agin Han where travellers were looked after for centuries by the Ottomans,' Hamza said as we parted company.

'Inshallah, I will come back to do that one day,' I said to them both, but what I really wanted to say was: don't forget those wonderful Novi Pazar traditions of welcoming travellers and outsiders from far and wide, be they Muslim, Christian, Jew or otherwise. I wanted to say: don't let that open, tolerant culture of the past be replaced by any new, closed ones masquerading as *Sunnah*. But I knew I couldn't be that candid with them, and so instead we hugged, took some final pictures and said our goodbyes and *salaams*.

The Grandfather of Muslim Europe

PRISTINA, KOSOVO

When Evliya visited the tomb of Murad I, he was unimpressed, to say the least. The Ottoman traveller describes how he and his highranking patron literally have to wade through shit, and when Melek Pasha's elegant robe is stained by human faeces, it is the last straw. The pasha reportedly flies into a rage, disgusted at the state of the tomb of one of their greatest sultans. Meanwhile, his nephew Evliya points out that Murad's murderer's tomb, on the other hand, is 'lit with jewelled lamps and scented with ambergris and musk' and tended to by priests who welcome visitors. The reason the 'infidels' come and shit in here, explains Evliya, is because there is no-one to stop them.

Hearing this, the pasha demands the tomb be cleaned up and hires locals to do so immediately. The shit is shovelled out, a well is dug, five hundred fruit trees are planted and 'a high wall with a lofty gate' is built around the mausoleum so that even 'people on horseback could not get in'. The *türbe* is furnished inside with silk carpets and ornate lamps, candles are lit and rose water is sprinkled. Melek Pasha then employs a family to live there as caretakers, building them a home and paying them an annual salary. The tomb is finally fit for a king.

Evliya and his pasha might well have left yesterday, such was the pristine condition of Murad's tomb when we arrived there from Novi Pazar. A black iron gate opened up to a courtyard surrounded by the pasha's stone wall. Despite two busy highways thundering past on their way to the Kosovan capital, Pristina, there was an air of calm and serenity inside the mausoleum's grounds. A black and white dog sat with his tongue hanging out in the shade of young fruit trees on an immaculately tended lawn. Grey paving stones led up to a white villa that would not have looked out of place beneath a Tuscan sun. A gold plaque said this was the 'Selamlik Building' or 'Cultural and Promotion House', built in 1896 and restored by TIKA, the Turkish Co-operation and Co-ordination Agency. The house was built as a visitors' building shortly after the site was refurbished by Sultan Abdulmejid I. After that the tomb was apparently restored one more time by the Ottomans before it fell into the custody of the Yugoslav authorities who also carried out a restoration.

I had seen TIKA's badge on the walls of several Ottoman monuments already on this journey. One of the Turkish government departments, TIKA was founded in 1992 with a view to support and develop 'Turkic' countries around the world that it shared a common 'language, history, culture and ethnicity' with. In the beginning this was mostly former Soviet countries, but after the turn of the century TIKA extended its work into parts of the Middle East, Africa and the Balkans. I had only seen TIKA's efforts renovating Ottoman heritage, but the aid organisation also built schools, trained doctors and brought clean water to communities in many of these areas.

A second gate led into the historic perimeter of Murad's mausoleum. Everything felt pristine and freshly scrubbed here. TIKA had firmly taken the baton from Evliya and Melek Pasha; Murad's tomb was once again in a condition befitting a king - one who might well be the grandfather of Muslim Europe.

When Murad I, the third sultan of the then-new Turkic Empire, fell at the spot we now stood on in 1389, he had taken his fledgling regional power into a new continent, grabbed coveted Byzantine territories, and turned the Ottomans into an international tour de force. Murad's expansionism put the new empire on course, over the next two centuries, to become the greatest Muslim dynasty the world had ever seen.

Murad died here during the pivotal Battle of Kosovo, which saw the Ottomans claim their first major victory over an allied European army. Their foes on the day were led by Serbian Prince Lazar, King Tvrtko of Bosnia, Vuk Branković (Lazar's son-in-law), Wallachian Prince Mircea the Great and a number of Albanian princes. Those aligned with the Ottomans included Constantine, Bulgarian Prince Kostendil, several Serbian princes that were rivals to Lazar, and a number of Anatolian Turkoman princes.

Evliya rather outlandishly claims Murad put 700,000 infidels to the sword, but historians believe there were around a fifth of that many soldiers at the battle in total. During the clash, the European allies initially had the upper hand, and it was only when Branković defected that the tide turned in favour of the Muslim-led army. It is unclear whether Murad died before or after victory was declared, but upon his death it was his son Bayezid who became the next Ottoman sultan and is said to have built the original mausoleum here on the plain for his martyred father.

How Murad died is a source of contention, with a host of myths and legends emerging shortly after. Evliya offers us one of the more evocative versions: victory had already been declared and, as Murad wandered on the battlefield, 'an inauspicious infidel named Koblaki' rose up from amongst the dead opposition soldiers and killed Murad before trying to flee on horseback. Ottoman soldiers chased after him but couldn't knock him off, until an old woman said they should strike the horse's hooves. When an archer did this, Koblaki was surrounded and had his throat slit.

Evliya says that the sultan's kidneys, liver and heart were then removed to prepare his body for transportation to Bursa, and buried on the spot where the *türbe* now stands. This was the very first Ottoman structure in Kosovo, and became a site of pilgrimage.

Murad, then, was the reason Islam made its way into Europe a second time. Ironically, this was happening just as the community from the first arrival was being squeezed out of Europe. Muslims had turned up in Spain as early as AD711 to found a flourishing society based on interfaith existence, one that accommodated Christians and Jews – something the Ottomans would also emulate. But, within the next century, the Spanish Muslim presence would come to an end when the last Muslim city of Granada in southern Spain was taken by the Catholic Monarchs Isabella I of Castile and Ferdinand II of Aragon in 1492. Many of the expelled Spanish (Sephardic) Jews would make their way into Ottoman territories. This meant Murad's victory ensured the continued presence of Muslims and Sephardic Jews in Europe; one that remains to this day.

The significance of the Battle of Kosovo and the Tomb of Sultan Murad was the reason I had wanted to visit Kosovo, but we had almost not made it. The unease that exists between Serbia and Kosovo had left us feeling uncomfortable.

This began with the Kosovo conflict in 1998, when the country's majority ethnic-Muslim Albanians refused to be part of the 'rump' of Yugoslavia, made up of Serbia and Montenegro. The Kosovans demanded political autonomy and, when this was refused, militant guerrilla group the Kosovo Liberation Army began carrying out attacks on Serbian police and politicians. Serbia responded with a programme of ethnic cleansing and large-scale massacres condemned by the international community. This displaced the entire Albanian population (nearly one million people), who sought refuge in neighbouring Albania and North Macedonia. Eventually, NATO carried out air strikes on the Serb military until it backed down and a peace accord was signed that allowed the Albanians to return to Kosovo, which was put under UN administration. The tensions continued right up until Kosovo declared independence from Serbia in February 2008.

However, at the time of writing, Serbia still refuses to acknowledge Kosovo as a sovereign state and is encouraging others to do the same. As a result, Kosovo is still not recognised by several countries, and this limbo has caused the new Muslim nation to be subjected to numerous economic sanctions and diplomatic difficulties.

Whilst arranging our car rental from London, for example, I was categorically told no company could insure us to enter Kosovo and we would have to purchase independent, local car insurance at the border, which we did in a bizarre scenario that saw me hand over cash to an uninterested vendor at the border for a blue certificate that said I could now legally drive in Kosovo. The dispute also meant that, once we were in Kosovo, if we left through another country we would be leaving Serbia illegally. Hence the reason we returned to Serbia later that day.

We entered the second set of gates to find Evliya's 'radiant shrine of the martyr sultan, Ghazi Khudavendigar' (devotee of God) almost exactly as he had described it: surrounded by several important graves in a well-maintained garden where roses were in bloom. The most impressive of these had tall, slim tombstones with delicate Persian inscriptions and bases inspired by Greco-Roman designs. Two women in long skirts and sleeveless tops walked in ahead of us and were greeted by an elderly woman in a patterned headscarf. She had been sat in a chair in front of a small house to the right of the inner court, the legacy of the caretakers Melek Pasha had installed to look after the tomb. The woman's family were descendants of a Haci Ali from Buhara, who was given the job in the middle of the 19th century. I watched as the two women pushed some notes into the hand of Haci Ali's descendant. She took the money and urged them to go left towards the entrance of the *türbe*, giving them instructions in a language we didn't understand. I took out some notes from my wallet and did the same. The woman, realising we did not speak Albanian, led us round to the door of the tomb, next to which stood an ancient tree bent over with age. The tree was clearly important, as it was now being supported by two thick metal poles. I wondered if it was one of those planted by Evliya and Melek; it certainly looked old enough.

Amani was eyeing it with intent and saw me shaking my head. Climbing trees has always been one of her greatest joys. We are lucky enough to live near Epping Forest on the outskirts of London and, as children, both girls had their favourite trees in there. Often, they would disappear up one, armed with a book, so that for the next half-hour or so, only a tiny face partially covered by a Jacqueline Wilson title was visible through the branches and leaves.

Anaiya was also eyeing up something – the tomb's resident cat. She was crouched down, stroking the thin black cat using a fallen leaf, just as we had agreed – no touching. Neither of them was keen to enter the tomb, so leaving them where we could still see them, Tamara and I headed inside the *türbe*.

Murad was also married to a Tamara; Kera Tamara, the daughter of medieval Bulgarian Emperor Ivan Alexander. Murad asked for her hand in marriage to guarantee peace between the two empires. It was common practice in those days for rulers to marry women from other ruling families and strengthen their ties, but the story of Tamara is interesting for two reasons: firstly, because Tamara did not convert to Islam and was allowed to remain a practising Christian; and secondly, because her marriage is remembered in Bulgarian folklore as a sacrifice she made for her people. Tamara's tomb is also in Bursa, next to her husband's second tomb.

My Tamara and I entered a small porch through a set of glass doors. Inside, it felt like a little greenhouse; a number of large beautiful plants sweated in the warmth created by the brilliant sunshine streaming through the glass. This included thick ivy climbing around the elaborately decorated entrance to the main chamber. Hanging from one corner of the porch was the red flag of Turkey and beneath this were scarves for women to place on their heads. As Tamara put one over her head, I could see a woman circumnavigating Murad's large purple tomb, the way Muslims do around the Kaaba. I nudged Tamara, who looked up and was genuinely shocked. We both were; neither of us had ever seen anything like this at any of the Muslim sites we had visited before. It clearly made Tamara even more uncomfortable than me because soon after this she decided to leave.

'I'm not sure about this,' she whispered as she walked out.

Amani would later tell me it was the look on her mother's face that prompted her to come in. She entered just as the woman was finishing her circumnavigation of Murad's wooden sarcophagus.

The woman then sat down at the head of the tomb beneath the large white turban. Her head was wrapped in one of the borrowed scarves, but her arms remained exposed in a sleeveless vest. As she sat reciting under her breath, the elderly caretaker returned with a cardigan and some books for her to recite from.

Amani and I walked around the room. Above us the *türbe's* dome had the most beautifully painted rose from which hung a chandelier; it was surrounded by Arabic inscriptions and a red and gold floral pattern. Light streamed in from windows on all four walls and I noticed the elaborate latter-day insignia of the Ottoman Empire hanging on one of them; it had two flags in red and green with crescents on them and was encompassed by weapons both modern and ancient. Crowned by a sultan's turban and topped with his *tughra,* various medals hung from the bottom. It was ridiculously busy. On the back wall, in a gold frame was the contrasting simple *tughra* of Murad, in gold on black.

'So that's why mum was a bit freaked out,' Amani whispered as we stepped back into the bright sunlight.

'Yes, it certainly wasn't the kind of ritual I had expected to see in a tomb for a sultan.'

'Shrines freak me out a little,' said Tamara as we headed back to the car.

Tamara's introduction to Islam had led to my reintroduction to the religion. This was via the conservative brand of Islam known as Salafism, which became popular in Saudi Arabia from around the 19th century and preaches a literal, uncompromising 'return' to a puritanical and 'pristine' Islam. Its advocates believe this version of Islam is the way the religion was practised by the Prophet and the first generation of Muslims in the 7th century, and therefore the correct and only way to practise Islam. Salafism sees saints, grave reverence and shrines as heretical, which is probably why such spaces made Tamara uncomfortable.

I, on the other hand, had grown up seeing all kinds of acts of reverence being performed at the shrine of Shah Jalal in Bangladesh. In fact, the stories of Murad and Shah Jalal had several parallels. Both were of Turkic origin and been credited with bringing Islam to a region where many local Muslims remain grateful for this. Both had achieved this by taking part in an epic battle – Shah Jalal's was with the local Hindu king, Gour Gobind. Although one had arrived as a missionary and the other as a sultan, over time both men had become saints to many. It was for this reason some people came to Murad's tomb, like they did to Shah Jalal's in Sylhet, with very different ideas about how to pay their respects to the sultan-cum-saint. We had come as tourists.

When World War I journalist Fortier Jones laid eyes upon Pristina, it was after a gruelling and stomach-churning trek through a mass of dying humans and animals between Mitrovica and the Kosovan capital – the result of the Great Retreat of 1916. It is therefore no surprise his description of the town is a glowing one. He described the 'ancient Turkish town' with its 'hundreds of minarets' as looking 'beautiful in the dusk' and claimed 'no place will ever seem so welcome again'. Bizarrely, Jones said he heard bells coming from the mosques as they approached the town, which at that point was heaving with refugees retreating from the massacre that had just taken place.

Jones was approaching in the depths of winter after a traumatic experience, and no doubt he was mistaken. Maybe it was churches he heard?

I could see no churches as we approached what looked to us also like a 'Turkish town'. The busy main road leading into the Kosovan capital mirrored the approach into Novi Pazar yesterday morning; it was also lined with mosques on either side. Most of them were brand new and would not have been here when Jones visited. Despite a secular constitution, Kosovo's population is more than ninety-five per cent Muslim. This makes Kosovo the most Muslim country in Europe.

We pulled up in a neighbourhood close to the Mother Teresa Cathedral, named after the late Calcutta-based ethnic-Albanian nun and Catholic saint. The location was very central and had a mix of run-down and modern properties. After parking the car, we passed a small mosque with a blue mirrored-glass front, a large central dome and three smaller ones. The restaurant we pitched up at had an outdoor area with comfy sofa-like seating and Wi-Fi. We were tired from our long drive and still had a gruelling return leg back to Serbia; food was the priority. I walked up to a counter with a large 'Hallal' sign, manned by a bearded hipster-type in a flannel shirt and skinny jeans. The girls wanted burgers, Tamara wanted risotto and I had a *pide* ghost to put to bed.

When Evliya and Melek Pasha came to Pristina, they found it to be a flourishing town where important Ottomans resided. This included a *kadi*, a steward and a commander of janissaries. Evliya also found it attractive, noting the one- and two-storey stone houses with tiled roofs and vineyards in the gardens. Back then, the most prominent buildings were the mansion of the local Ottoman *beg* and the courthouse and, like other prominent Muslim cities, Evliya notes there were a number of mosques, *madrasas*, *Hadith* schools, tekkes, fountains and *hans*. The Ottoman, who always offered a little history about the origins of the places he visited, claims Pristina was founded by the kings of Serbia, which might well be the case, as the first time the name was mentioned was in the middle of the 14th century by Byzantine Emperor John VI Kantakouzenos, who referred to it as a village in an area that used to belong to Serbian kings.

Our dinner predictably arrived on thick chopping boards and the girls' chips were served in mini chip-fryers. Tamara's risotto looked wonderfully colourful and my *pide* was the last to come out; I hoped this meant it had been freshly baked. Eventually, the smiling, bearded waiter laid down what was indeed a freshly baked pizza 'boat', with steam still rising from its centre. I examined the crust. It was golden with dark-brown patches and had a sprinkling of sesame seeds baked into it. But it was the centre that really made me smile. I had not ordered a *pide* since that first night in Sarajevo more than a week ago now, and could see it had been worth the wait. Tender chunks of delicately spiced minced meat sat in a shallow sea of melted ewe's cheese with a spiced tomato base and, in the middle, a solitary black olive. It had been sliced into five equal parts. I put the olive to one side and picked up the fattest slice straight from the centre of the 'boat'. Pinching both edges together like a sandwich, I shoved the whole thing in my mouth and sat back on the sofa. A warm sensation filled my mouth as the perfectly baked dough was engulfed in the delicious sauce, meat and melted cheese. A broad grin fell upon my face. Tamara noticed it.

'Good, is it?' she asked.

I nodded and continued to smile. It was like a culinary exorcism. The *pide* ghost was finally gone.

An Orthodox Town

NIŠ

If Novi Pazar was everything we hadn't expected of a Serbian town, Niš was: a busy, modern metropolis with only the faintest whiff of its lengthy Muslim heritage.

Named after the river Nišava, which runs through the middle of the town, Niš is where Rome's first Christian Emperor, Flavius Valerius Constantinus, was born in the 4th century AD. The Holy Roman Emperor, 'Constantine the Great' as he came to be known, later became a saint of the Serbian Orthodox Church and is whom the Byzantine capital Constantinople was named after.

Niš was destroyed by the Huns in AD441 and rebuilt by Byzantine Emperor Justinian I. The Ottomans arrived after the fall of the Kingdom of Serbia, around 1386, led by Sultan Murad I, whose tomb we had visited earlier that day. Niš then stayed under Muslim rule until 1878.

Sitting at the confluence of important roads that lead to Constantinople from major medieval cities like Vienna, Dubrovnik and Skopje, Niš was frequently traversed by pilgrims and traders. When 16th-century travelling pharmacist Reinhold Lubenau – part of the Habsburg Imperial Mission – stayed in one of the *hans*, he was pleasantly surprised by the hospitality of the Muslims. He and his horses were fed for free – as all travellers were – and Lubenau recalled with delight the piece of mutton, bread and delicious bowl of *chorba* (soup made from mutton stock and rice) he received on arrival.

Another Christian visitor that century was Vrančić, who was part of King Ferdinand I's delegation to Sultan Suleiman. For him, Niš was a 'fallen town' as it no longer belonged to Christians. Vrančić's comments appear in the diaries of German traveller Hans Dernschwam who was also in the delegation. Dernschwam was surprised to find Niš wasn't fortified but said it was in prime 'merchant territory'. Most medieval Christian observers though were negative in their assessment of Niš, and often described it as little more than a 'dilapidated' village.

Clearly things had changed by the time Evliya arrived in Niš on his journey to Sofia with Melek to take up his seat as Governor of the Eyalet of Rumelia, as he described a flourishing Muslim town with schools, tekkes, fountains, gardens and vineyards, where Christians also made up a large section of the community. Unsurprisingly, given the route Niš was on, Evliya said most locals were involved in trade in some capacity. A sketch made around this time in the mysterious *Leiden Sketchbook* – which depicts places on a journey from Vienna to Istanbul, probably by a pilgrim – reinforces this. It shows Niš with a skyline of minarets, surrounded by mountains. A main path leads into the town, past several *türbes*, close to the largest of the five mosques, the imperial one, commissioned by Sultan Murad II towards the end of the 15th century.

Today there are no minarets dominating Niš's skyline and Muslims make up less than one per cent of the city's population; a complete contrast to the Serbian town I had wandered through only that morning, with almost everyone here (ninety-eight per cent) claiming to follow the Orthodox Serbian church. I wondered what remained, if anything, of Niš' five centuries of Muslim heritage.

Our accommodation was right in the centre of Niš on the pedestrian-only Obrenovićeva, the main walking street in the heart of the city's shopping district, lined on either side by beautiful 18th-century, neoclassical buildings. We arrived late in the evening, exhausted by our long drive from Pristina. The City Center Guest House's location made it difficult to get near it in a car, and we found ourselves circling it twice before calling the host, Goran. I explained that it was late and that I didn't really want to wander through a strange new town at this time of night, but Goran said we had no choice but to leave our car on one of the surrounding streets and walk into the centre, where he agreed to meet us under the 'clock'. Reluctantly, we grabbed our overnight bags and wandered into the pedestrian-only centre of Niš.

The small green clock tower Goran had mentioned sat at the head of the busy Obrenovićeva, where many locals were still out enjoying the balmy summer evening. Some sat talking to friends on benches; others dined al fresco in cafés and restaurants that poured out on to the main walkway. As we waited for Goran to arrive, Anaiya suddenly became very animated.

'So we're gonna go shopping in there tomorrow, Mum. To eat our lunch and have some ice cream,' she squealed, pointing to a large, dark, glass-fronted shopping mall on the side of which were brands like Pull and Bear, Zara and New Yorker. It had been over a week since we had left the commercial centre of Mostar, the last major city to offer such familiar comforts.

'Sounds like a plan!' Tamara agreed, looking up at the multi-storey building.

Goran arrived to walk us less than fifty metres from the clock tower to the bottom of a beautiful four-storey 18th-century building, before cruelly revealing our apartment was on the top floor and there was no lift. We all groaned as Goran offered to carry some of our luggage up the wide marble stairwell with wrought-iron banisters.

On the way up we passed a small bar and a restaurant before Goran let us into two immaculately clean, spacious and modern air-conditioned rooms, cleverly built into the upper floor. After taking our passport details and handing us the keys, he bid us farewell.

That night, as Tamara and the girls settled in for another session of *Gilmore Girls*, I went for a walk to stretch my legs. It had been nearly six hours behind the wheel, including an hour at the border, where the guard looked at our British passports and smiled us back into Serbia – the first and last time a border guard would smile on this trip.

I didn't go far, stopping at a bench opposite bronze statues of two men in mid-conversation. The statues were at a table and had an empty chair beside them for tourists to pose in; this was art that involved the observer. Opposite were two old men, sat together deep in conversation. It was almost midnight, but they clearly had no intentions of going home yet. They were soon joined by a third man, who was much younger and out walking his dog, a big fluffy thing that sat obediently beside him as he nattered away. I got the distinct impression the dog knew the drill well.

I took a swig of the cold bottle of water I had picked up from one of the late-night vendors that sold everything you could possibly need on a Sunday night – water, cigarettes and beer – and reflected on the day.

It had begun in a Serbian town that was almost entirely Muslim and proud of its Muslim Ottoman roots, and then we had popped across a contested border to visit the tomb of the man who had brought Islam to this part of Europe. In both places, the local Muslim heritage had been embraced and presented positively. But now we were in a very different Serbia. Niš also had a long and storied

Muslim history, but one I suspected the town's majority Orthodox Christian population were unlikely to embrace, and probably viewed quite differently.

I was intrigued to see how, if at all, this heritage would be presented. Would it simply be ignored or rewritten? Would any of it be embraced, and how much of it had already been erased?

The next morning, as Anaiya sorted out the itinerary for her sister and mother, Tamara and I agreed a place and time to meet them all later. I then headed out for a day of exploring Niš, using an intriguing tourist app I had discovered the night before called 'Niš Talking'. The app not only revealed the places where there was still physical evidence of the town's Muslim heritage, but had integrated these into a trail called the 'Ottoman Turkish Occupation and Liberation Fight'. The trail would answer all the questions I had been mulling over the night before.

Niš's Ottoman Occupation trail began at the city's ancient fortress, which had originally been built in the 1st century AD and was the town's biggest historic attraction, covering twenty-two acres of what was now green and pleasant parkland. I arrived at the imposing main gate of the old fort on the bank of the Nišava to find it decorated with two distinctly Ottoman *mihrabs* carved into the brickwork either side of the arched entrance; they looked just like the traveller's *mihrabs* I had seen in the porticos of mosques all over the Balkans, but here they were clearly just decorative. Above them, two large tablets confirmed the gate's 18th-century Ottoman origins. Known by the Turks as the Stambul Kapije ('gates to Istanbul'), the impressive construction was extremely photogenic and I watched as tourist after tourist came up to it and framed themselves in the entrance arch, before asking a friend or partner to take their photo.

The first building inside the fort was the old hammam. Like the one in Novi Pazar, it was now a café, only a far more professional operation with the owners having spent a considerable amount of money refurbishing it. Today, it was closed, as was the small museum inside the old arsenal warehouse opposite. The app on my phone didn't offer any information on these three monuments, but it did direct me towards one dedicated to Prince Miloš Obrenović. This was a large, upturned stone bullet erected in 1902 to commemorate the Serbian prince's 'struggle for liberation from the Ottomans'. A national hero, there are numerous monuments dedicated to Obrenović all over Serbia, and a number of places and streets have been named after him, including Niš's wide pedestrian-only boulevard overlooked by our apartment.

Obrenović fought in the First Serbian Uprising in 1804 and then organised and led the second one in 1815, becoming head of the semi-autonomous Principality of Serbia. The first uprising came shortly after Belgrade was returned to the Ottomans by the Austrians, when a group of rogue janissaries, known as the Dahije, took over the Belgrade Pashalik. These rebels overturned many of the sultan's laws and began making life extremely miserable for the local Serbs, who tried to petition the sultan. The Dahije stopped the petition reaching Istanbul, and the final straw for the Serbs was when they began executing Serb noblemen and placing their severed heads in the town square.

The disgruntled Serbs gathered in the small village of Orašac and, backed by the sultan's forces, took Belgrade from the Dahije. Smelling liberation, the Serbs continued to take more and more territories and refused the sultan's orders to disband, instead seeking help from the Russians in St Petersburg, who promised diplomatic support. It was at this point the uprising became the Serbs against the Ottomans, with the Serbs now demanding the Belgrade Pashalik be run by one of their nobles. The Ottomans refused and the two factions went to war. The Serbs initially won a number of important battles – the first time Serb rebels had defeated Ottoman armies. Buoyed by their victories, the Serbs took Belgrade, slaughtering many of the city's Muslims and destroying its mosques and monuments as revenge for earlier Ottoman atrocities. By January 1807 they had declared Belgrade the capital of semi-autonomous Serbia.

The Ottomans backed off as they had more pressing matters in Istanbul; Sultan Selim III was murdered by Mustafa IV who was then quickly deposed by his brother Mahmud II, and soon after, the Russo-Turkish Wars began, with the Serbs choosing to side with the Russians.

The Serbs, however, experienced a crushing blow in May 1809 when a group of them was attacked by a large Ottoman army on Čegar Hill near Niš. A few months later, the Ottomans were marching on Belgrade to take back control of the Pashalik.

The second uprising began in April 1815 and was led by Obrenović, who managed to drive the Ottomans out of the Pashalik of Belgrade and ultimately come to an agreement that led to the formation of the Principality of Serbia in 1816, a semi-independent state governed by its own parliament and constitution with its own royal family: the Obrenović dynasty.

The furthest I made it into the fort was to the Bali Bey Mosque; one of only two 'mosques' still standing in Niš. The other was the Islamaga's Mosque, which was built in 1720 and apparently still in use. It sat five minutes from our apartment and when I visited *en route* to the fort, I found it closed with no sign of life anywhere. A white square building with a terracotta roof and a slim minaret, it looked just like hundreds of other mosques scattered all over the Balkans.

There was one other semblance of a mosque in Niš: the ruined minaret of the Hasan Begova Mosque, which stood on a small green patch, like a crumbling, old chimney stack, obscured by overgrown bushes and trees on Šumatovačka, the road that ran east from the Stambul Kapije. The minaret was badly destroyed: there was no pointed cone at the top, just a piece of metal sticking out of a big hole above the *muqarnas* pattern.

The Bali Bey, on the other hand, had no minaret – that was destroyed a while back – but it was the oldest 'mosque' left in Niš, dating to at least 1521, which means it would've been here when Evliya came to the city, and the Ottoman may even have prayed inside it.

Like the Altun-Alem Mosque in Novi Pazar, it was one of the only examples left in the Balkans of a mosque built using the cloisonné masonry technique – the same one used to build ancient Byzantine churches. This gave the mosque a distinct red-brick pattern throughout. It had a square base covered by a semi dome that rested on a brick *tambour*, and two smaller domes above a portico held up with Corinthian pillars. I stepped under its red brick arches and stared at the traveller's *mihrab*, its *muqarnas* pattern still intact after almost five hundred years. If Evliya had passed the Bali Bey as a traveller, he might well have stood right where I was standing now to offer his prayers.

The mosque's brown wooden door was locked shut, so I walked around the side, past the brick base of the destroyed minaret. Beside it there was a series of ruined walls that suggested other buildings were once connected to the mosque. This may have been a *madrasa*, *türbe* or *imaret* (soup kitchen). One of the more interesting features at the back were the upper windows. These had a series of circles, stars and crescents in them; a design I had not seen anywhere else in the Balkans. I peered in through the ground-floor windows, protected by thick iron grills. Inside, the walls had been rendered and painted a chalk white, and the floor was tiled over. There wasn't a single piece of furniture anywhere. On the wall hung a series of paintings: large nudes of a middle-aged woman. The Bali Bey was now an art gallery and I couldn't help but wonder if the decision to display nude art in a former mosque was deliberate. The city app said recent archaeological evidence showed the site was once used for 'Christian sacral purpose'; the mosque, it seems, may have been built on the site of a church. The paintings felt even more inappropriate.

It was a ridiculously warm day and, with the sun now reaching its midday zenith, the heat was unbearable. I sat down on a bench in the shade of a large tree and pulled out the cool bottle of water from my bag. I took off my brown 'paper' sunhat, placed it on the bench beside me and wiped the sweat from my brow. The hat looked as tired as I felt, having been sat on several times by accident. It was now on its second summer trip and holding up better than I had expected when I picked it up at the last minute from a discount store in London. Later, I was pleasantly surprised to discover it was woven from recycled paper.

There was no wind at all and the air felt stifling. The only noise I could hear were the shrieks of small children playing in a park somewhere further down the path. As I drank the water from the bottle, I noticed a man on a phone near the mosque-gallery. He was soon joined by another, slightly younger guy, and the pair of them wandered around the mosque taking pictures and posing for selfies. Just as they were about to leave, the younger one threw his shirt loosely around his head in a mock turban for his final pose, pulling a cheesy grin. I picked up my sad-looking hat and placed it back on my head. It was time to leave.

The next stop on the app's Ottoman trail took me back across the river to a synagogue. The description in the app read: 'The community of Sephardic Jews in Niš was first mentioned in the 1680s, since the Jews also settled in Serbia at the time after their exodus from Spain…' I wondered if the app was going to credit the Ottomans with offering the Jews refuge in Niš after they were kicked out of Spain. I could not see any other logical reason for including a synagogue on an Ottoman trail. But when I continued reading, the app offered no such explanation. It simply said the first synagogue was built on this spot in 1695 and that the current one dated from 1925.

I stared up at the sand-coloured building made in a modernist style, all straight lines and right angles. An unfurled Serbian flag stuck out over the entrance, giving it the look of an early 20th-century civic building. The only clue that this was a synagogue was the large Star of David and some Hebrew inscriptions over the entrance. When the building was constructed, Niš's Jewish community numbered around a thousand, but most of them were killed by the Nazis during World War II in a place not too far from the synagogue, a mere twenty minutes' walk to be exact. Niš's Red Cross Concentration Camp still stands on the other side of the city's fort as a reminder of the atrocities.

Today, only a handful of Jews live in Niš, which is why the synagogue, like the Bali Bey Mosque, is now an art gallery. Also like the Bali Bey, it was locked. I went to leave and noticed a small acrylic plaque stuck to a pillar of the entrance gate. It said 'Synagogue' in English and Cyrillic and had the date of construction. Beside this was a QR code. I scanned it with my phone, hoping it might tell me the story of how the synagogue's community came to Serbia. But it didn't. The page that loaded was only concerned with the modern building's architectural history. Like Niš Talking, it offered no insight into the story of how the Jews of Spain ended up in the Balkans. Any visitor to the synagogue in Niš would simply have to work that out themselves. I left feeling extremely disappointed.

The Sephardic Jews had effectively thrived during the seven hundred years of Muslim rule in Spain. Living in the relative harmony of *La Convivencia* with their Christian and Muslim neighbours, they had been allowed to practise their religion and even become upwardly socially mobile, especially during the early Umayyad period and in certain cities like Granada. It is true that some Spanish Muslim rulers were extremely intolerant and even expelled them from parts they controlled but, on the whole, historians accept that Sephardic Jews actively flourished under Muslim rule in Spain.

Even when the Catholic Monarchs first took over Granada, they initially promised to continue protecting the rights of Spanish Muslims and Jews and allow them to continue freely observing their religion. However, this did not last and, on 31st March 1492, they issued the Alhambra Decree, which demanded the expulsion of all Jews from Spain. The Spanish Jews were given just four months to convert to Catholicism, leave their country or face death. Knowing that in Muslim lands they were likely to be protected as 'People of the Book', most Sephardic Jews made for either Muslim North Africa or the Ottoman Empire. In fact, Sultan Bayezid II sent his navy to Spain when he learned 'People of the Book' were being expelled there and had them safely brought to his territories and under his protection. There, as part of the millet system, the Jews were free to practise their religion in return for paying certain taxes. Had it not been for the Nazi genocide of Europe's Jews, the Sephardic Jews of Niš would still be worshipping at their synagogue today.

I had left the Niš synagogue disappointed because it had refused to acknowledge the Jewish heritage of the Balkans in its entirety, and I suspected I knew why. To do so would be to acknowledge that Europe's Muslims through various empires in Spain and the Balkans had protected the continent's most persecuted religious group – the Jews – for almost twelve centuries. Something as a European Muslim I felt very proud of.

The last stop on the Niš Talking app's Ottoman trail was the Skull Tower, which happened to be on the road we would be taking out of Niš as we made our way to Skopje, the capital of North Macedonia and our next destination.

'It's a tower apparently built using the actual skulls of dead fighters,' I said to my three passengers as we passed a sign that indicated the 'Skull Tower' was to the right. I turned the car and entered a small bus terminal.

'Real skulls?' Amani asked, momentarily looking up from her book.

'Yes, real skulls of Serbians who fought against the Ottomans in the 19th century.'

'And they're inside?' Amani's eyes were widening.

Anaiya was flaked out beside her mother. They had spent the whole day wandering around looking at shops in the scorching heat and it had taken its toll. Both of them were going to pass on this one. My hopes lay with Amani.

'So, do you want to come?' I asked, trying not to sound too desperate.

'Erm… it's OK. I'm gonna stay here with Mum and Anaiya, thanks,' she said, returning to her book.

My efforts to tempt her with a gory, bloody monument had failed and I left hiding my disappointment. As I walked way, I heard the car door open.

'Dad?' Amani called out.

'Yes?' I said, a little too eagerly.

'Can you see if there is a shop and buy me a drink, please?'

'OK,' I replied, and, before I could add anything, the door slammed shut.

With a name like Skull Tower, I had half expected to be walking up to something resembling He-Man's Castle Grayskull, but instead, as I made my way towards the ticket office, two things became apparent: firstly, that the chapel housing the Skull Tower was actually quite pretty; and secondly, that it was closed.

Monday is a bad day to be a tourist in Serbia, apparently. It is the only day in the week when most tourist sites are closed, something I had failed to look up ahead of our trip. This explained why the museum inside the fort was also closed. I returned to the car deflated. The only skulls I got to see were the decorative ones near the entrance of the chapel and the souvenir ones in the window of the tourist shop, which was also closed. I was quite disappointed as I had been keen to visit this important piece of local history that revealed a more brutal side to the Ottomans.

The Skull Tower dates from the First Serbian Uprising and the Battle of Čegar, where Serbian forces were devastated by a large Ottoman army. According to Niš Talks, in the months following the battle the Turks collected 952 Serbian heads from the battlefield and skinned them to construct the gruesome fifteen-foot tower at the entrance of the city. The skulls were embedded on four sides in fourteen rows and were the Ottomans' way of deterring any further would-be rebels and, as visitors to the city discovered, it made for a gruesome welcome. In 1830, the French orientalist and poet Alphonse de Lamartine recalls seeing portions of human hair hanging 'like lichen or moss' from the bleached skulls, and hearing the mournful wind in their hollows.

Today only fifty-eight of the skulls remain. The rest are said to have been secretly taken away and buried in nearby cemeteries by relatives. The most important skull was that of the group's leader, Stevan Sinđelić, which is now kept in a glass case for display purposes. In the mid 19th century, local Ottoman governor Midhat Pasha actually got rid of the tower – or, at least, the skulls – because presumably he realised what a disgustingly evil thing it represented. Many of the skulls in the tower today were actually reinstated by the Royal Serbian Army after the country's independence to remind Serbs of the Ottoman oppression. It was during this period that a small wooden chapel was built over the tower, and in 1948, the tower was declared a Cultural Monument of Exceptional Importance. It is now one of the most visited sites in Serbia, but clearly not on Mondays.

The drive to Skopje was just over two hours through the South Morava river valley as it flowed from the top of North Macedonia near the Kosovo border towards Niš. It wasn't a long drive, but all three of my passengers eventually fell asleep, leaving me with the intermittent English songs on Serbian radio and my thoughts.

We had now been in three of the six countries we hoped to visit, and although so much of the journey still lay ahead, including a return to Bosnia, already I was beginning to see the impact this trip was having on my family and our understanding of what it means to be Muslims of Europe.

Tamara's reaction when she finally got to visit the Sufi lodge in Blagaj had been priceless, but the visit had also offered us a glimpse into the mystical traditions of indigenous European Muslims. Amani and Anaiya's disbelief at the Muslim 'choir' singing in the heart of Novi Pazar had left them, and us, stunned; none of us had ever seen such a thing before. Then there was our collective humbling by Mehrat, the candyfloss guy, as he continued a beautiful European Muslim traveller tradition in his own little way. Even the woman worshipping at Murad's tomb yesterday had been a valuable lesson for us all. It had left some of us feeling quite uncomfortable and in the process taught us that many of Europe's indigenous Muslims were going to be different to us, and likely to observe the faith in ways that might not be familiar. And that was OK.

My family were not going to join me in examining every tomb or mosque on this trip, nor were they going to be interested in talking to every Hamza and Adnan. For them, this was all just an exciting family adventure, and it was important it stayed that way, so that when we came upon European towns where everything was halal, and the sound of the *adhan* was as normal as the ringing of church bells, it would be an organic and natural experience – as natural and organic as the idea of a Muslim Europe.

PART THREE

NORTH MACEDONIA

Whose Heritage Is It, Anyway?

SKOPJE

I have to confess, before we came to North Macedonia, I knew very little about the country, except that it was really good at pissing off the Greeks.

'They have no fucking right to call themselves Macedonia, what the fuck is that about, malacca? They're stealing our fucking heritage, man, and it's bullshit, fucking bullshit!'

I remember listening to my Greek friend Ariston Diakos and thinking *surely it can't be that bad.* This was my default position every time someone banged on about the denial of their great historic culture (as I suspect it must be for anyone who has to listen to me bang on about the Muslim heritage of Europe).

But as soon as I left Skopje's old town and wandered into Philip II Square on the banks of the river Vardar, I began immediately reassessing things. Ariston, it seemed, had a point.

Described by one journalist as 'Pompeii retrofitted for the Las Vegas Strip', I now stood before a Disneyfied Hellenic fairground – though even Disney wouldn't have got it *this* wrong. At either end of the square, which wasn't officially allowed to be called 'Philip II Square' – we'll come to that later – were two immense fountains, the like of which I had not seen anywhere else on this trip. Each had a gigantic bronze statue rising from its centre.

The one that loomed directly over me was clearly Philip II, the father of Alexander the Great. Yet the official name of the statue was 'Warrior with accompanying elements'. The one further away, close to the Vardar's bank, was his wife cradling an infant Alex as he suckled at her perfectly shaped breast. In between were several other bronze monstrosities designed in the same Hellenic, neoclassical style. The mishmash, haphazard arrangement, set against a backdrop of historic Ottoman monuments, made it look like they were not really meant to be here – as if awaiting transit to a final destination.

I craned my neck to look beyond the river to the opposite bank, where the statue parade continued. Way off in the distance, in another square, the dramatic bronze figure of Ariston's hero Alexander sat astride a stallion up on its hind legs – the statue's official name: 'An Equestrian Warrior'. Almost every one of these had been put up in the last five years as part of a massive urban renewal scheme called 'Antiquisation', instigated by the now-deposed VMRO-DPMNE party, which some believe is trying to reinvent the country's heritage. Conservative estimates say the project, viewed externally as antagonistic and internally as divisive for ignoring the nation's actual Slavic, Albanian and Muslim cultures, is said to have cost North Macedonia over two-hundred million euros.

The only historically authentic thing in sight was the beautiful stone Ottoman bridge straddling the Vardar and connecting the two squares. A smaller version of the Mehmed Paša Sokolović Bridge we had seen in Višegrad, it also had solid, perfect arches that made it look as if it could last forever, which was more than could be said for the new Hellenic statues, many of them already oxidising aqua green. All of this was rather peculiar given Skopje's actual cultural heritage.

Although the city's name comes from a nearby settlement founded by the little-known Paeonian and Dardanian peoples, up until the 14th century Skopje was part of either Roman (Byzantine), Bulgarian or Serbian states. Even when Greeks did briefly hold sway here in the 13th century, it was the Romanised Byzantine Empire of Nicaea.

After that, Skopje became distinctly Muslim as the Ottoman city of Üsküp for the next five centuries, experiencing a golden age due to its strategically centralised position until the late 1600s. This was reflected in the city's highly skilled and diverse population of Turks, Armenians, Slavs, Greeks, Ragusans (Croats) and Albanians of varying Christian, Jewish and Muslim denominations.

When Englishman Dr Edward Brown visited in 1673, he described a flourishing Muslim town, with an excellent reputation for tanned leather. In the heart of the town, he found a lead-roofed central market, surrounded by trees and 'pleasant hills and dales', and claimed Üsküp was blessed with handsome monuments and houses, and a large number of beautiful 'Turkish churches' – mosques.

We had seen many of Dr Brown's 'Turkish churches' wandering through the old town that morning. Our favourite had been the beautiful Mustafa Pasha Mosque, high up on the hill where the city's famous sixth-century fortress was. Tamara and the girls found the stunning white interior with blue and red vegetal patterns particularly photogenic, as too the quaint wooden shelter of the *wudu* fountain at the entrance.

Later, as we wandered through the narrow alleyways paved with large cut stones, catching glimpses of pencil-thin minarets in the gaps between Ottoman-style dwellings, there was no denying Skopje still felt very much a Muslim town.

The city of Skopje, then, has no real connection to Alexander or his father, which made the statues I was now staring at seem all the more bizarre. In fact, the only real link the country has to ancient Macedon is that a small section of the south once fell within the boundaries of Alexander's kingdom.

This is why the Greeks, who see the Macedonian kings as part of their Greek-Hellenic heritage, were so incensed. Not that the VMRO-DPMNE cared. When asked by Britain's *Guardian* newspaper about the Greek grievances in 2010, a year before unveiling the 'Equestrian with Warrior' statue, then-Foreign Minister Antonio Milososki said, 'This is our way of saying [up yours] to them'.

Until very recently, North Macedonia had tried to use the name Macedonia without a geographic qualifier, citing the fact that it had historically been part of a region called Macedonia in the pre-Ottoman era. It was also known as the Socialist Republic of Macedonia during the Yugoslav years and, when the country's government peacefully transitioned to a parliamentary democracy in 1991, the Republic of Macedonia was born and the naming dispute began with Greece blocking the country's membership to NATO and the EU in protest.

This impasse lasted until 2018, when the social-democrat party SDSM came into power and an agreement was made to officially use the geographic qualifier 'North' in the country's name as well as halt any cultural or territorial claims over ancient Macedonia – hence the bizarre statue names. Unsurprisingly, the opposition party VMRO-DPMNE were not happy with these concessions and, should they ever be re-elected, things could get very interesting again.

I slowly walked over to a wooden bench and sat down. It was decorated with little bronze shields that looked like miniatures of the weaponry seen in movies like *300*. Tourists wandered past, carrying the same bemused look I'd had only minutes earlier. Some stopped and did their best to get the giant statues into the frame of their camera phones, shuffling backwards every so often.

I sat there wondering what Evliya would have made of it all. He and Melek had come through Üsküp on the same journey to Sofia for Melek's new post. It certainly would have been interesting as Evliya was amongst those who believed Alexander the Great is mentioned in the Qur'an as Dhu al-Qarnayn or 'he of the two horns' (18:83). This is the story of a man who reached the east and the west of the earth by God's favour and guidance and built a wall to keep the mythical Gog and Magog of Abrahamic traditions at bay.

Would Evliya have approved of Alexander being associated with Muslim Üsküp? He might well have, given his belief that Alexander was a monotheist, but I still couldn't imagine Evliya approving of the ridiculous statues I was staring at.

The sky was beginning to darken as the evening encroached. The banks of the Vardar slowly started to resemble a glittering classical theme park as choreographed light shows danced around the faux-marble porticoes and the pseudo-Hellenistic bronze statues.

I soon spotted some familiar tourists. Tamara and the girls had been to see an art exhibition inside the old Ottoman hammam and were now standing at the entrance to the square, scanning the area. I waved to grab their attention and Tamara waved back. Amani took out her white Polaroid camera. For a while, I watched as they wandered around looking a tad puzzled, but taking the necessary pictures for their social media feeds. In the middle, along the main walkway, a small wooden cart was being unpacked into a retro-record stand. Classic LPs by Michael Jackson, Led Zeppelin and Queen were carefully retrieved from storage boxes and displayed in neat rows. The owner was an old boy with long grey hair and a black leather waistcoat. After serving a customer, he set a Queen LP spinning and soon the distinctive voice of Freddie Mercury filled the air.

Tamara and the girls wandered over carrying Bangles and Cat Stevens LPs. My wife was an '80s baby, and we both loved 'The Cat' – who didn't? Amani held up her tiny Polaroid to show me the result. The statue of Philip II had been caught well against the light sky.

'What do you think, Dad?' she asked.

'It looks good, silhouetted like that, makes him stand out.'

'Yeah, but you can't see his face very well though… Erm, who is he?'

'He's Alexander the Great's father, Philip II.'

'Oh, right… I always thought he was Greek?'

'He was kind of Greek-Macedonian.'

'So he's from here?'

'Well, no, not exactly, he never actually came to Skopje, no.'

Amani looked at me, her face a picture of confusion.

'It's a long story,' I said, smiling at her, 'I'll tell you it on the way home.'

We were heading back to our car now, which was parked close to the medieval fort of Kale. The narrow paths leading up to the fort offered a great vantage point to look down on the old town and the square at the same time. The contrast was stark. They just didn't seem to fit together. On one side, an old Muslim town of minarets, mosques and hammams; and on the riverbank, huddled together, a random collection of Hellenic statues that looked like they belonged somewhere else entirely. It was easy to see why Ariston and his countrymen were so pissed off. This was like England sticking a giant bronze statue of William Wallace in Trafalgar Square and screaming, 'Fuck you, Scotland, he's ours!'

That evening, after a homemade meal of spaghetti bolognese served with a crunchy side salad, I left the family at the apartment to continue their *Gilmore Girls* marathon and returned to the square. I knew the story behind the North Macedonia-Greece fallout, but I didn't actually know what the locals thought. Earlier, as we passed the record cart, I had briefly chatted with one of the helpers. Seeing how tired Tamara and the girls looked, he had invited me back to hang out with him for the evening.

The cafés and bars overlooking the old town were now buzzing with tourists drinking cheap beer and smoking cigarettes. It was a lovely, warm summer's evening. I caught the faint waft of fruity smoke and heard the gentle rumbling of a shisha pipe. The alleys were so narrow and medieval-looking, it was easy to imagine them bustling with goods-laden carts coming up from the banks of the Vardar, as Dr Brown might have seen it. Down below, the darkness of twilight enhanced the light show now in full swing. The square seemed to be moving to a familiar rhythm. Was that Wagner?

'They play this shit all evening, man. Trying to slowly brainwash people. It's bullshit, man. This is not Vienna, this is not our nation's music!' Ertan exclaimed as he carefully placed a Rolling Stones LP back on to the cart. He was giving his friend Nesko, the old rocker, a hand for the evening. Ertan was heavyset and had long, black, curly hair, which he bound tightly in a ponytail. A local boy, Ertan's ancestry was Turkish. He was in essence the living Ottoman legacy of Skopje.

'Look around you, they are trying to pretend this is some kind of classical Greek, or western European town. That's not Macedonia, that's Vienna, Florence or Athens maybe. That bridge!' Ertan pointed – the ash from his cigarette fell to the ground with the sudden gesture. 'Those mountains. The Kale fortress. These are the symbols of Skopje.'

It was clear to me: Ertan also felt this was a Turkish-Ottoman town at heart.

I looked again at the statues and unfinished buildings, designed 'by numbers' from a 'how to' book on neoclassical art and architecture, as we left the square for a drive to the outskirts of town.

North Macedonia's desire to lay claim to an identity and cultural heritage more palatable to western Europe, which valued Greco-Roman culture above all other ancient ones, was interesting. We had seen various attempts to replace Muslim culture on this trip already, but so far it had been with others founded on religion, namely Orthodox Christianity. This was the first time it was with a non-religious ethnic identity, albeit one of questionable legitimacy. And yet it was easy to see why North Macedonia wanted to align itself with such a heritage and why the Greeks wanted exclusivity over it. At its height, the ancient Macedonian kingdom stretched from the south of modern North Macedonia all the way to Egypt and India. Alexander III, aka 'The Great', wasn't just King of Macedonia, he was also Pharaoh of Egypt, King of Persia and King of Asia. But he hadn't even been the 'ruler' of Skopje, which is why, like Ertan, I was highly cynical about the reasons North Macedonia was so desperate to adopt his legacy.

What was equally interesting was that to achieve all of this, Alexander had been no less a mass murderer, oppressor or cultural colonialist than any of the Ottoman rulers, yet across the modern Balkans, while many view the likes of Suleiman and Murad as cruel, barbaric occupiers, Alexander is lauded as a great military leader, a demigod even, for *his* colonial expansionism.

'There are two million people in Macedonia and this "project"…' Ertan spat out the words like he'd just bitten into something nasty, '… this project is costing hundreds of millions of euros. Who the hell is paying for it? Where did the money come from? It is dirty money. It's already several years late and we are now being told it will cost millions of more euros.'

Ertan wore red shorts, tired-looking trainers and a T-shirt that needed an iron – he was a self-confessed dope-smoking bum.

'There are no jobs here at all. Some people live on five euros a week here, do you know that?'

We stepped out of my car. The moon lit up a wide, grassy bank of the Vardar as it snaked past. Ertan had wanted to come here so we could talk freely, but also so he could enjoy his joint in peace.

Our trip to North Macedonia had coincided with one of the country's worst political crises – instigated by the revelation that the country's leader for the past decade or so, Nikola Gruevski, had been conducting espionage on a scale not seen since the Stasi. Leaked audio files had revealed levels of corruption, subjugation, death threats and spying that would've made La Cosa Nostra and Pablo Escobar proud. Everybody in the country was nervous and on edge. People like Ertan were worried about what they said and did in public.

We stood close to the water's edge, Ertan refusing to sit. With each puff, he glanced left and then right. It was not really necessary; he had picked a good spot, probably one he came to often. The few joggers, dog walkers and cyclists on the pathway were unlikely to catch a whiff; it was that far from us. The midsummer's night sky was clear and starry, and the evening air much cooler out here than in town. Ertan told me what happened the one time he wasn't so careful. The police had taken him in and threatened to beat him for not revealing where he'd got hold of the dope. The experience had left him wary. Even after putting out the joint, he kept nervously eyeing the surroundings. It was hassle he just didn't need, plus dope was expensive, especially for someone who had no real income.

Ertan was thirty-three years old and still living at home with his father and stepsister. Despite a mere four-year gap between us, he reminded me more of the students I taught than the adults I knew. After his parents split, Ertan's mother and sister moved to Germany. He visited them often and regretted not taking up the chance to move there permanently when he was younger.

'I was still in school when my mother left for Germany with my sister. My parents wanted me to finish my education here and by the time I did that, I was eighteen and could not legally be a child who qualified for German citizenship…' Ertan's voice trailed off. His eyes slightly glazed over; we both stared at the dark waters of the Vardar in silence. Something surfaced making bubbles, and a dog barked in the distance. I waited for Ertan to continue.

'It would have been great. I have good German friends and could have set up my life over there. Germany has jobs and opportunities, but I missed that chance… But it's OK, my father has sorted out a job for me in Prague. I'm really looking forward to that.'

'Great, what's the job?' I was happy to hear something positive lay on the horizon.

'It's in my uncle's pizza shop. I will go there and work for him. He has sorted out somewhere for me to stay too and then slowly I hope to get Czech citizenship. If I do, that will mean I have an EU passport.'

'Prague is a great city. Very beautiful,' I said, recalling my time in the Czech capital with Tamara on one of our weekends away.

'Yeah, man, it has great nightlife, beautiful women, and you can smoke weed there without any problems.' He laughed.

'When do you leave?'

'In two days' time.'

'Wow, that soon, huh?'

'Yeah. I'm really looking forward to it.'

Ertan's reasons for wanting to go Prague were as much about North Macedonia's uncertain future as anything else. Yet when he spoke about it, I was again reminded of students – the ones who fantasised about Amsterdam as if it were the Promised Land, just because you can smoke cannabis there. I wondered how much Ertan had thought it all through and whether he realised what lay in store. Was he *really* looking forward to it?

I didn't share my thoughts. I didn't want to spoil his enthusiasm. Besides, if nothing else, it would be an adventure for him.

We returned to Philip II Square to find Nesko head down playing air guitar to a young hitchhiking couple, Cristiano and Allegra. All three of them were getting stuck into a bottle of vodka that seemed to magically appear from the back of the stall. The couple were typical wide-eyed backpackers who couldn't wait to tell us all about their trip. We had covered many of the same places, which made the conversation flow easily. We compared notes on the beauty of Sarajevo's Old Town, the Mostar Bridge and the stunning Bosnian countryside. Cristiano told me about an old Bosnian house they had visited in Mostar that had an Ottoman exhibition inside, and I wowed them with pictures on my phone of Tamara's dreamy tekke in Blagaj. In between, we listened to Nesko's encyclopaedic knowledge of Balkan rock music.

Ertan disappeared momentarily to grab some street snacks: peanuts with raisins and the Ottoman classic, roasted sunflower seeds. He also thoughtfully grabbed a Sprite for me, which he handed over before sitting down in a stoned stupor. He then proceeded to pop sunflower seeds at a phenomenal rate as he listened to our stories.

The conversation moved from travels across the Balkans to the country's possible membership to the EU.

'I don't think western Europe has ever really accepted eastern Europe,' I said.

'You're right about that!' Nesko snorted.

'I think you guys disappearing behind the ol' Iron Curtain only increased the sense of being different from the west half of Europe,' I added.

'Yes… that I have to agree with,' Cristiano replied.

The group collectively shook their heads and Nesko handed over some change and a Bon Jovi record to a young woman in Doc Martens shoes.

As tempted as I was to divulge my theory that much of western Europe's xenophobia for eastern Europe was probably wrapped up in historic Islamophobia, I didn't. It had been a pleasant evening and I didn't want to dwell too long on a negative topic.

After a series of agreeing nods followed by thoughtful sips from our drinks, the group returned to the topic of travelling. Cristiano wanted to know if I had been to Portugal. I nodded, and told him about the articles I had written on the country's Muslim heritage. To my astonishment, he was not only excited by this but told me how he had recently discovered the name of a village near his parents' home town,

Marvão, was actually the Muslim name 'Marwan'. It had been named after the town's ninth-century Muslim founder. Encouraged, I began relating other Muslim heritage I had explored in Europe and asked Allegra if she knew there had once been an Italian-Arabic language.

The question made her stop rolling her cigarette.

'Noooooo,' she replied, her eyes widening. 'Tell me more!'

As I regaled her with the story of Sicily's Muslim past, I could see Ertan moving in closer. Nesko had turned the music off now, and Cristiano was also leaning in. For a split second, I was certain even the classical music in the square had stopped.

'Maltese is Arabic?' Allegra repeated in genuine disbelief.

'You mean, the Maltese people speak Arabic, and most of them don't know this?' asked Cristiano, his voice slightly muffled by the unlit roll-up in his mouth.

I nodded.

'Wow, man, just wow!'

'Yes, it's almost one third Siculo-Arabic, an ancient form of Arabic that developed in Sicily, where it was eventually replaced by Latin, but made its way to Malta in the early medieval period and became the basis of the modern Maltese language.'

'No way man, no fucking way!' Ertan exclaimed, the effects of his joint now wearing off.

I laughed. 'Yep, it's the only Arabic language recognised as an official EU language and the only one written in Latin script, not Arabic script… In fact, Tunisians, who also speak a form of Arabic descended from Siculo-Arabic and know Italian, can understand most of what Maltese people say, because the rest of Maltese is made up of Italian, French and English words.'

'Wow, just fucking wow!' Cristiano responded.

I explained to the group how a highly sophisticated and civilised Muslim culture emerged around the 9th century in Sicily, when Moors conquered the island along with Malta. Like their neighbours in Spain, they built beautiful palaces and nurtured the arts and learning in education institutes in their capital Palermo, which by the 11th century had become one of Europe's largest cities, so filled with mosques that when the Muslim Andalusian traveller Ibn Jubayr visited he said there were too many to count.

Even after they left, the Normans that took over were so enamoured by Muslim culture, they kept much of the administration in place and began speaking Arabic, so that for a century or so there were Norman Arabs in the south of Europe. It was their language that remains partially preserved on the tongues of the Maltese.

The guys were blown away imagining turbaned, learned men speaking Arabic, playing music, writing poetry, studying the sciences and producing great works of literature in the south of Italy. I was glad to have such a captivated, albeit slightly inebriated, non-Muslim audience.

The classical music had stopped playing now, the fountains and lights no longer danced. The large crowds from earlier had become a few individuals staring in silence at the 'Warrior' statue and his breastfeeding wife. I looked up towards the cross on the hill in the south of the city, shining bright against the velvet-blue sky. It had been a lovely evening with my new friends in Skopje, but now it was time to get back to my family. I stood up, hugged each one of them and exchanged details, before waving goodbye.

A Macedonian Imam

SKOPJE

The Sultan Murat Mosque sits on raised land east of Skopje's old bazaar, across the highway that dissects the city's two oldest districts. The roads here are littered with pot-holes and the houses more run-down. Many are unfinished, their red bricks only partially covered with cement. Squeezed in between them is the odd ancient stone house, now a sad, crumbling relic. The neighbourhood is quieter, with no tourists at all. Women in hijab walk past holding children in one hand and grocery bags in the other as young Macedonians drift in and out of local coffee shops. Cars are parked wherever there is space and large open bins emanate a stench as the August sun bakes their rotting innards. It is the last place you expect to find a royal mosque.

Skopje's only royally commissioned mosque was built by the deeply spiritual Sultan Murad II and for centuries, in spite of earthquake and fire damage, it was repaired, rebuilt and refurbished, as befitting an imperial monument and place of worship. Also known as the Hunkar Mosque – the mosque of the ruler – it now looks sad and neglected, like the neighbourhood that surrounds it.

The sky-blue paint of the frame around the doorway has mostly peeled off, and the inscription tablet above it has a lightning-shaped crack leading up to the wooden ceiling, where DIY-repair attempts jar next to the original yellow-and-green-painted wood. In its centre, a Star of David mould has an empty hexagonal rose awaiting the replacement of the opulent chandelier that once hung there. The two traveller's *mihrabs* under the handsome, multi-arcaded portico, held aloft by elegant stone columns, are barely decipherable; the once iridescent red and yellow floral patterns now faded and incomplete. The mosque's flat-hipped roof has several of its terracotta tiles missing, and along its western wall stands a typically slim minaret of finely chiselled stone with *muqarnas*-style decoration beneath its balcony.

The Sultan Murat was built at the start of Ottoman rule in North Macedonia, shortly after the civil war that threatened to split asunder the new imperial power. The war came about because Murad's fearsome grandfather, Bayezid, was captured by the Turco-Mongol ruler of central Asia, Timur (Tamerlane), and died in captivity without nominating an heir. Bayezid's sons fought it out for more than a decade, with Murad's father Mehmed I coming out on top and then one by one executing the three brothers that had challenged him. The significance of his victory, which once again united the Ottoman Empire, has not been lost on historians who have hailed Murad's father as the second founder of the Ottomans. Had he not been so ruthless, there would not have been an empire to continue with.

Similarly, upon Mehmed's death, Murad faced pretenders laying claim to the imperial throne, and had to do away first with his uncle and then his younger brother, both of whom had been encouraged to make their challenges by the Byzantine Empire. It was after this episode that Murad pledged to punish the Christian empire by taking its capital Constantinople, a promise his son would go on to fulfil.

Murad reigned twice during the 15th century, briefly giving the throne to his twelve-year-old son, Mehmed II, in 1444, before taking it back two years later following a revolt by the new military corps, the janissaries. His second reign lasted until 1451, but it was during the first he commissioned architect, Husein of Debar, to build this mosque.

Like most early Ottoman rulers, Murad modelled himself on the *gazi* – the pious Muslim warrior who only fought the 'enemies' of Islam – and, after several successful campaigns, was dubbed 'The Great', which might explain why, even when his mosque was destroyed, the empire kept rebuilding and caring for it right up until its collapse.

The stone inscription tablet above the door told me the first time this happened was in 1537 when a fire destroyed the mosque. This initial rebuild was carried out by Murad's great-great-grandson, Sultan Suleiman – surprisingly, there's no mention of Sinan. The mosque had to again be rebuilt after the Austro-Hungarians set Skopje ablaze in 1689. However, the current features and fading paintwork, clearly inspired by western European baroque-rococo, date from the mosque's most recent refurbishment in 1911, ahead of Sultan Mehmed V's visit to the city. It was clear from the tablet that this was a mosque the Ottomans had valued a great deal, resurrecting it on at least two occasions. Now they were gone; so too, it seemed, the desire to keep it alive.

I took my shoes off and entered a dark, musty hall. The interior looked as if it had not been touched since Mehmed V's visit over a century earlier. The floral patterns on the walls were barely visible and the wood on the window frames and ceiling, dry and brittle; several pieces already splintered. The *mahvil's* once-pretty, bulging balconies belonged in the classical theatres of Europe, and in the centre of the room hung a tiny chandelier, dwarfed by the scale of the vast prayer hall. Every time light passed through its cheap teardrops, it resembled a disco ball in an old, abandoned dance hall, somewhere in the north of England.

I walked over to the majestic green and orange *mihrab*. It had a moulded plaster crown of ostrich feathers above a sunflower. Two small urn-like shapes sat on either shoulder. Everything screamed neoclassical except for the latest addition: a horseshoe of grotesque, fluorescent tubular lights framing the niche where the imam stood.

This might have been a royal mosque, but now it was fit only for a pauper. It made me sad to see it in this state. How did a mosque built by a sultan known as 'The Great' come to be so neglected?

I positioned myself to the right of the *mihrab*, in front of a dark brown grandfather clock, to pray my usual two *rakats* for entering a mosque. Then I sat and listened. The room was almost completely silent, except for the ticking of the clock and the low, gentle snoring of a large man stretched out beneath the *mahvil*. He had been asleep long before my arrival, safe in the knowledge no-one would bother him until the *muezzin* made his call. To my left, through the broken shutters of a window, I could make out the family *türbe* of Ali Pasha of Dagestan, inside which were also the sarcophagi of his wife and daughter. The tomb had been built near a host of graves along the mosque's eastern wall. There was one other mausoleum on the site, a square structure of brick and stone built in 1556/7 along the southern wall. This was the tomb of a Bikiy Han, which one fanciful theory claims could be that of Beyhan Sultan, the sister of Sultan Suleiman, because she lived in Skopje in self-exile. Beyhan had fallen out with her royal family after Suleiman ordered the execution of her husband, the vizier Damat Ferid Pasha. She reportedly never forgave her brother or family for this. The theory also claims this is why the *türbe* is the largest closed Ottoman tomb in North Macedonia. There are a few issues though: as well as the tomb being dated two years earlier than the sultana's death, she is said to be buried in Istanbul in her father's *türbe* at the Yavuz Selim Mosque.

I wandered out of the gloomy interior into the bright afternoon sunshine. Before me was yet another reminder of Skopje's significance during the early Ottoman period: the city's red-brick clock tower. This tall, handsome, octagonal monument had a beautiful arched double *tambour* topped by a lead onion dome. Originally a wooden structure, it was built in the second half of the 16th century, when Üsküp was important enough to become the first Ottoman city to have a clock tower. Like the mosque, it had undergone several rebuilds and, although the clock's faces displayed the correct time, it was unsafe for visitors to climb up the tower and, much to my dismay, the small wooden door at the base was firmly padlocked.

I sat down on a bench near the mosque's stone fountain, which no longer flowed from the top. Silver taps installed around the base are now used to perform the ablutions. It was late afternoon and although I had to meet Tamara and the girls soon, I decided to hang around for just a bit longer. The *Asr* prayer was imminent and maybe, I told myself, I might come across someone who can tell me more about the mosque and why such an important and historic monument is now in this sad state of neglect and disrepair.

Two days ago, we had visited the Mustafa Pasha Mosque on Kale Hill on the other side of town. We had come upon a mosque visibly gleaming from its recent renovation by TIKA. It was true the Mustafa Pasha was closer to the touristic centre of Skopje, but it was still a mosque built by a mere pasha. This was a royal mosque beside one of the empire's first clock towers. Our jaunt through Philip II Square had shown me where North Macedonia's heritage priorities lay, but that didn't explain why even TIKA had ignored the Sultan Murat Mosque. Was it really just down to the fact it was on the 'wrong side' of town?

Behind me, on a bench overlooking a neat lawn, sat two middle-aged men in deep conversation. One held a green water hose that he directed towards different sections of the lawn, some of which had been scorched yellow by the summer sun. He had a thick black beard, whilst his companion was clean shaven and slightly older. Both men had their shirtsleeves rolled up to their elbows as if preparing to perform *wudu*.

The men smiled warmly when they noticed me, lifting their hands in unison and offering a loud *salaam*. I returned the greeting, also lifting my arm. They then continued with their conversation.

'TIKA have promised to renovate. They came recently to assess the mosque and the clock tower and were supposed to have started work on both already, but we have heard nothing since,' Imam Rajaab explained, the bearded man who had *salaamed* me earlier. I had accosted him shortly after he led our small congregation of twenty or so worshippers in the mid-afternoon prayer. I had hoped he might speak a little English and be able to tell me more about the mosque. To my utter delight, the young imam spoke perfect English.

As we made our way out of the dark hall back into the sunshine, he stopped at the mosque's entrance and turned to face the faded paintings above the door frame. Pointing to the one on the left, Imam Rajaab explained it was a picture of the elegant Suleymaniye Mosque in Istanbul, built by Sultan Suleiman twenty years after he rebuilt this one. Deemed the finest example of Ottoman architecture, it was constructed by Mimar Sinan – I had found the Sinan connection – and identified easily by its four elegant, slender minarets. The reason it had been painted on the mosque, explained the imam, was because historically the Suleymaniye had almost a mythical status in Ottoman culture.

When Evliya Çelebi described the stunning mosque in his home town, he went into extensive detail about the mystical significance of each architectural feature, and the 16th-century Ottoman poet, Sai Mustafa Çelebi, often compared it to the holy Kaaba in Makkah.

The other picture was of an Istanbul neighbourhood, said Imam Rajaab, admitting he didn't know which one or why that particular scene had been featured. He did, however, point out that the mosque in that picture was probably built by an Ottoman royal. I asked him how he knew this and he said because it had two minarets. The Suleymaniye's four meant it was a sultan's mosque whereas two means it was built by lesser royals, like a prince or princess. All other mosques were only allowed to have the one minaret.

I asked if that meant the Sultan Murat might have had four minarets in the beginning, but the imam couldn't say. Apparently, nobody knows for sure what the original looked like and the minaret rules, said the imam, were most common during the era of Sultan Suleiman. The pictures were painted during one of the rebuilds, he explained, reminding me that when the mosque was first built, Istanbul wasn't even an Ottoman city. The images had been framed in raised red and yellow stonework and were in desperate need of restoration. Most of the Suleymaniye's domes had lost their paint, revealing the white plaster underneath, and the other picture had a large crack cutting through the bottom right corner.

'You don't really sound confident about TIKA doing the renovations,' I said, when the imam had finished explaining the pictures to me. 'Why would they not want to fix such a significant mosque?'

The imam wasn't much taller than myself and had a warm, round face. After hearing my thoughts, he fell silent and began stroking his thick beard.

I waited.

Some of the congregation had stayed behind to do further prayers and were now making their way out. As they passed us, they shook each of our hands before touching their breasts.

The imam waited until the last person had left.

'One of the reasons this mosque has been neglected in the past...' He seemed to hesitate, looking for the right words. 'One of the reasons is because some members of the congregation in the past here were a bit outspoken'.

His reply wasn't what I had expected.

I asked if those individuals had been at the prayer he had just led, wondering if that was why he had waited for everyone to leave.

He shook his head.

'What are they outspoken about?'

'The country's national Islamic organisation. These individuals believe the organisation is working with the government and not for the Muslims of Macedonia.'

I was tempted to ask what he thought. Did he agree with them? Was the organisation doing enough for Muslim Macedonians?

But I chose not to. I wanted him to continue speaking.

'Islam is still weak in Macedonia,' he said, pointing to the size of the congregation at *Asr* as evidence.

It was Friday, the Muslim holy day, and once upon a time that would've meant the weekend here in Skopje. Not any more. Yet, despite this, the city's large Muslim presence always turned out in numbers for the weekly *Jumua'ah* prayer, said the imam, but the rest of the week, the attendance was poor.

'It is the same in London, where the Muslim population is also big. Most of us find it difficult to attend the *salah* in the week, with work and busy family lives, but on Fridays our mosques are full. Maybe it is just because both our societies are not Muslim ones?'

The imam agreed before telling me he was actually not from Skopje, but a small village about twenty kilometres out of town. The next prayer at sunset was going to be the last he would lead for the day before returning home. The imam revealed he was trying to leave his role at the mosque and was actively seeking a permanent replacement to take over. Until that happened, his daily routine involved driving in for the midday prayer and staying until sunset.

'It is just not worth my time, staying to lead *Isha* prayer or coming early for *Fajr*. Sometimes for *Fajr* or *Isha* there might be just one man at *jama'at*. It is just not worth it.'

It's the same in England. The earliest and latest prayers always attract the lowest numbers, when people would rather sleep or pray at home after a long day at work. Those that attend are usually the elderly, for whom, in retirement, the five daily prayers offer structure to their day. The mosque is also an important social space for them.

Imam Rajaab felt the distance he had to travel to lead a handful of men every day just wasn't worth his while, but I wondered if his desire to leave also had something to do with the 'outspoken' individuals he had mentioned earlier.

Who were they and what kind of things had they said?

The imam was reluctant to discuss this and I didn't push him. Instead, I asked what other challenges Macedonian Muslims faced.

'There are around 1,500 converts a year in Macedonia,' began the imam, whose dark skin and sharp, aquiline nose made him look central Asian, even though, like most Muslims in Skopje, he was ethnically Albanian. 'Mainly they are women, often because they want to marry Muslim men.'

'Is it difficult for them, when they convert?' I asked.

'Very. New converts, especially the men, always get interrogated – first by local police, then national police, and then special police. This happens to them many, many times when they first come to Islam,' he said.

'That sounds awful. Are their families supportive?'

'No. Usually their families abandon them and this means they can become very isolated and lonely. It is not an easy path for Macedonians that choose Islam.'

I explained that my wife was a convert and how we spent a lot of time with members of the British convert community, where we had heard similar stories.

Imam Rajaab smiled.

Then, lowering his tone, he told me the fate of a convert village girl who wanted to marry a Muslim Macedonian.

'When her father found out, he was so angry and upset, he shot her.'

The revelation stunned me into silence. The imam let it sink in.

'Not to kill her, but to maim her and scare her not to become Muslim. He then disowned her.'

'Did she relent?'

'No, she remained Muslim, but her life became very lonely.'

We were now sat at the benches close to the fountain. One of the taps dripped because of poor plumbing. Around the edges of the fountain there were bars of soap in colourful plastic dishes. I stared at them for a while before asking the imam what other challenges he faced here at the mosque.

This time his anecdote was a personal one about a local man he knew for many years as a warm, kind-hearted individual. Someone whose company he enjoyed and trusted enough to take him along on journeys across Europe to visit different Muslim communities.

'Then he began watching videos online and reading *Takfiri* material.'

Takfiri material refers to interpretations of Islamic texts that have a preoccupation with establishing who is an apostate.

'He slowly became radicalised. Now he doesn't even attend our mosque any more.'

'Why?'

'He says everyone here is a *kafir* [disbeliever]. He is now a very harsh and angry person who talks very negatively about non-Muslims all the time.'

It is a story many Muslims including myself are familiar with, and so I wondered what the imam's response to this had been. Had he stayed in touch or cut the man off?

'I continue to talk to him, but he is increasingly isolating himself from the community.' The imam shook his head and looked skyward.

It was almost time for his last congregation of the day, but before then he had time for one more example of local radicalism.

'The other day, when these Malaysian missionary brothers were giving a talk about how to interact with non-Muslims at the mosque, a man gets up at the end and says that all Muslims should unite to kill all the non-Muslims.'

There was a wry smile across Imam Rajaab's face as he told me his response.

'I said to him in front of everyone, "And then what? You end up in hell yourself?"' He laughed. 'The man looked shocked. He didn't know what to say. Some of these people, they say these things and they have no idea what they are talking about.'

I asked Imam Rajaab what the answer was.

'Education!' he exclaimed, before getting up and pointing to a building near the entrance to the mosque complex. 'In there reside several young boys,' he told me. All of them had come from far and wide, including one that had travelled all the way from Kosovo. They were here to spend their summer studying with the imam and learning about the *proper* teachings of Islam – instead of picking things up online and from random individuals. Every day, Imam Rajaab sat with them for a couple of hours and taught them the role the Qur'an and the *Hadiths* play in Islam; how they are meant to be used to decide the way a Muslim should live their life.

'I hope if they understand how Islam should *really* be interpreted from these sources, they will educate their friends and family, and people will not fall into the same problems.'

The route from the Sultan Murat Mosque back to the main road took me down a narrow, cobbled alleyway, flanked by houses on one side and, on the other, on a raised plinth, the recently refurbished *türbe* of Ishak Bey, the city's 16th-century governor, whose father was Pasha Yiğit Bey, Skopje's Ottoman conqueror.

Further along, I came upon Skopje's oldest tree, a huge, gnarled sycamore in the courtyard of the Gazi Isa Bey Mosque – named after Ishak Bey's son, Skopje's third Ottoman governor who went on to found the cities of Novi Pazar and Sarajevo. The tree is said to have been planted when the mosque was built in 1475 after the great Bey had died. It is smaller than the Sultan Murat, but much better looked-after, appearing in a good state of repair. It looked quainter, with two large, equally-sized central domes – a unique design for its time – and several smaller ones above the front portico. It is also more popular, judging by the number of old men sitting around in the green garden waiting for the *Maghrib adhan*.

That evening, after riding the cable cars up to the spectacular viewing platform next to the giant crucifix that overlooks Skopje, we ate dinner al fresco at a restaurant where I asked for a Greek salad only for the waiter to half-jokingly remind me that around here it was known as a 'Macedonian salad'. Afterwards, we went for a walk through the old bazaar and ended up at the Kapan Han, built by Isa Bey in the late 15th century, where Evliya and Melek Pasha rocked up with their large entourage and beasts. Back then it was the Isa Bey Han, becoming the Kapan much later because of the large scales (*kapan*) the inn used to weigh foreign merchandise. Located at the southern tip of the old bazaar, the scales would have been convenient for merchants to weigh their goods before entering the city's bustling markets.

The Kapan was one of the better examples of a caravanserai we had come across on our trip. Despite undergoing major renovation, the *han*'s original features were still there, including the forty-four lodging rooms connected by a set of stairs that were built wide enough for horses to be led up by merchants and travellers. The *han*'s design was cloisonné masonry, just like the mosques in Novi Pazar and Niš, and was square-shaped with a central courtyard where a tall silver birch grew. The *han*'s shape and thick exterior walls made it easy to secure and keep out any would-be thieves through the night. These days, most of the former rooms are occupied by local businesses aimed at tourists like us.

One of these was a shisha café in what used to be the stables. We walked in to find it decorated with old pictures showing the *han*'s gradual resurrection from a dilapidated ruin to the hip, modern hangout it was now aspiring to become. The Kapan was one of three *hans* in Skopje's old bazaar; all of them, I was pleased to note, had been restored and given a new lease of life. The 16th-century Kuršumli An, at the opposite end of the bazaar, was originally built by a wealthy local *muezzin* called Muslihudin Abdul Gani and is now part of the national Archaeological Museum, whilst the 15th-century Suli An to the east is now home to the Academy of Art and the Old Bazaar Museum. I wanted to see them all, but we had run out of time.

It was our last night in Skopje, and we sat playing cards and drinking coffee. After we finished a few games I reclined on a cushion to puff away at an apple-flavoured shisha. The girls connected their phones to the Wi-Fi in the café and Tamara read a book.

Skopje had been one of the Ottomans' major cities in Europe, and the sheer wealth of historic Islamic monuments still scattered across it today reinforced that, making it feel like a 'Muslim Rome'. Despite the best efforts of some to assign a new cultural identity to North Macedonia's capital city, it remains very much the Ottoman Üsküp at heart.

The Fool's Tekke

TETOVO

We would never have come across the Ali Pasha Mosque if we had not arrived in Tetovo absolutely famished. The Sufi lodge we were looking for was on the edge of town at the foot of the Sharr Mountains and the chances of finding food there felt slim, so we decided that before we went in search of Macedonian mystics we would first go in search of lunch.

Roughly fifty kilometres west of the capital Skopje, close to the mountainous border with Kosovo and Albania, Tetovo has the feel of a provincial town. Our route took us through a local market where piles of vegetables were laid out on rickety, old wooden carts. Large red and green tomatoes, bunches of spring onions and sacks of dirty potatoes, fresh from the ground, stood next to ancient scales with iron weights. As locals browsed, brown and white goats nibbled at rotting vegetables behind them. Whenever they got too close to the fresh produce, the vendors would shoo them away. The market was on a road surrounded by grey low-rise blocks, beyond which were the patchy green slopes of the Sharr mountain range. The rest of Tetovo seemed to be mainly two- and three-storey houses with exposed red brickwork, like the ones I had seen in the poorer Sultan Murat Mosque neighbourhood in Skopje. The sheer number of these made me wonder if the local Albanian population – Tetovo sits along North Macedonia's 'Muslim' western corridor, home primarily to ethnic Albanians – was actually quite fond of this unfinished 'builders-on-a-tea-break' look, where exposed lumps of grey cement could be seen between the red bricks and grey breeze blocks. It was as if all of Tetovo had forgotten to budget for plasterers and renderers.

With only croissants sustaining us since leaving our apartment in Skopje, we stopped at the first place that looked like it could offer us food: the ambitiously named Burger Palace – a strictly no-frills fast-food joint, outside which the headless torso of a lamb was being slowly roasted over a charcoal fire. It was as we were turning in to park up for the Burger Palace that Tamara spotted the Ali Pasha Mosque.

Despite its diminutive size, the Ali Pasha was spectacular; the walls a patchwork of neat, colourful squares with painted star-shaped patterns, like those on the backs of playing cards, only more dazzling in iridescent reds, oranges and greens. The mosque windows were housed in dark wooden frames and floral patterns that tumbled out of Greco-Roman urns – the European baroque-rococo influence was again apparent. Had it not been for the grey stone minaret, it would have been difficult to tell this was a mosque at all; there was no dome or any other obvious indicators, except for a white circle painted on to the wooden lip of the roof on all four sides. Inside these was the Arabic phrase *mashallah* painted in a style so naïve the artist had missed out the 'letter' *hamza*. I suspected this was because it was done by a painter and not a scribe who knew Arabic well. *Mashallah* literally means 'God willed it' and is used by Muslims all over the world as a term of praise. Many superstitious Muslim cultures also believe it is necessary for protection against the proverbial 'evil eye' being cast upon the thing or person being praised. In this case, that was the stunning paintwork of the Ali Pasha; a mosque unlike any other we had seen before.

It sat on the edge of a small green, opposite the town's old hammam, close to the River Pena. In its well-kempt garden, small fir trees, roses and sweet-smelling flowers grew around a stone water fountain, and along the western wall there was a large *türbe* housing the tombs of the mosque's original founders who, unusually for Muslim societies, were two local sisters, Hurside and Mensure. They had built a mosque here in 1475. However, the reason it was known today as the Ali Pasha Mosque was because, after the two sisters' mosque was destroyed in a fire in the 17th century, two local pashas, father and son, Receb Pasha and Abdurrahman Pasha, built the current one in the 1830s, during a period when Ottoman art became more elaborate and highly influenced by European styles, especially the baroque movement. The elaborate patterns and art that cover the mosque's walls are the reason it is also known locally as the Šarena Džamija – the decorated mosque.

Legend has it the pashas hired skilled painters from the town of Debar to the north – a place noted for its artisans – who needed thirty thousand eggs to complete the painting of the stunning little mosque.

We were genuinely impressed, but sadly the doors to the mosque were locked and so, after taking their fill of photos, Tamara and the girls headed off to look for a stationery shop – Anaiya needed supplies for the scrapbook she was making about our trip – and we decided we would all meet back at the mosque when they were finished.

I stood at the back of the garden near the tiled perimeter wall. The mosque looked even more impressive with the early afternoon sunshine hitting its gleaming white walls. They made for a wonderful backdrop to the pretty little garden, and for a moment, with its slender pillars and Latin decorations, it looked like a small Tuscan villa had been transported into the centre of Tetovo.

I walked over to the mosque's portico, where a man was now quietly praying. Trying not to disturb him, I peered in through one of the grilled windows beside the entrance. The lights were off and, although I could just about make out the outline of the mosque's *mihrab* in the dark, it was impossible to see what it actually looked like.

'You have to go and look inside,' said the man, who had stopped praying. 'It is very beautiful inside.'

'I'm sure it is if the outside is anything to go by, but the doors are locked.'

'Yes, they keep it locked except for prayer times, but if you ask the old men at the front, one of them will let you in.'

I looked towards the gate, and could just make out two elderly, bald heads, one with a crown of white hair shaped like that of a Franciscan monk, and the other as smooth as a baby's bottom. The men were in deep conversation.

'Look…' I began, turning to the stranger. 'Would you be kind enough to ask them for me, please?'

The man was clearly about to start another round of *salah* and I felt guilty making this request, so I offered an explanation.

'I don't speak Albanian, and I don't think they will understand me very well.'

'No problem,' he said with a smile, before disappearing behind the gate.

I quickly checked the battery life on my camera and my mobile phone.

'He is coming,' the stranger said, reappearing almost as quickly as he had left. 'But be careful, they are very grumpy old men.' He smiled and began raising his hands for the *Takbir* before I could even say thanks.

An old man with a sour look on his face rounded the corner. I *salaamed* him, but got no reply. Instead, he headed straight over to the door, pulled out a large set of ancient-looking keys, unlocked it and walked inside. I scurried in behind him.

'Two minutes!' he growled, heading over to the light switch.

I looked up in absolute awe. The flick of the switch had transported me to a strange chapel somewhere in Florence; rich, stylised yellow and red floral patterns covered every inch of wall in the baroque-rococo style – not a single blank space was visible anywhere. Neoclassical shapes and patterns that belonged in cathedrals, framing a lamenting angel here or a frowning saint there, instead housed delicate paintings of Islamic sites from across the globe. I spotted the Kaaba in Makkah and the Prophet's tomb from Madinah. It was actually a little unsettling at first; I felt confused as I stared at the surreal and mesmerising array before me.

The mosque had an internal dome painted in a dizzying and familiar pattern. My mind searched for where I had seen it last. That was it! The cathedral in Córdoba, Spain. However, unlike the cathedral, there was no stucco or plaster work here; the Romanesque pillars, the red floral wreaths, the urns on the bulging *mahvil*, were all two-dimensional works of art. Even the intricately patterned rose for the central chandelier was painted on. It was as if a Muslim had visited the Renaissance and decided to paint their own version of what they had seen.

I could've have spent hours in that tiny mosque, examining every inch and trying to decipher the artwork, but I had only two minutes. Right on cue and without even acknowledging me, my grumpy host walked over to the lights and switched them off. And just like that I could no longer see the magical Pasha's interior.

The paintwork of the Ali Pasha Mosque was a fine expression of an art form that first emerged in the Ottoman Empire during the Tulip period – the relatively peaceful years between 1718 and 1730 – and takes its name from the tulip craze that took hold of Ottoman court society. The Tulip period marks the moment the Muslim empire began to look admiringly towards Europe. The ruling sultan at the time, Ahmed III, was a poet who loved calligraphy and cultivated the arts and literature. It was Sultan Ahmed III who oversaw the opening of the first-ever printing press in Istanbul. During this period a distinct style began to emerge in the empire's arts, culture and architecture, one that paid homage to European artistic styles by marrying classical Islamic elements with baroque ones – in that respect it was a uniquely European Muslim artistic tradition. This style became popular long after the *actual* Tulip period ended, which is why so many surviving Ottoman monuments display this influence. I had first encountered it at the Tombul Mosque in Bulgaria, but we had seen remnants of the style on the walls of the Koski Mehmed Pasha in Mostar; the Sultana Valida in Sjenica; the Sultan Murat in Skopje and at that magical tekke in Blagaj, yet none of them came close to the way it was manifest here at the Ali Pasha Mosque. This was truly a rare Ottoman gem; those thirty thousand eggs had made one hell of an omelette!

Tetovo is the unofficial capital of the Albanian-Macedonians and it is here that the calls for Albanian cultural autonomy in North Macedonia have always been heard the loudest. In fact, even during the communist period, local Albanians agitated for Tetovo and other Albanian majority territories in the country to be joined with Kosovo. On the eve of Yugoslavia's collapse, the town's Albanian majority took to the streets demanding secession from what was then the Socialist

Republic of Macedonia, and unity with neighbouring Albania. They then boycotted the referendum that led to the country's independence and as a result the country's Albanians were almost entirely excluded from government representation. Fiercely proud of their ethnic and religious roots, during the Bosnian and Kosovo wars the city took in thousands of Muslims fleeing the conflicts in their countries, and reportedly became the rear supply base for the Kosovo Liberation Army.

Tetovo means 'Teto's place'. According to legend, this is because a mythical figure called Teto cleared snakes from a village at the foot of the Sharr Mountains and that place came to be known as his village. The Ottomans, however, knew it as Kalkandelen, which means 'shield penetrator' in Turkish. This was because Tetovo's blacksmiths were the region's premier weapon makers. Before the arrival of the Ottomans in the 14th century, Tetovo had been little more than a small rural settlement. It was the Muslim empire, recognising the town's strategic location, sheltered by the looming Sharr mountain range, that made it into an important business and trading town. As Kalkandelen witnessed economic growth, it began to attract more and more people from the surrounding countryside and the population grew dramatically during the Ottoman period when several of the town's most beautiful monuments were built, including three *jama'at* mosques and seven local ones, as well as several hammams – one of which still stands opposite the Ali Pasha Mosque. Tetovo is also home to one of the most impressive Sufi lodges in North Macedonia.

There was a strange atmosphere in the Arabati Baba Tekke. As we parked up inside the fort-like complex, walled in on all four sides, I couldn't help but notice the Saudi Arabian flag inside the main office at the entrance. As far as I was aware, Tetovo did not have a Saudi community. Most Saudis are fiercely conservative Sunni Muslims who consider any practice of Islam based on non-literal theology to be deviant. Sufism – with its focus on the inner, more spiritual interpretation – in their eyes would be just downright heresy. The Arabati Baba Tekke, as the name suggests, is a Bektashi lodge. Bektashism's liberal interpretations of Islam combined with its Shia roots would make it beyond heretical to most Saudi Muslims. In fact, I doubt many would even consider it Islam. All of which made the green and white flag inside the office very peculiar. Something was definitely afoot.

Unlike the welcoming atmosphere at the Blagaj Tekke, here men at the entrance stopped and interrogated the drivers of any cars that tried to come in. When they stopped us, our English accents and the fact that we were quite obviously a family of tourists meant no interrogation was necessary and they simply waved us in.

We parked beneath the historic *musafirhan,* a stunning 18th-century traveller's guesthouse. This classical Ottoman structure of two floors had a wonderfully uneven wooden balcony decorated with carved floral motifs. We all gasped as we exited the car and would've loved exploring inside it, but the heavy lock on the door made it clear it was off limits.

The Arabati Baba Tekke was built sometime in the 16th century and was also known as the Sersem Tekke, which means 'Fool's Tekke'. This is because it was reportedly founded by a Sersem Ali Baba, who was no ordinary baba. He had started off life as one of Sultan Suleiman the Magnificent's most trusted viziers and was also his brother-in-law. However, one day, Ali Baba reportedly had a powerful dream that affected him so deeply – the legend doesn't explain what this dream was about – that he made the decision to turn his back on the wealth and riches of Ottoman courtly life. Instead, he decided to devote himself to religious contemplation and meditation as a Bektashi dervish. To start his new monastic life, the vizier travelled far from Istanbul, arriving at the foot of the Sharr Mountains, near Tetovo, where he spent the rest of his life. Around the time of his death in 1569, either Ali Baba or one of his disciples – Harabati Baba (hence the Arabati name) – founded the lodge here. Helpless and angry that he would be losing one of his greatest aides to a life of solitude and asceticism, the great sultan is supposed to have famously said to Ali: 'If you will be a "sersem" [fool] then go!' And that is the reason the tekke was known as the Fool's Tekke.

Today, the unique complex of richly ornamented pavilions represents the best-preserved lodge in North Macedonia. On the site is a fountain, guest quarters, dining room, dervish dwellings, and a mosque – all added over the course of several centuries around the original *türbe* of Sersem Ali Dede, the founding baba. Some of the most impressive parts of the complex were commissioned by local governor Receb Pasha and his son Abdurrahman Pasha – builders of the Ali Pasha Mosque – in the 18th and 19th centuries. In fact, Receb Pasha was also a dervish and buried at the tekke as well.

We headed straight for its centrepiece, the *şadrvan,* an ornately decorated raised platform made of intricately carved dark wood oriented towards Makkah. Most likely dating from the pasha's period, the *şadrvan* was split in two parts by a pair of delicately carved wooden doors and looked as if it could've been sat somewhere in the hills of northern Thailand; I half expected bald monks in saffron robes to appear.

At the centre of the *şadrvan,* in an area for relaxing called the *divanhane,* was a seven-sided marble fountain that gives the platform its name (*şadirvan* is Turkish for the ablution fountain of a mosque), but the main space, the *semahane*, was a raised area for prayers and *dhikr*. This was left deliberately open to the elements, so that the dervishes could sit beneath the stunning, patterned wood ceiling, listening to the world around them as they carried out their worship. It really was a thing of absolute beauty and, though we felt privileged to be able to explore it, as it sat there empty, I couldn't help but wonder if it was still in use.

'This is a nice lodge, but it doesn't have the same feel as the one in Blagaj,' Tamara remarked as we sat on one of the wooden ledges.

'Maybe it's the weird welcome at the entrance. Also, there's no-one here that seems to be using any of the spaces, in Blagaj the dervishes were welcoming us in,' I agreed.

'Yeah, I dunno… there's a strange feel to the place, right?' Tamara looked up towards the Sharr Mountains where a large bird, maybe an eagle or a falcon, was circling over its prey.

'I know what you mean; it doesn't feel right, like it's missing something.'

There was an emptiness hanging in the air inside this tekke. Where were the worshippers? Where were the dervishes who had built this fabulous complex and gave the lodge meaning? The lodge was missing its soul.

In the northwestern corner of the walled tekke was a tile-roofed building with grimy glass walls. I peered inside through the gaps between the dirty curtains: dusty furniture sat piled up in the corner of a large, darkened room where the carpet resembled the type you find in a mosque; straight rows of arabesque arches faced Makkah, but nobody had prayed here for quite some time. Several panes of glass were broken. Had there been violence here?

Walking past the broken glass, I came upon a tomb draped in a green funeral covering with yellow Arabic inscriptions and protected by metal bars. Around the edges, visitors had left monetary offerings and on the wall were two beautiful paintings of mosques. I suspected it was the tomb of Receb Pasha and that the artwork had most likely been done by the same artists from Debar that had painted his stunning mosque in the town.

Next to this was a small wooden farm gate that led to a whole other section of the tekke, hidden behind a roundhouse built using the *bondruk* technique of thin red bricks and wood. In the middle of the roundhouse sat the most important tomb of all – Sersem Ali Dede, the brother-in-law of Sultan Suleiman, and reported founder of the lodge. This was clearly the tekke's historic centre.

I stood for a while staring at the dusty tomb. I had found yet another connection to the great sultan. For so long, Sultan Suleiman had been just another mythical Muslim hero: a distant, otherworldly figure of the east, like the companions of the Prophet or the Mughal Emperors of India. The first time I became aware of Sultan Suleiman was when my brother, also a 'Soleman', had told me he had been named after a great Muslim ruler. I don't remember my brother telling me much else, but I do remember my Western-educated mind conjuring up an image of the great sultan as a distant orientalist's fantasy, someone so far removed from my world he might as well have been Tamerlane or Genghis Khan. Yet already on this journey I had found so much to connect me to medieval Islam's great Caesar – Suleiman was literally referred to as *Kayser-i-Rum*, the 'Caesar of the Romans'.

During his reign in the 16th century, the Ottoman Empire achieved its absolute zenith as the most powerful and influential state in the world. Ottoman technology, art and architecture reached new heights and the empire witnessed a degree of economic and political stability, peace and religious tolerance rarely seen after this point. It became a major player across Europe and for the first time was recognised as the actual caliphate of the Sunni Islamic world. It was after this period that Ottoman sultans began carrying the titles historically reserved for the rulers of the Muslim *ummah* (community). Suleiman was therefore caliph, *Amir al-Mu'minin* ('Commander of the Faithful') and Protector of the Two Holy Mosques (Makkah and Madinah). In the 16th century, the sultan known as 'the Magnificent' in the west was the most revered man on earth.

This journey had brought me face to face with 'God's Shadow on Earth' – another of his many titles. It was Suleiman who had commissioned the magnificent bridge at Mostar; it was his great vizier who had commissioned the one in Višegrad and his chief architect who had built it. It is Suleiman's mosque in Istanbul that has been painted all over Muslim Europe as a mythical place on a par with the other holy places in Islam.

For so long, Suleiman – like Sinan, Sokollu and Evliya – had been a mystery to me; another name from that 'other' history I was told had nothing to do with Europe's one, yet here I was travelling through Europe with my family, encountering places and people that tangibly connected him to the continent's cultural landscape and its Muslim heritage, my Muslim heritage. The more I learned about Sultan Suleiman on this trip, the more I realised he was Muslim Europe's Alexander.

Shortly after our Balkan trip, news filtered out of Szigetvár in Hungary that the 'lost' tomb of Sultan Suleiman the Magnificent had been found. Suleiman had died whilst leading a siege on Szigetvár Castle in 1566 and, as with Murad in Kosovo, his organs had been buried there and a *türbe* built over the grave. The location of the *türbe* was lost after Hungary was taken from the Ottomans by Austria in the 17th century. Plans are now underway to turn the site into an open-air museum. Muslim Europe's Alexander had also been buried in Europe.

Sersem's tomb had a concrete base, wooden top and a soft green and white hat at the head, like those worn by the Bektashi babas. It sat in a sunken space, with a number of silver candelabras at the front covered in wax dripping. Parts of the *türbe*'s walls were missing and next to it was another tomb with an impressive decorated stone sarcophagus – most likely that of his famous disciple, Harabati Baba. It was in a bad way: cracked and damaged, hinting at vandalism.

Behind both of these, past a series of wooden posts blackened by fire, was a long row of tombs housed in green, Toblerone-shaped wooden boxes, each with its own green-and-white baba hat. The entire complex looked in desperate need of repair.

Some of the fire damage probably dated to 1948, when the complex was set alight by guerrillas from Yugoslavia's communist party who wanted to ban all religious activity in the country. The communists turned the Arabati Baba Tekke into a tourist complex, complete with a discotheque. Religious activities were only restored at the tekke after the collapse of Yugoslavia and following a sit-in led by two babas, Tayyar Gashi and Tahir Emini, in 1995. However, in 2002 armed local conservative Sunnis stormed the tekke, demanding it be converted into a conventional Sunni mosque – despite never historically functioning as one. The invaders were allegedly part of the national Muslim organisation, the Islamic Community of Macedonia (ICM), and, as the official body for the Muslim community of North Macedonia, they claimed the tekke belonged to them because the Bektashis were an Islamic sect and fell under their umbrella. In response, the Bektashis tried to sue the government for failing to restore the tekke to their community at the end of the communist period – something that was done across the country for privately owned property and land originally seized by the communist government. The reason the Arabati Baba Tekke was overlooked was because the 1990 law applied only to private individuals and not religious communities.

The tekke remains a disputed territory with ICM members reportedly squatting in the lodge and slowly trying to take over more of the buildings. When we visited, they had also taken control of the small 'mosque' on site. It was these guys who were flying the Saudi flags at the front, and it was this tension we had sensed in the lodge.

Ali Reza spoke almost no English, which wasn't such a bad thing, judging by the wheezing noises he made every time he tried to speak. He was, however, very relaxed when he saw me enter his section of the tekke. And with the little English he could muster, Ali explained that he was an initiate of the Bektashi order, and this little corner of the tekke was still theirs, complete with offices right next to the tombs of their babas, including that of the sit-in baba, Tahir Emini, the one who had managed to reacquire the tekke for the Bektashi. He was also the last of the babas to be buried at the complex, having passed away in 2006, and it was the only tomb in the complex with a large bouquet of white lilies by the headstone.

Ali was around fifty years old and balding at the front. His greying hair was light and fluffy and looked as if it could be blown away by a strong gust of wind. Dressed in a bright blue polo shirt, he had a thick handlebar moustache that gave him something of an Americantrucker look. Ali didn't smile much – he mostly just wheezed, as he was very overweight – but he was kind and welcoming and I was really pleased to have finally met a Bektashi here at their tekke.

Upon realising my interest in the tekke, Ali hauled himself up and headed towards the glass doors of the office, indicating I should follow. The room was wonderfully cool and quiet, except for the low hum of the air-conditioning unit. It resembled the clubhouse of an amateur football team, the walls completely covered with framed pictures and awards. However, the awards were not for sporting achievements and the pictures were not local sporting heroes; they were mostly of three highly revered Shia figures: Imam Ali, the nephew of the Prophet Muhammad, and his sons Hasan and Husayn.

As well as these major Shia figures, the wall was also furnished with pictures of several famous Bektashi babas, past and present, including Tahir Emini, and older, historical ones whose illustrated profiles appeared on round plates or as wood carvings. There were also pictures of famous Bektashi tombs from around the Balkans, including two I had visited in Bulgaria: Demir Baba in Sveshtari and his teacher Ak Yazili Baba, close to Balchik on the Black Sea.

Ali Reza pointed to a photo of a heavyset man wearing a white prayer cap. Like Ali Reza, he had a thick moustache and a large nose that made him look like Obelix from the Asterix comic books of my childhood. He then pointed to himself.

I stared blankly. Was that him in the picture? There was definitely a resemblance.

'Brat,' he said, again pointing at himself.

Did that mean 'me'? I wondered.

Ali Reza could see I didn't understand and thought for a while, wheezing heavily as he did.

'Brother!' he finally exclaimed with some triumph.

'Ah, your brother!'

Ali's brother, it turned out, was also a dervish of the Bektashi order, and clearly someone Ali was very proud of, as he was of the wall in general, beaming with pride every time he saw me admiring something on it. I wondered if others ever visited the space. I was genuinely fascinated by it. It offered a real insight into this much maligned and forgotten religious community that I had known almost nothing about before I came to the Balkans.

Having shown me the wall, Ali Reza brought out a book, which he placed on a wooden stand like the ones Muslims use to read the Qur'an. The book was green and had an enigmatic face made out of Arabic calligraphy on the front. I immediately recognised the cryptic depictions as the same ones I had seen on the ceiling of the Bektashi tombs in Bulgaria. The face was round and bald, with large, full lips and earrings. It reminded me of the laughing Buddha in Thai culture. The two-volume book, printed in Istanbul, was called *Bektasiligin Icyüzü*.

'Bektashi pray,' said Ali Reza, pointing at the words that I didn't understand. 'Bektashi pray,' he repeated, cupping his hands to indicate the words were Bektashi prayers. I looked again at them. They were in Latin script but not in a language I recognised.

Outside, the *adhan* for *Asr* was being called from somewhere within the tekke. I asked Ali Reza where the mosque was. He pointed in the direction of the small mosque opposite his part of the tekke but then made a cross sign and an angry face. He also shook his head as if telling me I shouldn't go there. This was because the mosque, like the lodge office near the *musafirhan*, was run by the ICM, who the Bektashi were fighting for the tekke.

The Ibadet Hane Mesci, the lodge's mosque, was a square building with a small porch where the dervishes used to pray – now it is used by the local Sunni community. Nobody entering the mosque paid any heed to the Bektashi side of the tekke or the tombs of the babas.

Inside, a blind wooden dome sat over the main hall. The interior was exposed stone with the top half painted entirely white, muting the intricate plasterwork patterns – a stark contrast to the lavish decorations seen around the rest of the lodge. In the centre of the wall that faced Makkah was the *mihrab*, which according to the Bektashis was something the Sunnis had introduced. The Bektashis knew this building as the *Kubali Meydan*, a space used for their ceremonial prayers which had no need for a niche because the space had never been used as a traditional mosque.

On my way out, I paused to admire the Blue Tower close to the mosque. Also known as Fatima's Tower, it was yet another one of the tekke's standout features: an elegant two-storey building, modelled on the classic *chardak* – a traditional Balkan house. Constructed with a solid stone base, it had an ornate wooden upper floor and was painted blue. It was wonderfully quaint and, like the *şadrvan*, dated to the period of the pashas. In fact, the story of how it came to be is linked directly to Abdurrahman Pasha, who built it for his sickly daughter, Fatima. Fatima suffered from tuberculosis and the pasha had hoped by staying on these holy premises, in the company of dervishes and surrounded by the sound of their daily worship, her condition might improve. I'm not sure if this worked for Fatima, but the legend, like so many aspects of the Arabati Baba Tekke was quite beautiful. For how long though, I wondered. The damage and vandalism I had seen suggested the sectarian battle for ownership of the tekke was also slowly destroying it. In that regard, I hoped Ali Reza and his community's defiant stance continued. As the obvious guardians of the tekke's heritage, they appeared to be its natural inheritors and the ones most likely to preserve its stunning historic monuments. As Bektashis, Ali Reza's community was used to being marginalised and pushed to the very edges of history. Both the Ottomans (towards the end) and the communists were guilty of this. Though this was clearly not the case during Evliya's time; when Evliya came across two Bektashi dervishes in northeast Africa, he described them as 'lovers of God' and 'brothers' and he had clearly gone out of his way to visit their lodges, like the one in Blagaj.

Now, it seemed the types of intolerant attitudes Imam Rajaab had described to me in Skopje were becoming an issue across North Macedonia.

The Bektashis and the Balkans are as intertwined as Islam and Europe; one has clearly enhanced and informed the other's cultural tapestry and heritage, and there is just no getting away from that.

PART FOUR

ALBANIA

Taken by Albanians

VLORË

My notebook shows two significant entries for the border crossing from North Macedonia into Albania. The first says 'angry', because our satellite navigation did not recognise our destination in Albania. In fact, it didn't recognise Albania. This was after I had repeatedly told the rental company in Sarajevo Airport that it was an absolute must all the countries we were visiting were on the navigation system. I had actually pulled out a list and asked one by one if the navigation unit covered them. The guy at the desk had assured me it did. Yet as we approached the border near the western bank of Lake Ohrid, our navigation screen showed nothing on the other side – just a blank green space where the country of Albania should have been.

The second note I had made was about the poster at the checkpoint: it showed a child behind a wire fence. The poster was a warning to would-be child sex traffickers. It was on a wall near the border guard and I was worried the girls might see it, but fortunately Amani had her nose deep inside a book and both Anaiya and Tamara were fast asleep.

There had been six hundred cases of human trafficking in Albania the previous year alone. Many of these were women and young girls trafficked for sex and prostitution. Usually, they were girls duped into false marriages and the promise of a better life abroad by organised gangs who would then move them around Europe like commodities.

The gangs were also involved in other violent and serious organised crime, including drug smuggling and firearms trafficking, making the prospect of escape from their clutches almost impossible.

The female border guard who examined our passports was a middle-aged woman with curly hair and a face that could've turned the milk in a cup of tea. It was the first time we had seen a female border guard and also the first one to be truly suspicious of us. After thoroughly interrogating me about our reasons for entering Albania, she then asked if I knew any Albanians, all the time carefully thumbing our passports. I cheerfully explained I had a friend in Vlorë. But instead of reassuring her, this seemed to make her even more suspicious and she lowered her head again to see who was in the vehicle with me.

After several awkward minutes slowly flicking through all the pages of every single passport, stopping to examine the odd stamp, she reluctantly handed them back to me and finally waved us into our fifth Balkan country.

The poster at the border and the suspicious guard had brought back some creeping doubts I had been fending off ever since we announced we would be visiting Albania. I had been determined from the start not to give in to the popular image of Albania as somewhere dangerous and full of criminals, but it wasn't easy. First there were the car hire companies that had refused to even let their vehicles cross into Albania – we eventually found one that did. Then there were my Albanian friends, many of whom said they felt 'it wasn't safe' for non-Albanians. Yet when I asked them why, they seemed to have no answers except to say there were a lot of 'bad people' there. I pointed out there were a lot of bad people in England too, which just made them laugh.

Even human trafficking was a bigger problem in the UK, according to the latest government figures. I found it strange that, in spite of this, it was Albania with the reputation for trafficking, and wondered how much of this was down to the Hollywood blockbuster trilogy, *Taken*, where the main villains are gangs of Muslim Albanian human traffickers. The damage to the public perception of Albania by the movies was so great that the Balkan country felt the need to launch a tourism campaign to counteract this called 'Be Taken by Albania', with one of the main strategies titled 'Hey Liam'. This featured videos by campaigners directly addressing *Taken* star Liam Neeson and asking him to come and see for himself how amazing Albania really is.

This is nothing new for Europe's second-most 'Muslim' country – around sixty per cent of Albanians are Muslim. Historic xenophobic and Islamophobic depictions of the country by Western travellers are also often to blame for Albania's depiction as a hotbed of crime, hostility and barbarism.

Take the descriptions of Albania by E. F. Knight in his *Albania: A Narrative of Recent Travel*, published in 1880, which offers little empathy for local customs or beliefs and shows Knight to have the kind of Victorian attitude the Brits often displayed when describing natives in their colonised territories: inferior, barbaric and uncivilised. Encountering a social order in the highlands of Albania, where local clans avenge crimes based on a set of ancient and highly intricate codes that Knight clearly does not understand or appreciate, he suggests this is little more than some kind of 'wild and savage' behaviour. Two decades later, in her 1909 book *High Albania*, Edith Durham reinforces this by depicting the country as lawless.

Even American writer Rose Wilder Lane, who claims to be enamoured by Albania, is unable to hide her conviction that as a white American woman, she is further along the evolutionary ladder than the Albanians. After learning about the local belief in the *Ora*, a protective spirit possessed by every human being, during her 1921 educational mission for the Red Cross, Rose writes in her book, *The Peaks of Shala*, that the Albanians are 'living still in the childhood of the Aryan race' whilst she is a 'daughter of a century that is, to them, in the far and unknown future'.

Following the collapse of communism, attempted democracy and the debacle of large-scale, fraudulent get-rich-quick schemes in Albania, Robert Carver turns up when the country is on its knees in 1996 and reinforces all the Western expectations of Albania in his *The Accursed Mountains*, by claiming it has returned to the 'lawlessness' witnessed by Durham a century earlier.

Liam Neeson's trilogy is merely at the front of a queue of xenophobic and Islamophobic representations of Albania that has solidified the negative perception of the country and its people.

Driving through Albania, the thing that struck me the most was the lack of visible mosques. We had seen more minarets in the North Macedonian countryside then in Albania, which was very strange given that, of the two nations, Albania had the larger proportion of Muslims, and was historically a place filled with mosques – as British painter Edward Lear reported in the middle of the 19th century.

The reason for the dramatic disappearance of mosques is down to the four decades of rule by paranoid communist dictator Enver Hoxha after World War II. Hoxha violently clamped down on all religious activity in Albania. Between 1944 and 1967, almost all of the country's churches, mosques, monasteries and tekkes were destroyed or shut down as he declared Albania the world's first atheist state. Prior to that, Albania had been part of the Muslim Ottoman Empire for almost six centuries, with more than thirty Albanians serving as the empire's prime ministers – grand viziers.

We were headed to Vlorë, where my British-Albanian friend Idar spent his summers. He was the caretaker at the school I worked in and when I told him about our trip through the western Balkans he had insisted I come and spend some time there with his family. We were now less than an hour from Vlorë and decided to stop for a late lunch just short of the town of Fier by pulling into a large Renoil service station. The service station was almost as big as some airport buildings we had seen in the Balkans. Most of it was outdoors beneath a large steel roof. The seating was stylish and comfortable and we found ourselves surrounded by young, wealthy Albanians drinking coffee and eating the freshly baked pizza from the on-site clay oven. A squad of waiters stood to attention and at the back three delighted kids bounced up and down on a large trampoline while their parents sat close by.

Our young waiter had a cocky swagger about him. Above his lip were the beginnings of a moustache and he was the only member of staff with his shirt undone to the third button. He struck me as the kind of guy who in between taking orders slicked his hair back using the comb from his top pocket. He reminded me of a young Fonz from *Happy Days*, only not as cool, and much shorter.

'Do you take cards?' I asked him.

'No card, only cash,' he replied in an instant.

'OK, do you know where I can get cash from a bank machine?'

The wannabe-Fonz looked confused and turned to his colleague who was manning the pizza oven. The pair of them had a brief conversation as the latter translated my request to our waiter, who then said, 'No bank.'

'No bank?' I repeated, slightly incredulous that such a big service station would not have at least one cash machine. 'Are you sure?'

'No bank, but mister, if you have euro, I give you lek,' he said, smiling.

I wasn't sure.

I looked the waiter up and down. I had spent the last ten years teaching cocky teenage upstarts like him in London and suspected he wasn't being wholly truthful. So, after placing our order, I headed back to the main road to see if I could spy an ATM sign. I didn't even have to leave the vicinity of the Renoil when I spotted a large, shiny building with a covered ATM machine.

'Cheeky little bastard!' I muttered under my breath as I headed over to withdraw some Albanian lek for the week ahead. Despite the lie, I decided to give the waiter the benefit of the doubt. Maybe he thought I wanted an *actual* bank.

The pizzas in the Renoil were the best we had eaten so far in the Balkans. They had perfectly crisp, thin crusts and just the right balance of ingredients to cheese. The influence of their Italian neighbours was such that even a service station in Albania could make better pizza than most restaurants in England.

When it was time to pay our bill, our waiter came over and did something rather strange. He asked that I tally up the total from the receipts myself. I took this to be a local peculiarity and did as he asked. The total came to around 1,500 lek: about ten English pounds. I handed the young man a 5,000-lek note. The waiter wiped his brow and headed back to the front of the service area to get our change. When he returned though, he only handed back 3,000 lek. Normally, I wouldn't check my change; if it looks about right, I tend to accept what is given, especially with all the different currencies I had been dealing with and how cheap things were in the Balkans. But as we had only just stepped into Albania and I was still trying to figure out what everything cost, I decided to count the change and noticed it was 500 lek short.

'Must be a mistake,' I said to Tam, who nodded and continued reading something on her phone.

I looked for the receipts to check, but they were now gone, and so I called over the young waiter and explained that there may have been an oversight. The young man gave me an exasperated look before turning to the pizza baker to translate for him.

'He says, he asked you to count the receipts so you would know how much the bill is, and he doesn't understand why you now think it is wrong,' explained the pizza baker.

I had to admit he was good. His confident, languid mannerism had me fooled, and as the missing money amounted to only £3.50, I walked away thinking it probably was my mistake after all.

'Everything OK?' Tamara asked, noting the confused expression on my face.

'Yes, come on, let's go, I think it was my mistake. You know what it's like with all these different currencies.'

But no sooner had we got up then a voice called me from the back of the kitchen. It was the pizza baker, and it was quite apparent he was trying to stay hidden. How strange I thought, as he urged me to go over.

'Look, don't worry about it, my friend, maybe it was my...' I began, but the baker cut me off.

'Please, my friend, tell me what you had to eat and drink. I am the manager here and the owner has sent me to come and see you,' he said in a hushed tone.

Slightly confused, I listed the items and could see the manager mentally tallying it all up.

'That should come to 1,500 lek,' he confirmed. 'Now, please tell me, how much did you give the waiter?'

'I gave him 5,000 lek, which is why I was expecting 3,500 lek back, because I counted 1,500 lek in front of him'

'Yes, you are right, he should've given you back 3,500 lek. Please may I have the change he gave you?'

I handed the manager the money. Thanking me, he disappeared into the back of the shop and I went and sat back down with Tamara and the girls, who wanted to know what was going on. But before I could finish telling them, the manager was back, closely pursued by our waiter, who went straight up to him and said something in Albanian in a tone that suggested he was not happy. The manager ignored him and I tensed, expecting him to turn to me, but he didn't. He didn't even look at us. Instead, he just walked back to the front of the service station. When the manager knew the waiter was gone, he gave me back my original 5,000-lek note and then spoke very softly, with sadness in his voice.

'I have spoken to my boss, and he said you are not to be charged for anything. We are very sorry for the trouble you have had,' he said, keeping his head slightly bowed the whole time. I was suddenly struck by immense guilt.

'Listen, I'm really sorry to cause any problems…'

Again the manager cut me off.

'No, you must not apologise, sir, my boss is very grateful you told us. We need to know these things so that we know if it happens to other customers. Please forgive us.'

'Please let me at least pay for what we did eat.' I pleaded, but the manager wouldn't budge.

'No, sir, we cannot take your money now, please, you are our guest now.'

I realised that maybe this had happened before, and thanked the manager.

'I won't forget how honest you have been. This is our first day in Albania, and I was worried it had started with a bad experience, but already you have shown us the hospitality and kindness of your people. Thank you.'

'Where is this person?' I looked at my phone for the umpteenth time.

We were sat outside Cream Caffe on Bulevardi Vlorë, the main road that ran through the centre of the coastal town. It was a modern-looking street with lots of boutique stores, cake shops, supermarkets and cafés. Cream Caffe was where Emma had asked to meet us to hand over the keys to her apartment. The problem was I didn't know what Emma looked like. Her image on Airbnb was one of those 'arty' pictures where the person is looking away. I was communicating with her via WhatsApp, and her most recent message said she was nearly here. I scanned the passing traffic. Vlorë was home to a lot of prosperous Albanians. Everyone that walked past was dressed well. The town had the air of a holiday resort. Men in sunglasses and smart leather sandals sat outside coffee shops as pretty young women sauntered past.

There was still no sign of Emma. I looked at the phone again.

'Hei where are u', read the latest message.

I decided to call her. The girls were on to their second game of Scabby Queen. It was early afternoon; we had been driving for most of the day and just wanted to get into our apartment for the evening.

'Hi Emma, we are at the coffee shop, Cream Caffe, are you here?' I asked, looking around the coffee shop, where two girls sat showing each other their phones.

'I'm just outside,' she said.

I looked up and a young girl with short curls in jeans and a T-shirt walked in holding a phone to her ear. I waved to grab her attention. Emma was not what I had expected at all. The profile picture on Airbnb, even with the head turned, looked like someone much older.

'I'm sorry for being late.'

'That's OK,' I lied, relieved she had finally arrived. We had been waiting for nearly an hour. 'I'm Tharik, this is my wife Tamara, and these are our daughters, Amani and Anaiya.'

'Hi,' said the girls, looking up from their game of cards.

I ordered an espresso for Emma and waited for her to present me with a key. But when I brought the espresso over, Emma explained that she didn't have the key and the person who did would phone her soon. We could then go and get the key. Emma seemed honest enough, but I was very confused.

As we waited for the call, Emma told us more about herself. I listened, expecting things to become clear. Emma didn't live in Vlorë herself, she worked for an accountancy firm in the capital Tirana, which was a three-hour drive away. She explained that there was no work in Vlorë and, after graduating, she had been left no choice but to take a job in the capital, where she rented a small apartment during the week. It wasn't ideal, but it was better than a lot of people who were struggling to get any kind of job in Albania. Emma came back most weekends to spend time with her parents in the home she had grown up in.

'So whose apartment are we staying in?' I asked.

'Someone I know through a friend,' she said, a little hesitant. I flashed a look at Tamara.

We had booked this apartment for three nights because it was close to Idar's house and the centre of Vlorë. The person who had posted the property was called Emma, and when we switched from communicating via the booking app to WhatsApp, I had assumed I was still speaking to the host, but apparently not.

'Emma' was now on the phone. She spoke in Albanian briefly. 'OK, we can go and get the keys now,' she said.

Leaving Tamara and the girls at the café, the two of us drove off. 'Emma' was polite, intelligent and clearly quite innocent, so I decided to find out what exactly was going on as we sat in the car together.

'So, you are not the owner, but your name is also Emma?' I asked as she directed me towards a road that ran parallel to the high street and the coast.

'No, my name is Eda. Were you calling me "Emma"? I thought you were saying "Eda"!'

'Ah, I see,' I said, as we both laughed and one part of the puzzle became clear.

'So, who are we getting the keys from then?' I asked.

'I'm not sure, I think it is the owner's brother.' Again, this response didn't fill me with confidence. My confusion was now turning into genuine concern. The car radio was playing traditional Albanian music as Eda signalled for me to pull up next to a couple of tower blocks.

'Wait here,' she said, heading out of the car towards two men standing near a bench. One of them handed her some keys and, after a brief exchange, she returned.

'OK, so if there is any problem with the apartment, he said you can call me and he will come and fix it for you,'

'Great,' I said, still wondering who 'he' was.

As we drove back, I didn't ask Eda anything else. It was quite apparent she either didn't have the answers or didn't want to tell me and although this made very uneasy, I also didn't want to jump to any conclusions. Maybe this was just the casual manner in which things were done around here, I told myself.

After picking up Tamara and the girls, Eda stayed in the car to direct us to the apartment. We left the boulevard and turned on to a road badly in need of repair. I could see everyone was exhausted and decided that we would stay in the apartment for just tonight and rethink things in the morning. The route took us past tired blocks of flats with crumbling façades where people sat outside cafés and grocery stores. After passing a launderette and a small tailor, we turned into a housing estate that looked just like the ones I had grown up on in the East End of London. As our shiny white Megane slowly came through, mothers sat outside ground-floor flats stopped chatting and looked up, and small boys halted their game of street football so we could pass. I smiled and nodded at them, remembering the days when my friends and I would do the same. The boys smiled back. It was now getting dark and, as the street lamps came on, we could see that several were not working.

'Go slow, I've got to remember where exactly it is,' Eda said, as two boys wearing fake Barcelona football shorts stood and stared with a ball at their feet. I now suspected Eda had never been to the flat at all.

A mother with a headscarf was scolding her daughter for getting her frock dirty as we pulled into what felt like the darkest and quietest corner of the estate. The car's headlights momentarily lit up windows along the ground floor before I switched the engine off. We were parked behind a car that had been in the same spot for so long there was moss growing on its back tyres.

The apartment was two flights up and when we arrived at the door, Eda remained uncertain. I kept throwing glances at Tamara, who looked equally bemused. When she put the key in and it turned, I sensed Eda's relief. The door opened on to a large apartment with clean marble floors and a huge central living space. There was a big double room with two beds for the girls, and an even larger master bedroom with an en suite and a balcony that had a grill across it.

I told Tamara I would go and grab the rest of our luggage and see Eda off.

Downstairs, I shook Eda's hand and said goodbye before heading to the car and grabbing just the one bag. The noise of the children playing football was very faint now. Somewhere in a flat a baby was crying, and I could see the flickering images of a TV set through one of the windows. I looked up at our block, it was eerily silent.

As I walked up the two flights of stairs, all my earlier anxieties came flooding back. Whose house was this? Who was the guy with the key? Who else had a key to this place? Why didn't Eda seem to have any convincing answers? And was I just feeling this suspicious because we were in Albania?

I was worried that being tired might be clouding my judgement. So I stopped and thought for a moment. This was not about where the apartment was; I had grown up in similar housing estates. What was bothering me was that I didn't know who the hell owned this property, or why so many people were involved in its rental. That, I decided, was legitimate grounds to be concerned, regardless of where we were.

By the time I got to the top of the stairs, I had made my decision. We were not going to stay here tonight, or any night. There were just too many uncertainties.

I walked in to find the girls excitedly exploring their room, deciding who would take what bed as Tamara opened up the windows to air out the place. She turned to look at me holding just the one bag.

'Where are the others?' she asked.

'I don't think we should stay here,' I said.

Tamara looked confused, and then a little alarmed. 'Why, has something happened?'

'No, nothing has happened; I just don't feel comfortable with this set-up, whatever it is.'

'What do you mean?' she asked.

'Well, I thought we were meeting the owner to get the keys, but instead this young girl turns up who can't properly explain her connection to the owner, and then tells us she doesn't know where the keys are. We then go to get keys off some random people she again doesn't seem to know very well… I mean, who else has keys? I don't even know if the person who *really* owns this house knows we are staying here. What if someone just turns up, and we're not meant to be here?'

I could hear myself beginning to sound a little manic as I said this all out loud for the first time, but Tamara understood.

'OK, if you don't feel comfortable then we won't stay here. To be honest, I agree something feels a bit off,' she said very calmly.

'So, it's not just me then? Good. I wanted to stay here and believe everything was fine, but too many things don't add up and I just don't want to take any chances with our family. Let's go and find a hotel for the night and we can sort out what is going on with this place in the morning.'

'That's fine, but what shall we tell the girls?' she asked.

'We'll tell them the truth.'

And we did. We agreed it would be an important lesson for them too, and so we explained how the set-up felt strange, and although nothing bad had *actually* happened, I was going with my gut feeling. This was an important instinct on the road in foreign lands, we told them.

'If something doesn't feel right, you should avoid it,' I said. 'Even if it means a little more hassle and effort, the most important thing is that you feel secure and safe.'

The girls understood. We could see they were a little worried and very tired, but they trusted us. We had been travelling with them from almost the moment each of them had been born, and they knew our family's safety was always the priority, regardless of how weird and wonderful the adventures became.

It was getting really late now and we were very hungry, so we headed back to the centre of town, where we found a crêperie next door to the Cream Caffe. As we tucked into savoury crêpes for dinner, I managed to book a one-bedroom apartment with a sea view at the Hotel Nacional Vlorë. It was perfect for one night and would give us the time needed to rearrange the rest of our time in Vlorë.

The Nacional was a ten-minute drive to the south of the city and when we arrived, we were greeted by a bemused team of receptionists who could not find our booking. None of them spoke English. Eventually, an extremely glamorous woman in a red dress and high heels came out from the back and explained that she was the owner but had no booking confirmed in my name. I asked her what she did have.

'I'm sorry,' she said, looking genuinely sad. 'I have nothing, maybe next door...' she began, before sending her bellboy to check. He returned looking just as sad. It was the weekend in peak season, there was nothing they could do, she explained.

Tamara was looking online and not having much luck either. There was only one thing for it: we would have to do things the old-fashioned way and physically visit each hotel along the seafront. The woman at the Nacional agreed this was the best option given how late it was.

Our first night in Albania turned out to be our most uncomfortable. We visited several places, most were either fully booked or 'stank of fish' according to Anaiya, who helped with room inspections. We ended up staying in a large family room with four beds and an en suite in a place that resembled the kind of roadside motel fugitives in American movies stayed in, only this one was yards from the gorgeous Adriatic. We didn't care though. It was clean, had a friendly receptionist and, most importantly, felt safe and secure.

A Beer with a Muslim

LLOGARA NATIONAL PARK

The sun glistened in the waters of the aqua-green Adriatic, which resembled a million shimmering jewels. Amani and Anaiya's heads bobbed up and down near the shore where their mother lay stretched out on a towel, a sun hat and large sunglasses covering her face. It had been a wonderfully relaxing day on the small beach just south of Vlorë, where Idar's daughter, Liri was spending the summer with her new baby and her mother-in-law. Idar had met us in the morning dressed like a Sicilian don in a smart striped shirt and white cotton trousers. I was so used to seeing him shuffling around in overalls with a large set of keys swinging by his side that at first I hadn't recognised him sat in the hostel garden. His attire had reminded me of the suits we had to wear when we went 'back home' to Bangladesh as children. Our parents dressed us in these so that when we stepped off the plane, we looked every bit the wealthy foreigners our relatives imagined we were.

'I still can't believe your wife, an English woman that is so nice and respectful. And she became Muslim.' Idar's face was very serious as he sat beside me in the shade of two large olive trees. 'You know, Terick,' – he had trouble pronouncing my name – 'I still can't believe this!'

I laughed but also felt sad. Idar had never met my family before, and it seems he had also never met a nice 'English' person, or one that was Muslim. I was again reminded of my youth. I too had spent

191

my early years wondering if 'English' people were actually nice. I had suspected they could be because of the wonderful primary school teachers we had, who showered me with affection. Then there was Eileen, my 'English Ma', as she came to be known. Eileen was an elderly East End woman who had lived in our block of flats long before us Bangladeshi migrants came along. She didn't have much time for the others, but she loved me. Whenever I was playing outside, she would call me over and offer me ice cream, chocolate and all kinds of little treats. If she popped down to the market, she would come back with a cheap football for me to play with. Eileen lived alone – her only son, Douglas, had moved away – and so I knew she was lonely. We were a poor immigrant family and treats like ice cream and chocolate were a rarity, as too was a new football to play with. Maybe she felt sorry for me or maybe she just wanted the company, but up until I left primary school, Eileen was the only nice English person I knew that wasn't a teacher. It took years for me to realise that this wasn't normal, and that the kind of hostile white people I had grown up around in run-down East End council estates were not actually representative of wider British society.

Since moving to England from Albania, Idar had only ever lived in Dagenham, where, as an eastern European immigrant, he was experiencing the same hostility my family did in 1980s east London – which is why he too believed there were no nice English people.

I explained this to Idar and said that 1980s Tower Hamlets was probably not that different to Dagenham; the British National Party's first ever London council seat was won in an east London ward in 1993, and the next one in a Dagenham ward in 2004. I assured Idar that all he was suffering from was a classic case of underexposure to British society. Idar listened carefully and laughed.

'Would you like a drink?' he asked. I gave him a thumbs up and sat back on the hard plastic chair. It had been a hectic few days, and it felt good to spend time relaxing with a friend and his family. I had met Liri before I met Idar. She had been in one of my first A-level classes at the school I taught at and when she got back in touch after finishing university, she told me the school's new caretaker was in fact her father. So the next time I saw Idar, I introduced myself. We have been friends ever since.

When Idar returned he had two bottles in his hands, I couldn't see what they were because of the bright sun and grabbed one from him. Holding it up to look, I realised he had bought me a bottle of Corona.

'Idar.' I laughed. 'I don't drink beer.'

'No? You want something stronger?' he asked.

I was confused. 'No. No, not at all. I mean I don't drink alcohol.'

Idar looked at me. Now he was confused. 'Why not?' he asked.

'Because I'm Muslim,' I said.

'But so am I and I drink beer,' said Idar without the slightest hint of irony, as if there was nothing wrong with this statement. I was even more confused now. I knew many Muslims that liked a drink. I had even seen Idar drinking beer at the end-of-term staff parties, and just assumed that, like some of the Muslims I had grown up with, he drank alcohol but knew it wasn't permissible in Islam. But Idar's response suggested he didn't. So I asked him why.

'As a Bektashi,' he explained, 'drinking is allowed as long as you don't get drunk.'

'I had no idea,' I said. 'Before I came to the Balkans, I knew nothing about Bektashism.'

'Yes, we are more modern in our beliefs.'

'But you know most Muslims don't drink alcohol, don't you?'

Idar shrugged his shoulders and nodded, before grabbing the beer from me and heading back to the bar.

That afternoon, Idar decided he wanted to take us out for a traditional Albanian dinner in a place he knew high up in the mountains.

'It's very beautiful, Terick, very high in montains,' said Idar as his British-registered black BMW wound its way up the stunning mountain roads of the Llogara National Park. Every time the car lurched around a hairpin, the hand of Fatima hanging from the rear-view mirror swung from side to side. The bright sun appeared to wink at us as we passed thick forests of pine. Soon these gave way to a more arid landscape of scrub and rocks.

After a while, as we neared the summit, Idar pulled into a car park close to the mountain's edge. I looked around for a restaurant, but couldn't see one. We parked next to a yellow JCB digger, and Idar led us across the road to a brand-new viewing platform – it was his little pre-dinner surprise. The panorama overlooking the shimmering blue Albanian Riviera was breathtaking.

'Wooooah!' gasped the girls.

'This is stunning, Idar,' Tamara said. 'Thank you for bringing us here.' She loved a good view, and this was a fabulous one. Idar had a grin on his face as he pulled out a cigarette, the small silver bracelet on his right arm twinkling in the sunlight.

We were looking out towards Greece and could see the island of Corfu in the distance. Several other people, particulary young couples, had also made the trip up and were busy taking pictures. One guy in red shorts and a white T-shirt bravely posed for a photo on top of the concrete semicircle at the edge of the mountain. A couple beside us had their arms tenderly around each other as they stood admiring the view. We looked down at gentle green slopes making their way to the water's edge. Some had small clusters of white houses on them. The sea looked perfectly still from up here; we could make out the silhouettes of cruise liners that were touring the nearby Greek islands and the whole of Vlorë. It was easy to see why it had historically been such a great natural harbour.

Vlorë became the most important Ottoman city in Albania after the Muslims captured their first Adriatic port in 1417, giving it the name Avlonya. To promote commerce in the region, at the start of the 16th century the Ottomans settled a number of Sephardic Jewish families here to live beside the existing Christians, before adding more of them over the next decade or so. In fact, in the first century of Ottoman rule, almost no Muslims lived in Vlorë.

The city became the base for several Ottoman operations, including Suleiman the Magnificent's Corfu expedition in 1537. Suleiman stayed in the town for over a month and built a fortress, which was so impressive Evliya regarded it as one of the finest Ottoman castles in southeastern Europe. Suleiman also developed the castle of Kaninë and built a mosque, but none of these have survived. However, the 16th-century Muradie Mosque in the town centre is attributed to him and said to have been built by Sinan. This might well be true as Evliya called it the 'Sultan Suleyman Mosque' and said an inscription on it identified the founder as a certain 'Yakub, sheikh of the devotees', but it was Suleiman who had turned it into a congregational mosque. The inscription, written by a 'Hasbi', is dated to 1542. Given the trajectory of Sinan's career under Suleiman, there is every chance the mosque could be one of his early works.

Evliya described Vlorë as an open settlement full of 'prosperous' stone houses, built in the meadows among gardens and orchards with fruit and olive trees. By the time he visited, towards the end of his travels in the Balkans, Muslims were also living in Vlorë. Evliya counts nine mosques, three *madrasas* and five *maktabs*. A Venetian army conquered the town shortly after his visit, and when the Ottomans reclaimed it, Vlorë entered a period of decline. Forgotten for the next few centuries, the town became something of a backwater. The, Austrian diplomat, Johann Gorg von Hahn, visiting it in the middle of the 19th century, described it as a miserable and decaying place.

It wasn't until the turn of the 20th century that Vlorë became relevant again. On 28th November 1912, the town's most famous son and the father of modern Albania, Ismail Qemali, declared the country's independence from the balcony of a two-storey house in Vlorë. Born into a distinguished Albanian family, Qemali had a successful career as an Ottoman civil servant. However, after falling out with the authorities, he was sent into exile and later caught up in an abandoned plot to overthrow the Ottoman Sultan Abdul Hamid II. After this, Qemali turned his focus towards the cause for an independent Albania, and when he raised the twin-headed-eagle flag from that balcony in 1912 with the Assembly of Vlorë, it brought to an end five centuries of Ottoman rule in Albania.

The delightful little family restaurant Idar took us to for dinner was back down the mountain road in a place with far more trees and where the air was much cooler. We sat outside on large wooden tables and chairs, and the girls played on swings in the restaurant's little play park. The food was traditional Albanian mountain fare, explained Idar as he placed the order. The girls opted for something more recognisable from the menu, choosing pasta dishes. As we waited for the food to arrive, I joined Amani and Anaiya for a game of blackjack and Tamara and Idar got to know each other better. Liri had just recently had a baby, making Idar a grandfather, and Tamara wanted to know how that made him feel. She also asked about how often he came back to Albania. Idar said he tried to come every summer.

Eventually, the kind waitress turned up with our starters: a huge communal bowl of local mountain yoghurt known as *kos* and a tomato, olive and cucumber salad. This was accompanied by a plate of semolina-type mash that had been mixed with chopped-up offal – I hated offal but politely gave it a go. I kept getting mouthfuls of kidney, salty and bland, and eventually gave up being polite. Our main dish looked delicious, three large plates of slow-roasted meat on the bone. The waiter who brought this over took the time to explain in Albanian exactly how the lamb had been cooked, acting out the roasting method for our purposes.

'Oh my god, Idar, this is way too much food,' I said, assessing the amount of meat on each plate.

Tamara had ordered a risotto and was planning to only 'taste' the traditional meal, so it was left to me and Idar to eat three plates of meat. I felt bad as I knew there was no way we would get through it all, and suspected he had ordered extra in the hope everyone would tuck in. The meat was delicious, but again quite bland with only the slightest hint of salt and no seasoning. As we all got stuck into the veritable feast, I told Idar how blessed and privileged I felt that he had brought us all up here for this wonderful experience. We were sat under beautiful pine trees, looking out to a delightful mountainous vista surrounded by locals and eating a traditional Albanian meal, and he had made it all possible.

The food Idar ordered for us was reminiscent of what Edith Durham, a British relief worker and ethnologist, was fed on one of her sojourns to Albania in 1908. Like my daughters and Tamara, she too wasn't keen on *kos* and was also served a ton of meat, though hers was accompanied by maize bread and pilaf rice. A product of colonial Britain, Edith's description of the local Albanians is typically disparaging. She describes them as eating 'like wolves, tearing off the meat, bolting great lumps – apparently whole – and flinging the bones behind them.' In fact, much of her account of the local Muslim culture she and her companion, a Franciscan monk, encounter is negative. The only time Edith is positive about her description of the Albanians is when they drink *rakia*, the local brandy, to honour their Christian guests. During this little ceremony, they also praise Christ, she says, before remarking, 'I know no Christian village anywhere that would be similarly considerate of Moslems.'

The Town 'Addicted to Prayer'

GJIROKASTËR

The drive to Gjirokastër would take two hours and presented the perfect opportunity for Idar and me to *really* get to know each other. In England, he was my favourite caretaker in a team of three at the school. As a result, our relationship had mainly been a working one, with just the odd fleeting conversation that went beyond discussing broken windows and missing cupboard keys. We started to become close after I helped out Liri, first with her university dissertation and then with her husband's passport application. Something Idar had never forgotten.

'You are a good man, Terick,' he would say, as he saw me leaving the school car park.

Idar's house, like an old-fashioned school caretaker's, was on-site, beside the car park. Some days when I was running late and couldn't find a space, he would see me about to drive out to look for on-street parking and urge me to put it in one of his private spots. If I needed something done at the school – a minor maintenance for my room – Idar would personally see to it, even bypassing the online reporting system if necessary, ensuring my job didn't get lost in the queue with all the others. I didn't ask him to do this, just like he didn't ask me to help Liri.

At the end-of-term parties, I would always make the time to sit with Idar and his team, just as I did with the IT guys, the kitchen staff, the admin team and the teaching assistants. That was the closest Idar and I ever got to *really* socialising and it was in those moments I would get a glimpse of his life, one I knew well: the story of a migrant father moving with his family to a place far from their homeland in the hope of a better, more secure life.

As we headed northwest out of Vlorë along the SH76, which snaked through the mountainous interior, Idar asked if he could light a cigarette. I nodded and he pressed the button to bring down the window. The sudden roar of passing wind drowned out the Albanian music playing on the radio. Idar pulled out a duty-free Benson and Hedges cigarette and a small matchbox. He struck a match and cupped his hands to protect the flame from the vicious wind, successfully lighting the first of many cigarettes he would smoke on the trip. Taking a long drag, Idar began to visibly relax. Outside, the bright mid-morning sun was casting cloud-shaped shadows on to the slopes of the surrounding hills, beyond which lay the Korab mountain range. I asked Idar if he had always lived in Vlorë before his move to England.

'No,' he said, shaking his head. 'I grew up in a village high up in the montains that is so far even today you can only go by foot.' Idar took another long drag, being extra careful to blow the smoke out of the window.

As a young boy, he loved maths more than any other subject. In those days, school in Albania started at 9am and finished at 2pm. There were five lessons and only two breaks.

'We had so much respect for the teachers in those days. I remember if I saw my teacher walking through the village, I would run and hide, because I didn't want him to think I wasn't practising what he had taught me that day.'

'Wow, can you imagine the kids at our school doing that?' I said. We both laughed.

Progress at Idar's school was on merit; students only moved up if they passed their tests. In maths, this was not a problem, explained Idar, winding the window up to stop the rushing wind wreaking havoc with the little hair he had on his head. 'I was top of my class in maths, but geography!' Idar snorted and smiled, a glint in his eye as he remembered. 'Geography, I really didn't like. For geography, always I was in the low class!'

The scenery outside was now entirely rural. All around us there were tall mountains; we had entered the Korab range proper, and nestled in them were small villages, just like the one Idar had described growing up in. There was very little sign of life along the route. Most of the flatland was being used for agricultural farming. Every now and then we would pass one of the local farmers, tools and lunch in hand, wandering along the roadside. Hearing the car, they would stop to watch it pass, squinting in the bright August sunshine. It was the school holidays and so some of them were accompanied by their grandchildren who had been sent out to the villages for the summer by their busy city-dwelling parents.

I asked Idar to tell me more about his childhood. Who were his friends? What did he do with them? Did they ever get up to any mischief?

Idar finished his latest cigarette and flicked the butt out of the window. He then waited for the lingering smoke to leave the car before slowly closing it. They did get up to mischief, he said, like all children, but one day that innocent mischief took away his best friend. Idar wasn't there at the time and was told the story afterwards.

'He had been playing in the fields and came across an unused grenade, left over from the war when the Italians had invaded. He didn't know what it was and picked it up. The grenade exploded, killing him instantly. I found out when his funeral was announced. It was a very sad day.'

I glanced across. Idar didn't use his friend's name and I didn't ask what it was. He was staring straight ahead towards the mountains in the distance. I waited to hear more. But Idar had finished telling the story.

'What about other friends?'

'I haven't seen most of them in over twenty years,' he said, pausing to think. 'All I know is that one of them is now somewhere in Italy.'

My father had also grown up in a remote, rural village and, like Idar, he used to talk about his teachers with great reverence. He had also lost contact with most of his school friends. Some had died during the Bangladesh War of Independence and others ended up scattered across the globe when they had migrated in search of better lives

Idar hadn't always dreamt of leaving Albania. As a boy growing up in a communist state, he didn't know that was even possible. He had grown up dreaming of one day working for the government, everyone did. He fulfilled that dream when he was made head of catering at one of the branches of the state oil-drilling company.

Idar's childhood coincided with Albania's most brutally repressive regime under Stalinist dictator Hoxha and his successor, Ramiz Alia, until 1990. An advocate of anti-revisionist Marxist-Leninism, Hoxha's forty-year rule is remembered for regular murderous purges, elitism, ruthless power, repression and the creation of one of the most oppressed, restricted and isolated countries in Europe. Little wonder that as soon as it came to an end, the likes of Idar and his friends immediately fled abroad.

Strangely though, Idar remembers it differently.

'Life was good; everyone had enough. Not too much, not too less, just enough. The government made sure everyone had enough. For example, if you have too much animals on your farm, the government will take away what you don't need and give it to somebody who needed it. It was fair, no?' The question was rhetorical. Idar was summing up the 'communal' part of the philosophy.

'All these montains, they were full of farms.' Idar used the tip of his latest cigarette to point to the barren hills we were now passing. 'All of this, full of lemons and oranges. Now look!' He kept scanning the tops of the green hills and mountains; he was right, there was nothing growing anywhere now. The Korab mountains rise impressively over the Aoös Valley through the interior. This is a fertile region traditionally renowned for its citrus fruit and winegrowing culture, but not any more.

Hoxha inherited an impoverished country battered by the fallout of empire and a mismanaging monarchy, and it was true there was progress in several key areas during his reign. Albania's literacy leapt from a mere five per cent to nearly one hundred per cent; the country became agriculturally self-sufficient; the first railway was built; ancient loyalties deemed socially divisive (religious, clan and regional) were reduced; education, health and women's rights were improved; and Hoxha maintained Albania's territorial integrity whilst diversifying the economy through a Soviet-style programme of industrialisation.

Idar recalls how Hoxha tried to protect the country's rural culture and stop Albania becoming too urbanised.

'You were not allowed to move to the city unless you had a very good reason, like if your dad got a job there or something. Only one person in the family was allowed to go to university.'

'Who went from your family?'

'My brother, he is now structural engineer.'

That didn't sound particularly fair to me, nor the restrictions placed on villagers who were not allowed to head into the towns and cities in search of a better future; they were stuck and had to be satisfied with their lot, unless the state gave them permission to do so. It sounded very strange to me but Idar was very matter-of-fact about it, like he understood the rationale and maybe even believed the narrative to justify it.

'We knew something was going wrong with the communist idea around 1971,' he said, as he tried to light another cigarette using the one he had just finished. He was now chain-smoking, not because he wanted to – although he probably did – but because he had used up his last matchstick and we hadn't passed anything resembling a shop for about half an hour.

Idar said it was around this time stories begin to circulate of people being unlawfully imprisoned and tortured by Hoxha. There were rumours that some even went missing, but he confessed his sheltered life – growing up in a mountain village – meant he actually knew very little about the reality of Hoxha's brutal regime. All he knew was that things began to go downhill after the 1970s, though he wasn't sure things were any better today.

'Now, look at it all. It is owned by greedy individuals and rich people who are as corrupt as the state…'

It's not a surprise that Idar felt things got worse by the 1970s; unlike other dictators in the region such as Yugoslavia's Josip Tito, who became less hard line the older they got, Hoxha became more extreme and paranoid, and as he did, he took it out on his people. It is believed that one in every three adult Albanians had by that point been interrogated by Hoxha's secret police, the Sigurimi, whose behaviour was akin to the Soviet KGB and the Stasi. Those deemed politically deviant simply disappeared after brutal torturing and imprisonment. Executions of political enemies were the norm in Hoxha's world, where thirty-four thousand were imprisoned and more than six thousand were murdered for political reasons. This was at a time when Albania's total population numbered only three million.

The other thing Hoxha did was make the practising of religion illegal in the country. Hoxha – whose family name ironically comes from the Turkish for teacher of Islam, *hoca* – closed or destroyed all of the country's two-thousand-plus mosques and churches in his bid to make Albania the world's first official atheist state, which was why we had hardly seen a mosque on our drive.

Enver Hoxha was born in a small Ottoman town called Ergiri in 1908. Today Ergiri is known as Gjirokastër.

'Terick, you drive really good,' said Idar. 'I hate driving in Albania. Actually, I can't even drive these cars.'

'What, small cars?' I asked.

'No, cars with wheel on this side,' he replied, pointing to the steering wheel.

'But ... but you're Albanian!'

'I know, but I passed my test in England, so I can only drive with wheel on this side.' Idar snorted as he said this and we both laughed out loud.

Outside we could see the rushing waters of the River Aoös. Our drive was now in its final half-hour as we turned into the town of Tepelenë to find the SH4 highway to Gjirokastër.

Tepelenë was where one of Albania's most intriguing characters had been born: Ali Pasha, also known as the 'Lion of Yanina', a man whose legend was so great in the west, he became the archetype of the 'oriental despot'.

Pasha was an 18th-century warlord whose father was murdered by local chieftains when he was just a child. Brought up by a ferocious and vengeful mother, Pasha became a notorious bandit roaming the very hills we were now passing through. His victims were often those serving the Ottomans, who ruled the region at the time. After constantly losing goods to the notorious bandit and his gang, the Ottomans, ever the pragmatists, decided it might be better to bring Ali on to their side and so made him the *dervendji-Pasha*: a role that meant he was now in charge of the very mountain passes which, until recently, he had been raiding. Ali could now have his own little army to see to it that law and order was maintained. It was an astute move. Over time Ali rose through the Ottoman ranks, proving himself to be a ruthless and ambitious leader, and was eventually appointed pasha of the sanjak of Ioannina around 1788. Over the course of the next forty years or so, Ali's reputation as a despotic and fearsome warlord grew as he increased his territories like an independent ruler, taking advantage of a weak Ottoman government. In time Ali held sway over much of what is today Albania and large swathes of Greece.

Interestingly, as well as being a fearsome warlord, much of Pasha's success has been put down to his religious tolerance. A follower of Bektashism, Ali Pasha actively supported the local Greek Christians and Sunni Muslims and was also politically savvy, making several alliances with western powers including Napoleon Bonaparte of France and the British. A young Lord Broughton, on a Balkan tour in 1809 with his friend Lord Byron, tells an amusing story about the gift Ali Pasha received from Napoleon. The anecdote offers a wonderful insight into both the insecurities and ambitions of the notorious warlord.

Broughton and Byron were staying with the pasha at his citadel in Tepelenë, and on their last day the warlord, who was over sixty years of age at this point, proudly showed them the rifle gifted to him by the French emperor. The two Englishmen were suitably impressed when they saw the short rifle with a silver stock, studded with 'diamonds and brilliants'. Broughton remarked that it was a 'handsome gift'. However, the pasha's secretary, their translator for the visit, told them the truth: when the gun was given to Ali Pasha by Napoleon, it was very ordinary looking with a common stock. Ali Pasha had the silver and ornaments placed on it himself, so it would look more like a royal gift.

When Ali Pasha's ambitions to become an independent ruler became apparent to the Ottomans, Sultan Mahmud II decided to call time on the warlord's career, and in 1822 he was killed by Ottoman troops following a violent battle at the monastery of St Panteleimon on Lake Pamvotis in Epirus, northern Greece. After the battle, the Ottoman soldiers carried his head back to the sultan where, despite his status as a rebel, Ali Pasha was granted a funeral with full honours and buried in his state capital of Ioannina, in modern-day Greece.

To this day, he is seen as something of an Albanian hero because of the way he stood up to the might of the Ottomans. The fort at the top of Gjirokastër was one of Ali Pasha's many abodes.

After Tepelenë, the highway followed the valley floor as closely as the river Drino, passing the mountains of the Kurvelesh region on the right, which Evliya claimed came from 'Quraysh': the name of the Prophet Muhammad's tribe. This is because the Ottoman believed the founding tribe of the Albanians were Qurayshi from Makkah. Evliya tells the story of how one of the Qurayshi tribesmen, Jabal-i Alhama, accidentally put out the eye of an Arab *beg*, who went to the Caliph Omar and demanded Jabal's eye be put out too, citing the Qur'anic 'eye for an eye' verse. The caliph agreed and Jabal fled with three thousand of his tribesmen, pursued by the caliph. They all apparently ended up in Albania, settling in the very mountains we were now passing, hence the name. Evliya even claims that Jabal is buried in the Albanian town of Elbasan to the north. When I told Idar this story, he laughed and said:

'See, I told you we are Muslims!'

Soon the silhouette of Gjirokastër began to emerge in the distance. Nestled high up in the mountains, overlooked by Ali Pasha's huge fort, Gjirokastër's beautiful 17th- and 18th-century Ottoman houses cascade down the slopes like a medieval mirage.

We turned off the highway close to an eight-storey building with pink balconies, beneath which locals sat in the sun sipping coffee on lime-coloured patio furniture.

'This is Gjirokastër,' Idar announced, with a degree of triumph.

'Yes, it is, but you know I have come to find Ergiri!' I said, and we both laughed.

Ergiri was the Ottoman name for Gjirokastër when the Muslim empire ruled this part of Albania for five centuries between 1417 and 1913. Inhabited since the Bronze Age, the area around Gjirokastër was historically the abode of Greek people, and became the home of roaming Albanian nomads in the 14th century, just before the arrival of the Ottomans. At that time, it was known as Argyrocastron and Argyropolis – from the Greek words for 'silver', 'castle' and 'city' – probably because of the silvery-grey rock widely used to build the town's houses and the main defensive fort at the top. The fort is the oldest part of the town, with some walls dating all the way back to the

6th century. The rest of the old town dates to its days as Ergiri and is home to the finest collection of classical Ottoman-era country houses in all of Albania.

Evliya was more specific about the town's origins, claiming it was founded by the son of a certain Greek King Philip. He also believed Ergiri may have been home to Venetians at some point, as he came across the image of St Mark, Venice's patron saint, on a number of buildings. Evliya described Ergiri as a beautiful open town, spread across eight hills and valleys overlooked by the fortress with slate-roofed houses made of stone. Each one had a tower and a courtyard surrounded by a white granite wall. The houses also had vineyards and gardens.

As the tiny white Megane struggled up the steep cobblestoned roads of the 'city of stone', Idar was staring out of the window, cigarette in hand, mouth agape, admiring the stunning Ottoman houses scattered all over the busy hillside. Gjirokastër still clearly had the charm of Evliya's Ergiri, for this was the longest he had gone without taking a drag from a cigarette.

We were heading for the town's original Ottoman bazaar area, rebuilt in the 19th century. This, according to my guidebook, was the prettiest of all the neighbourhoods, and was overlooked by Ergiri's only surviving mosque, the Memi Bey or Bazaar Mosque.

In Evliya's day, the town was a deeply religious place where people were 'addicted to prayer'. Home to at least fifteen mosques, Ergiri was where would-be Islamic scholars of *Hadith* came to train at one of the three *madrasas* that specialised in this field. There were also tekkes for three different Sufi orders and four shrines dedicated to famous Muslim saints in the town. Sadly, all of this was destroyed when local boy Hoxha ran Albania. It is believed the only reason the Memi Bey survived was because it was already listed as a cultural monument – the communists used it as a training hall for circus acrobats who would hang their trapezes from the mosque's high-domed ceilings.

The wheels of the car were starting to slip and I was thankful when we turned a corner and the thick minaret of the mosque came into view.

'Thank God for that. I don't think the car could've gone up much further!' I said, turning the engine off.

'Yes, these roads are very small and veeery steep. I'm glad you are the driver,' Idar laughed.

Putting the gearstick into first, I turned the wheels in towards the pavement and pulled up the handbrake. Idar immediately set off in search of a lighter. We had parked in the shade of the mosque's minaret, which now towered over me. I looked up at the circular balcony that broke up its pencil-like shape, noting the *muqarnas* pattern. The front of the mosque, which was built in the 18th century around the same time as local bandit leader Ali was made an Ottoman pasha, had two sets of stairs symmetrically leading up to the main courtyard. A wire-framed grey gate marked the entrance to the portico held up by Romanesque arches beneath a roof of grey slates, just like the ones covering the town's historic houses.

Behind the mosque, trees and bushes led up the slope of the mountain where in the distance the walls of the city's fort could just be made out. To the left, framing the valley floor, was one of the bazaar's original lanes. Once the bustling heart of a medieval market, today it was lined with shops that had colourful awnings and sold fridge magnets, Gjirokastër T-shirts and miniatures of the town's fort. A handful of tourists milled around inside, their silhouettes framed by the climbing bougainvillea the owners had trained over the tops of their stores-cum-houses. Gjirokastër was easily the most beautiful place I had been in Albania and I could see why even Hoxha declared it one of only two 'Museum Towns'. The other was Berat, one hundred kilometres to the north. It too was an ode to classical Ottoman architecture and the only other historic town not subjected fully to the communist-version of modernisation that saw mosques, synagogues, churches, Sufi lodges and monasteries closed and torn down, along with many other important monuments. These were replaced with the ugly, functional buildings that are the hallmark of communist architecture; as a result, both Berat and Gjirokastër's old towns are now protected UNESCO World Heritage sites.

I sat on the stone steps of the ancient mosque and waited for Idar to return. The air was much cleaner up here and the views over the valley, now drenched in glorious sunshine, were spectacular. I tried imagining what kind of bustling town Ergiri would have been, filled with Greeks, Turks, Aromanians, Roma and, of course, Albanians.

Evliya wrote that the Muslims of the town had a deep love for the Prophet Muhammad's nephew and son-in-law, Ali, and his family. Apparently 'Ya Ali!' was one of their favourite turn of phrases – this might explain the historic popularity of the name in the area. Ergirins also spoke Persian and would curse the Umayyad caliphs, Muawiyah and Yazid, the latter responsible for the murder of the Prophet's grandson Husayn, the third Shia imam. This suggests many of the town's residents probably observed a form of Shia Islam. The disdain for the Umayyad caliphs extended to the clothes they wore and the food and drink they consumed; locals refused to wear the colour blue, eat *zerde* (sweet, rice pudding) or drink *boza* (low-alcoholic malt drink), which they thought had been invented by Muawiyah. However, Evliya said this did not stop them enjoying a drink: 'they shamelessly drink wine and other intoxicating beverages, such as the one called *reyhania* [modern *rehani*]'. In fact, whenever there was a religious festival to be celebrated, regardless of faith, the locals would all dress up in their finest clothes, get extremely drunk and spend the day dancing. The historic blurring of religious lines I had seen across the Balkans was also apparent in Ergiri, according to Evliya; it didn't matter whether it was the day of St George, St Demetrius, the Persian new year – Nowruz – or the days of Eid, the (Muslim) 'lovers go hand in hand with their pretty boys and embrace them and dance about in a manner of the Christians'. This behaviour was something the Ottoman found to be 'quite shameful' as it was apparently the 'characteristic of the infidels', though in his typically accepting way he also wrote that 'it is their custom'.

Evliya makes one other curious observation in Ergiri, and this is about the local habits when it comes to mourning their dead, which he claimed could sometimes go on for up to one hundred years after the person had died. This mourning was done by gathering every Sunday in a house and hiring professional mourners to weep and wail for the dead. Evliya found this practice so unbearably noisy, he dubbed Ergiri 'the city of wailing'. As is his habit, he offers a fantastic and hilarious anecdote about this local obsession. The story goes that one day whilst having sex, a man happens to remind his wife that the next day is Sunday – the day of mourning. This suddenly brings to mind her seventeenth husband (Evliya doesn't tell us what number her current husband is) who died in a naval battle against the English. The woman then rather insensitively decides, whilst 'tearing out her hair' and still in mid-intercourse, to detail how much she misses him and what great sex they used to have. Needless to say, her current husband's penis goes limp and the poor fellow regrets bringing up the day of mourning at all. Evliya ends this story with his tongue firmly in his cheek by suggesting this was why the town's menfolk all walked around looking so sad and mournful!

This influence of Shia Islam and the pluralist practices of Gjirokastër's historic townsfolk was yet another example of religious coexistence in the Balkans. But it was no longer a surprise to me.

It was becoming increasingly clear that the religious landscape of this region was once a complex, multi-layered and fluid one – virtually every town we had visited so far had historic examples of this and some even had modern ones. Ottoman Sarajevo had clearly not been an exception, it had been the norm, which is why Evliya's writing continues to be so matter of fact in its description of the coexistence of Muslims, Christians and Jews in the places he visited.

It seems that not only did people of different faiths in the Balkans historically coexist, but the lines between their religious and cultural practices were blurred far more regularly than popular history would have us believe. It was also becoming clear to me that the overt Muslim identity of places like Višegrad, Niš and now Gjirokastër has been deliberately destroyed and reduced to a footnote by those writing the new and alternative narratives. As a result, anyone visiting Gjirokastër today would have no idea that it was once a Balkan centre of Islamic scholarship and Sufism, a place where students of theology and spirituality came to study from all over.

I was roused from my musings by a crackling over the mosque's dated tannoy system as the local *muezzin* prepared to call the *adhan*.

Allahu Akbar. Allahu Akbar. Allahu Akbar. Allahu Akbar…
(God is Great. God is Great. God is Great. God is Great…)

Ashhadu an la ilaha illa Allah. Ashhadu an la ilaha illa Allah…
(I bear witness that there is no god except the One God. I bear
witness that there is no god except the One God…)

The elderly voice filled the valley with praise for his lord just like
the *muezzins* of old had done for almost five centuries here, except
for those forty years when its most famous son ruled the country. The
adhan was not as sing-songy as I had heard it in other parts of the
Balkans; the old man's voice was more deliberate. I leant back on the
stone walls and realised this was the first time I was hearing an *adhan*
in Albania.

Soon I spied a familiar figure, leaning forward as he walked up
the steep cobbled lane, puffs of smoke billowing from his mouth. Idar
was grinning from ear to ear. He had found a lighter and was proudly
showing it to me as he walked. It was red and black and had 'Shqipëria'
written on it, the name by which Albanians refer to their homeland.

'Right, you ready now?' I enquired.

Idar nodded, his grin barely visible through the smoke.

'Up we go to the fort then!'

above Tharik, Amani, Tamara and Anaiya on holiday on the island of Rhodes in Greece in 2010

below left Tamara at the Blagaj Tekke, in Bosnia and Herzegovina (page 45)

below right Amani and Anaiya enjoy a swim in the Adriatic off the Croatian coast (page 275)

above Worshippers sit in front of the traveller's *mihrab* beneath the portico of Sarajevo's Gazi Husrev-beg Mosque (page 18)

below left View of the Stari Most from the Koski Mehmed Pasha Mosque in Mostar (page 29)

below right The Blagaj Tekke at the mouth of the River Buna (page 45)

above left The gifted Sebilj in Sjenica (page 71)

above right Helpful Hamza and Darjan from Novi Pazar in Serbia (page 90)

below The female Muslim 'choir' performing in Novi Pazar (page 76)

above The Tomb of Sultan Murad I near Pristina, Kosovo (page 100)

below left Macedonian Muslims
walk ahead of Skopje's 'Warrior with
accompanying elements' statue
(page 128)

below right Detail of Skopje's Ottoman
clock tower (page 145)

above Stunning painted detail of the Ali Pasha Mosque's dome in Tetovo (page 155)

below Tomb of Sersem Ali Baba inside Tetovo's Arabati Baba Tekke (page 162)

above Idar and Tharik examine the menu at the restaurant in the Llogara National Park near Vlorë (page 191)

below left The house the Pasha built (Zekate House) in Gjirokastër (page 219)

below right The *mihrab* at Berat's Bachelors' Mosque featuring the Suleymaniye Mosque painted on the left (page 224)

above Dollma Tekke inside Krujë's fortress with its mountain backdrop (page 251)

below Mirza inside the Osmanagic Mosque in Podgorica (page 259)

above left Ibrahim Babic Effendi in his library in Zenica holding a 600-year-old book on Islamic jurisprudence (page 280)

above right Mevludin looks out from the fort at Travnik (page 284)

below A mosque and minaret in the Bosnian mountains

The House the Pasha Built

GJIROKASTËR

The climb up to the fort was worth it for the views alone. Gjirokastër really was a very handsome town, and as Idar and I leant on the stone walls, as much to catch our breath as anything else, we stared out in silence over an old town that still looked like it belonged in the pages of Evliya's *Seyahâtnâme*. I could see the many 'gardens and vineyards' and 'magnificent townhouses' he had described, maybe even whilst standing on this very spot. These were framed by the surrounding hills and valleys. The only missing places were the numerous Muslim buildings and monuments he reels off: the Mosque of Hizir Aga with its stonework minaret; the Mosque of Hadji Murad with its fountain of sweet-tasting water; the Halveti Tekke where Evliya had to bury one of the boys in his retinue; the many *hans*, fountains and *madrasas*, all gone. Thankfully though, Gjirokastër's charm had remained.

'I have to give it to you guys – somehow, despite Hoxha being anti-Muslim and tearing down all the mosques, tekkes and *madrasas*, you've preserved this fabulous Ottoman town, Idar.' I said after a little while, playfully slapping his back.

Idar didn't respond, he just nodded and kept staring out over the historic town. 'I didn't know there is place like this in Albania, Terick…' he eventually said, pausing for a moment. I could see he was quite emotional. I hadn't seen Idar in this light before. This was not the matter-of-fact guy I had worked beside all these years, the hardy man who just got on with things accepting them for what they were. Idar pulled out a cigarette and lit it with his new patriot's lighter, letting out a short, violent smoker's cough.

'I am going to come back with my family,' he continued. 'They need to see this, they need to know Albania is beautiful and has so much history.'

Idar had originally wanted to take us all towards the Greek border and the resort town of Sarandë. With views of Corfu and holiday-brochure hotels overlooking a shore lined with thatched parasols, it was easy to see why he chose Sarandë. I had been tempted; there was even a mosque to investigate right beside the ruins of a 5th-century synagogue, but when Tamara and the girls saw it meant a round trip of six hours, they understandably opted to relax locally. Idar had looked visibly disappointed when I had suggested the alternative: the two of us heading inland to Gjirokastër instead. He had heard about Gjirokastër but had never visited and wasn't convinced at first. Ironically, Sarandë now lay just over an hour's drive through the mountains behind us, but I sensed Idar was quite happy to stay here.

'Thank you, Terick,' he said, finishing his cigarette by stubbing it out on the fort's wall.

'For what?'

'Thank you for bringing me here and showing me my country's history.'

I felt a tad embarrassed by this, and wasn't sure at first how to respond. 'Sometimes when we are from a place we can't always see some of the beautiful things the way someone from outside might see them,' I eventually offered, hoping he didn't feel patronised.

I also wanted to say it was probably because European Muslims didn't value their past and heritage the way they valued a sandy beach with blue waters, where a repetitive bassline played from a nearby bar, but I sensed it wasn't the right time.

'You are a good man, Terick,' Idar said, now grinning, as we headed towards the fort's castle.

We didn't spend a great deal of time in the castle. Although it had a long and storied history dating back to the 5th century and had been substantially expanded by Ali Pasha in the 19th, I found very little to hold my attention.

As we wandered through the empty tall-arched corridors, vast ramparts and inner quarters, the only information I found about the pasha was a small board that explained his expansion had included a now-destroyed double-tiered aqueduct, impressively depicted by Edward Lear in an 1848 painting. The castle's curators had focused on the communist resistance to the German occupation and it was therefore mainly dressed with 20th-century military paraphernalia, including automatic cannons, a military tank and statues of Albanian communist soldiers. Idar got very excited when we came outside to discover the shell of a captured American plane now used to commemorate the communist struggle against the Western imperial powers.

During Evliya's time the fort was home to the imperial Sultan Bayezid II Mosque, a large mosque with finely decorated ceilings and two hundred two-storey stone houses with slate roofs. None of this remains today; however, there are two *türbes* on the site that reportedly date from this period, which unusually the Ottoman does not list amongst the tombs he encounters in the town. These belong to two Bektashi babas, Baba Sulltani and Baba Kapllani, and would no doubt have been highly revered by Bektashi devotee Ali Pasha during his time here.

The tombs were entered through a small wrought-iron gate tucked in between two high walls of the castle, not far from the main entrance. Idar and I stepped through it to enter what felt like a little green oasis; ivy grew around the trunks of young trees and potted plants lay scattered all around the stone *türbe* that had been rebuilt over the tombs after the communists destroyed it. Candle wax dripped on to the floor in small niches set into the walls of the *türbe*. This was an active site of worship, and Idar, a Bektashi himself, was clearly moved by it, falling silent as we walked around the site.

A small set of steps led up to the *türbe's* entrance through a large, stained pine door. We both tried to open it but it was locked. I pointed to the doorstep to show Idar the collection of silver coins someone had left at the entrance. He nodded as we both peered in through an opening. Two small tombs sat side by side inside a room painted entirely white, both decorated with white pieces of embroidered cloth and bouquets of flowers. At the head of the tomb were three white stone steps. The lowest step had silver coffee pots and plastic water bottles with flowers in small vases, and the highest step had a number of frames and more flowers in vases. There was also a small wooden plaque with a gold plate that had 'Allah' and 'Muhammad' written on it in Arabic. On the floor were small patterned prayer rugs. The flowers were fresh and the tomb was neat and tidy. The communists might have razed this place to the ground before, but it had once again become a place of reverence for the locals.

I left Idar in quiet contemplation looking into the tomb and wandered around the side of the *türbe,* passing stones blackened by the flames of candles and noting the colourful ties attached to some of the plants and the branches of trees, just like the ones I had seen near the *türbes* of Bulgaria.

The *türbe* was a hidden little corner of the castle complex; had we blinked we might well have missed it, and I was glad we hadn't. This felt like the only spot in the fort that still had any real link to its Muslim past. It was also the only place I could imagine Ali Pasha in; coming here, maybe in moments of doubt, or to seek solitude away from the hustle and bustle of castle life and spend a little time in this tiny green oasis in the company of the revered babas.

Parjon Anastasi used to play for the local football team, Gjirokastër Klubi Sportiv. But that was a long time ago, during the Hoxha years, in 1978 when the team was called KF Luftëtari. These days Parjon is known for a different reason: he is the proud owner of the Zekate House, the finest Ottoman town house in all of Gjirokastër, built by none other than feared warlord, Ali Pasha of Tepelenë, in 1811. Not that you would know it – as befitting an ex-pro, Parjon greeted us at the entrance to the fabulous historic house wearing a pair of German Adidas football shorts, a white vest and sandals. It was not quite how I had expected a man looking after a national treasure to be dressed.

Clinging to the side of the mountains, overlooking the magnificent slopes of the valley, the Zekate House is an impressive stone structure with two tall arched entrances and is spread across four levels. Parjon led us in, explaining that the lower floor was where the stables and cistern were kept. It was the upper floors that we really wanted to see, he said, showing us the way in before leaving us to explore.

'He will meet us for a drink after,' translated Idar as Parjon waved goodbye and headed back to the modest house near the entrance that he shared with his wife, probably to watch reruns of World Cups, or so I imagined.

The Zekate House was a real treat to explore; exposed wooden beams ran along the walls and ceilings, framing delicately painted decorations. All the large rooms had divan-like low seating that ran around the edges and stunning decorated Ottoman fireplaces. It was easy to imagine the elders of Ergiri gathering in these rooms, maybe one or two puffing away at a hookah fired by coals from the flaming brazier, as they sipped on thick coffee to discuss the matters of the day.

'Wow, this place is gorgeous,' I said, pointing out the delicate floral patterns on the cone-shaped chimney breast over the fireplace. These were in the Tulip baroque-rococo style, like the patterns we had seen all over the Balkans.

Idar just nodded. For the first time on the trip, he was holding something other than a cigarette in his hand: his phone, which he was using to take as many pictures as he could.

I indicated I was going upstairs and Idar nodded from behind the camera. Parjon had dressed the rooms up there in the same minimalist style. Rich, patterned red carpets lay in the middle, complementing the elaborate floral patterns on the walls. The most impressive room was the one where the men of the house would sit and enjoy their coffee and smoke their pipes. This had a fabulously intricate wood ceiling with a beautiful, large, octagonal red-and-gold rose where an expensive chandelier would have once proudly hung. Now there was just a single energy-saving bulb. The room also had a small balcony above the wooden entrance and resembled the layout of a tiny mosque; even the windows were stained glass.

My favourite spot though was on the uppermost level, which opened up on to a spectacular balcony with a purpose-built reclining platform. This had been designed so that anyone lounging there could do so enjoying the dramatic views of the valley.

Ali Pasha built the house as a gift for Parjon's ancestor, Beqir Zeko – hence the name – one of his most trusted men, and no doubt the fearsome ruler spent many hours relaxing with Beqir and other friends in the house. Earlier, at the castle, I had tried to imagine the great pasha residing there and struggled, but here was a place I could see him in. As I climbed up on to the platform and leant back on the soft mattress and backrest, imagining what it might have felt like to be an actual Ottoman pasha, I was reminded of one of the most famous paintings of Ali Pasha, by French painter Louis Dupré, called *Ali Pasha of Janina Hunting on Lake Butrinto*. It shows a bearded Ali reclining into plush cushions wearing luxuriously thick robes, a bejewelled dagger hanging from his waistband and a long smoking pipe in his mouth. Despite being on a lake, in a boat, he looks completely at ease with not a care in the world, which was exactly how I felt as I sat on that rooftop surveying the valley floor.

The Zekate House felt like a fitting place to end our trip in Gjirokastër. It was one of houses that had helped put the town on the UNESCO World Heritage list.

'Too many Albanians, they do not know these beautiful places,' Idar said as we sat in the courtyard, near Parjon's little annexe.

'Yes, it is such a shame,' I said, sipping the coffee the ex-footballer had brought out for us.

Parjon, who spoke no English, then told Idar about the difficulties of sustaining such a stunning relic with virtually no support from the government.

'The family has to pay for all renovation themselves, he says.'

'The government doesn't help at all?'

'Hmph!' Parjon understood that statement and shook his head.

'No,' Idar translated, though there was no need. 'Our people don't value our own heritage.'

I shared Idar's frustrations about Muslim heritage and how little we as a community seemed to care for it. Idar knew this. But the more this journey through the western Balkans went on, the more I began to appreciate the odds that were stacked against us, certainly in Europe. The efforts to deny, erase, rewrite and simply do away with our continent's Muslim heritage had been so aggressive and so comprehensive that even those living in Muslim countries no longer knew it.

Parjon – who owns one of Ergiri's most beautiful historic monuments, for example – had no idea that his town was once said to be 'addicted to prayer', or that scholars and dervishes came from far and wide to study in its institutes, and meditate in its Sufi lodges. And if he didn't know this living here, what chance did Idar or I have? How can we care about something we don't even know is there?

I looked out over the climbing vines towards the urban slopes of Gjirokastër, crowned by the large fort at the top of the hill. High above, two falcons swirled, looking for their dinner. The majestic silhouette of the Zekate House had an orange glow around the edges from the setting sun behind it. It really was a marvellous sight, I thought as I sat there, thoroughly grateful I could come and see such a place in the company of my friend.

After we bid farewell to Parjon, Idar and I walked to the car in silence, both of us lost in our own thoughts. I put on the radio and soon the car was again filled with the sound of Albanian music, though the beats for this song suggested it was modern Albanian pop. Idar wound down his window and lit up a cigarette. I could see he was thinking about his conversation with Parjon.

'It makes me so angry, Terick!' he said after a while, almost with gritted teeth.

'What does, Idar?'

'Our government doesn't give a shit about our history.'

It was getting late now and we were both hungry, so on our way back to Vlorë we stopped at a beautiful traditional roadside restaurant. The quaint wooden eatery had an open veranda that overlooked a small lake. As we ate a meal of grilled fish with freshly cut potato chips, the lights of the restaurant came on one by one, their reflection twinkling in the dark waters of the lake.

I raised my glass of Sprite and thanked Idar for spending the day with me exploring the heritage of Gjirokastër. Idar smiled and lifted his beer.

'No, Terick, thank you for showing me *my* heritage.'

A Fairy-Tale Ottoman Village

BERAT

'Should we wait for the rest of the congregation?' I asked Firbent as I lined up beside him.

'No, there will be no-one joining the *jama'at* now,' explained the twenty-six-year-old imam who had just given the *adhan*. 'Maybe for *Isha* or *Maghrib* there will be some people coming for the *jama'at*, but not now.'

I was in a small mosque at the foot of Berat's Ottoman Muslim quarter, part of the town's stunning UNESCO World Heritage site, which climbs all the way up the cliff side to an ancient fortress at the top, like Gjirokastër, only the hillside is steeper, the pathways narrower and the houses much more concentrated. The mosque I was in was called the Bachelors' Mosque, because it was where the single men plying their trade in the bazaar used to pray. But the bazaar, like the pious bachelors, is long gone. Today the mosque's only regular attendee is its imam, Firbent, who normally prays the *Dhuhr* (mid-afternoon) prayer alone. My presence had doubled the size of the congregation, but there would be no-one else joining us. Like Ottoman Gjirokastër, Ottoman Berat is no more.

I came upon Firbent when I wandered into the Bachelors' Mosque to find him sat in front of the colourful *mihrab* reciting from an open Qur'an. As I finished my two *rakats* – maybe sensing my presence –

Firbent closed the Qur'an and stood up. He then put his hands to either side of his head and began calling out the *adhan*. A tall, slim figure, the imam had a beautiful, melodious voice that suggested he had been trained classically. He then gave the *Iqama,* saying the words quicker and in a lower voice before taking up his position a few inches in front and to my right. This is the convention when there are only two people performing a congregational *salah*. If another person were to join mid-prayer, they would simply touch me on my shoulder. I would then take a full step back to make a new row and the person joining would stand beside me, ensuring we were both positioned directly behind the imam. During the four *rakats* I prayed with Firbent, nobody came.

After shaking his hand and thanking him for leading the prayer, Firbent told me a little bit about himself.

'I studied for nine years in Bursa,' he explained.

'The old Ottoman capital… in Turkey?'

'Yes, it is a really special town. I really enjoyed being there.'

Bursa was the first Ottoman capital from 1300 to 1360, when the founder of the empire, Osman I, and his son Orhan had ruled. It was also where the body of Murad I was buried, whose other tomb we had visited in Kosovo. According to Firbent, Bursa remains an important place for Islamic scholarship.

I then asked Firbent about Berat, and why he felt no-one came to the prayers.

'Berat is actually predominantly Muslim,' he began. 'Around seventy per cent of the people here are, I would say.'

'But they are not practising?' I asked.

'Well, some are Bektashi, and those that are Sunni prefer their own mosques, and yes many do not pray regularly.' Firbent looked sad as he said this.

He wore trousers and a polo shirt with thick yellow and pink horizontal stripes. I didn't get a chance to ask who employed him or if his job was a salaried one, as I sensed Firbent was eager to continue his *salah* and complete the *Sunnah* prayers. So instead I stepped back and watched. The Bachelors' Mosque was a small one. There was no *mahvil* or even a *mimbar*; there was just the *mihrab*, next to which stood Firbent, cutting a sad and lonely figure, arms folded across his chest, silently reciting. The mosque walls had once been richly decorated with colourful paintings and patterns that now desperately needed restoration. Again, the patterns were clearly of the Tulip era. As in the mosque in Skopje, one of the paintings was of Istanbul's Suleymaniye Mosque, easily identified by the four slim minarets around its main dome. But here it had pride of place right next to the richly decorated *mihrab*. The painting on the other side of the *mihrab* was more difficult to identify: two rows of domed terraces, one above the other. Both murals were framed by baroque-rococo-inspired floral patterns in red, yellow and faded blue. Along the top was a neat line of Arabic inscription that once went all the way around. Built in 1828, the mosque looked every bit the relic from a bygone era, as did its 'Ottoman'-trained imam, praying alone – a shepherd with no flock. Both felt out of place and time, as if Berat no longer needed or wanted them.

It was a very different story when Evliya Çelebi came to Berat in 1670. He describes the 'Albanian Belgrade' as an attractive, large, open town covered in vineyards, roses and vegetable gardens full of nice stone houses and several splendid mansions spread across seven hills. Like Gjirokastër, Evliya came across a town renowned for its mosques, institutes of Islamic studies and Sufi lodges. Evliya says in those days there was a 'great demand' for the learning of religious sciences in Berat, a place where he counted more than thirty congregational mosques – each with its own learned 'professor' able to teach the religious sciences – and numerous local ones, as well as five *madrasas* training *ulema,* five *hans* and at least three *tekkes.* This is not to say that Berat was an entirely Muslim town; there were almost as many churches and several synagogues in its Christian and Jewish neighbourhoods. Nor was the population all Albanian – Evliya reports meeting Greeks, Turks, Bosnians and Serbs in yet another depiction of that famous Ottoman version of *komšiluk.*

His Berat was the home of poets, scholars and writers 'possessing vast knowledge', as well as viziers, deputies and learned men. These were brave *gazis* that were neat and clean. In fact, the Ottoman was so impressed by the townsfolk of Berat, he compares them favourably with the clan of the Prophet Muhammad, the Quraysh.

Having said goodbye to Idar and his family the previous night, we had left Vlorë early in the morning for Berat and, as we now walked around the old town, we were finding there was still a lot of Evliya's Berat left to see. After finishing my prayers in the Bachelors' Mosque, I met back up with Tamara and the girls and headed up to the town's fort. Wandering through the narrow, cobblestoned alleyways of the Muslim quarter, each one barely wide enough for two donkeys to pass, we saw lemon trees peering out from behind snow-white walls and bougainvillea climbing over exposed wooden beams; there was beautiful flora in almost every nook and cranny. Tamara and the girls were taken by the stunning wooden doorways, some of which were extremely photogenic, like the ones in the medinas of Fez or Tunis.

The climb took half an hour and left us a little short of breath. The worst part was the last leg, which veered around a stone wall and up a steep incline. But it was worth it. The views from Berat's old fort were spectacular. We could see as far as the mountains to the south, which looked dramatic and otherworldly as the sun streamed through the clouds and on to the slopes. To the right was the new riverside walkway, busy with tourists enjoying the August sunshine: some sat in the shade of the recently planted trees and watched, whilst others enjoyed the excellent local coffee sitting under parasols the colours of the Italian flag.

Evliya also arrived to find that part of Berat had been recently constructed – the city's governor Hüsein Pasha had built a shiny, new bazaar of a hundred shops with streams of water flowing through it. This made the market area so clean that 'a man could sit down on the road and let himself be enraptured by the surrounding beauty'. The bazaar was also home to a magnificent clock tower with a bell so big ten people could fit inside. Its beauty left Evliya speechless: 'the clock tower is so wonderful that it cannot be described; it must be seen to be believed'. Sadly, like the bazaar, it is no more.

Beyond the shiny new walkway – paid for using UNESCO money – the old town gave way to what Hoxha's architects had added to the landscape: a smattering of mid- and low-rise tower blocks in various shades of greys and pastel colours. The pedestrian-only walkway ended where these started. To the right, across the smart stone bridge over the Osumi river, looking marginally less photogenic than the old Muslim quarter, was Gorica, the area Evliya knew as Koru Varos: a collection of two hundred or so houses that was historically home to the town's non-Muslim Greek and Albanian families.

Berat's old fort predates the Ottoman conquest in 1412, going all the way back to at least the 3rd century BC, when it was burnt down by the Romans. It was then developed by the Byzantines and later, local despots in the 13th century, which is the period that most of the fort today dates back to. Evliya describes it as built like a 'candlestick on a steep and bare cliff', where the 'foundation stones of the gate are as big as the body of an elephant'. Such stones, he wrote, 'can only be found in Hebron near Jerusalem and in the fortress at Bender' (modern-day Moldavia). He found Greeks living in the houses outside its main walls and inside, just like the larger fort in Gjirokastër, several houses and a now-destroyed mosque dedicated to Sultan Bayezid II.

'I really didn't expect this place to look so Ottoman,' Tamara said as we began making our way back down the hillside. It was nearly lunchtime and we were hungry.

'Neither did I, it really is quite amazing how much has survived,' I said.

'Was Gjirokastër like this?'

'Yeah, it was, although it had much bigger houses and was not as picture-postcard as this hill, which looks like a fairy-tale Ottoman village because of how close together the houses are.'

'So this is what an Ottoman town would've looked like, Dad?' Amani asked, negotiating an uneven step as we got nearer the bottom.

'Yes, it's certainly a good example, but obviously lots of the buildings and monuments have been removed or damaged since that time, but yeah, as good an example as we're probably gonna see on this trip,'

'Ott-o-man. That's such a funny word,' Anaiya laughed.

I knew there was something different about the Lead Mosque the minute I entered it. Unlike the Bachelors' Mosque, the interior had been completely repainted a plain snow white. There was none of the vibrant Tulip art inside this mosque. This one also had a healthy congregation. I had pitched up just short of the sunset prayer to find several young men already patiently waiting for the *adhan*.

After performing my two *rakats*, I sat down and looked around for a *tasbih*. Normally these are positioned all over a mosque, hung on hooks close to where people might sit or lean, but in the Lead Mosque they were conspicuous by their absence. *Tasbihs* look like the Christian rosary beads and are used by Muslims all over the world to aid in *dhikr* by praising Allah using three different superlatives thirty-three times each. This is why each set has at least thirty-three or ninety-nine beads and is essentially an aide-memoire. I've always found the *tasbih* extremely useful and they are popular in many Muslim cultures. However, some conservative Muslims discourage their use.

'They are not from the *Sunnah*, that is why you will not find any in this mosque,' Edlir explained, when I asked about the *tasbih*.

Edlir had noticed me sitting in the mosque. I was clearly not one of the regulars and so he approached me to make conversation. He spoke surprisingly good English and explained that the reason the mosque didn't have the prayer beads is because there was no evidence the Prophet ever used them, and as they assisted with worship it would be wrong for us to now start using them.

Once the prayer began, I noticed other things that felt familiar to me as a former resident of Saudi Arabia, like the way certain men folded their arms when the prayer began or how high above their ankles they wore their trousers. Most telling was the insistence to stand with toes touching and the fact that before the *Iqama* there was no recitation of *surah al-Ikhlas* or dua as I had encountered in other mosques across the Balkans. Here the young men resembled those I had met with Hamza and Darjan in Novi Pazar. They had unkempt, scraggly beards and were led by a young imam also with a large beard, wearing only a small skullcap. The classical attire of a Balkan imam was nowhere to be seen in the Lead Mosque. This all pointed to one thing: this was a mosque for adherents of the Salafi brand of Islam popular in Saudi Arabia. I was a little surprised by this, as Albania was a place I had always associated with liberal Islam.

After the prayer I sat with Edlir and two other friends, one of whom reminded me of the character Compo from the classic British sitcom *Last of the Summer Wine*: scruffy, cheeky and very animated. Like Compo, he was quick-witted and knew how to make you laugh. Then there was Kasim, who had also lived in Saudi Arabia. Kasim had studied in the University of Madinah – one of the leading schools of Islamic scholarship in the kingdom. He had also spent some time in Cairo, Egypt, and was fluent in Arabic. This meant I could tell him to use an Arabic term when his English failed him. English was his fourth language after his native Albanian, Arabic and French.

Kasim had some form of physical disability, which made one side of his body appear slightly paralysed. His left arm was bent inwards and he seemed unable to use it. He was a heavyset man, with a friendly face and a lovely gentleness about him. I warmed to him very quickly and so, when he and Edlir asked if I wanted to grab a bite to eat with them, I was only too happy to accept.

The three of us left the Lead Mosque and headed towards the main road. Edlir and Kasim were going to take me to one of the town's halal eateries. I asked if halal food was easy to come by in Berat and the two of them nodded. I then asked if it was possible to have any food delivered to my family who were resting in our very own Ottoman house, high up in the hills.

'Don't worry, the restaurant will deliver to them,' Edlir said.

'But it is in the old historic town, where the roads are very narrow, and I am not sure what exactly the address is.'

'It's OK, as long as they can ride a motorcycle up there, it is fine. They can get a motorcycle on the road near the house, right?'

'Erm, I think so...'

It's one of the things I love about small-town communities: everyone knows every street and alley regardless of whether they have actual names or not. All I had to do was call the property's owner and give the phone to the delivery guy, and the moped was off, whizzing up the narrow, cobblestoned pathways. It didn't matter that the lanes had no formal names or that the houses all looked the same to me. The driver knew exactly where to go. Within minutes I received a text message from Tamara thanking me for sending up the chicken pizzas, fries, fizzy drinks and bars of chocolate. She also told me the driver had kindly removed a giant grasshopper from the doorway, which had apparently taken them hostage.

The guys at the pizza joint all wore T-shirts emblazoned with 'Medina Pizza Hallall' – a nod to the holy city in Saudi Arabia. Some also had large beards, and *salaamed* us as we entered. We grabbed what Kasim said was a local delicacy – a salami, tuna and cheese toasted sandwich – and headed for the banks of the Osumi river. Both men refused to let me pay for my food, making it clear that as *musafir* I was their guest.

It was a balmy summer's evening, which made sitting by the riverside with the cool air bouncing off the waters a great choice. The three of us made our way towards the walkway that had been teeming with tourists during the day.

'This is where the old Ottoman bazaar used to be,' Kasim explained as we settled on a wooden structure resembling a small open-air stage.

I nodded and took a bite of the thick, crispy toastie. The thought of meat and fish in one sandwich wouldn't have normally appealed, but I wanted to try something local and went with Edlir and Kasim's recommendation. I was glad I had; this was delicious.

'Berat was an amazing Muslim city once,' Edlir said.

Both men had been born in Berat and were very proud of their country's Muslim heritage, something I had not yet come across in Albania, so it was very refreshing. I pointed this out to them, explaining that often the Ottomans were viewed as invaders by their fellow Balkans.

'*Alhamdulillah*, they gave us Islam. This is an amazing gift, even if they did invade,' Kasim said.

'Without them, what would we be following now?'

Edlir nodded sagely as we all took bigger chunks out of the sandwiches while they were still warm.

The Ottoman market both men described was one of Evliya's favourite places to hang out in Berat. He wrote that it was where friends and lovers spent the day chatting up the 'handsome young' male workers and that this wasn't seen as shameful. In fact, the boys' parents were proud of the fact that their sons were being courted in this way. Evliya's description suggests that here in Berat, just as in Ergiri (Gjirokastër), during his time men and boys were engaged in more than just platonic relations.

Nor was this the only social norm Muslim Berat had in common with Muslim Ergiri; when Evliya describes the habits of the 'polite and elegant' poets and scholars of Berat, he admits, like the Ergirins, they are 'given more to carousing than to piety'.

I wondered what Edlir and Kasim, who both confessed an ultra-conservative brand of Islam, might have made of these reports. How would they feel about the very liberal and tolerant positions on alcohol and male same-sex relations the Ottoman-era residents of their town reportedly had? I wondered if they already knew what Evliya had written.

My experience of Muslims who took their lead from Saudi-educated scholars told me they certainly would have been uncomfortable with this, which is probably why I chose not to bring it up.

The lights of the Ottoman houses appeared to twinkle as they looked down on us from the hills on either side of the Osumi. No one property stuck out: their design and colours were almost uniform, yet not a single one was identical to its neighbour either. The houses here were not as grand as those in Gjirokastër. They were smaller, more compact and just one or two storeys high, reflecting the modest wealth of the original inhabitants.

'You have such a beautiful town, so much of this Muslim history is not known outside of Albania.'

'Hmmph…' Kasim snorted, taking a big mouthful of melted cheese and bread. 'Forget outside Albania. I am a history teacher and when I teach Albanian history, I cover the Ottomans in just two lessons… That's almost five hundred years of history being covered in two lessons. Can you believe that? Two lessons.' There was a resigned tone to his statement.

An intelligent and wise man, Kasim was held in high regard by his peers, who all displayed a reverence for him. After we had sat chatting in the mosque and the time came around for the evening prayer, it was Kasim who had led that one.

'Instead…' he continued, 'Albanian history is based mostly on a legend – Skanderbeg – that is mostly made up.'

I asked him what he meant.

'Five hundred years of Ottoman influence on our country and I teach it in two lessons, discussing the Muslim empire negatively and this 'legend' Skanderbeg who lived for only sixty-five years or so. I have to teach as if he is some kind of superhero, when most of his story has been made up. It is mostly a lie!' Kasim laughed as he said this, and Edlir joined him. It was obvious he had heard this before.

Tamara had been reading up on Krujë, Skanderbeg's medieval capital, and we were planning a short trip there. Kasim's take on the great Albanian hero was therefore quite intriguing.

Skanderbeg was born Gjergj Kastrioti in 1405 to a noble family in the medieval central Albanian Principality of Kastrioti. He was one of the earliest of the anti-Ottoman Balkan 'freedom fighters'. Like Ali Pasha, Skanderbeg also served in the Ottoman army, having joined either as a hostage or *devsirme*. His displays of bravery and skill for the Muslim empire led the Ottomans to nickname him 'Iskender', as in Alexander the Great, which may have also been a nod to the fact his mother's perceived origins were North Macedonian.

Skanderbeg quickly became a very successful and loyal janissary, helping Sultan Murad II win a number of important battles for which he was rewarded with the title of Bey. This is where his name Skanderbeg comes from: the combining of 'Iskender' with 'Bey' or 'Beg'.

However, by 1443 Skanderbeg had became disillusioned by the Ottomans and deserted, taking control of large parts of central Albania and making Krujë his capital. Over the course of the next two decades or so, Skanderbeg united many Albanian noble families under his banner and successfully held off the Ottomans, defeating them in a number of famous battles. The Turkish Empire only regained control of the lands he had taken after his death. His plucky ability to withstand the might of the Muslim Empire led to Skanderbeg being immortalised by later writers of Albanian nationalist history. Over the centuries since his death, the story of Skanderbeg has been somewhat enhanced – like that of Ali Pasha – elevating the local warlord into an almost mythical and saintly figure, cast into the role of valiant, oppressed Christian leader up against the tyrannical Muslim imperialists.

For Kasim, the Skanderbeg 'myth' was a classic example of how his history had been rewritten to present the Muslims as the enemy. He was a history teacher and it concerned him greatly that Albanians were being brought up to admire someone like Skanderbeg and completely dismiss any of Albania's great Ottoman personalities. For him, there were two Skanderbegs: the real historic person, and the mythic national hero he had to teach kids about.

I found this idea fascinating and we spoke at length about other such examples, not just in the Balkans but across Europe. I told them about the curious story of the patron saint of Spain, St James, the mythical figure of local Catholicism dubbed the 'Moor-slayer' or 'Muslim killer'. There was just one problem: there were no 'Muslims' when St James was *actually* alive.

'What?' Kasim nearly choked on the fizzy drink he had bought to wash down the sandwich.

'*Yani*, he was a *sahaba* of Isa *alay sallam*,' I said, switching between Arabic and English phrases as I explained that St James had been a companion of Jesus Christ and died in AD44, long before Islam was announced by the Prophet Muhammad.

'Why...? How...?'

'This is where it gets really outrageous,' I said.

St James was dubbed the 'Moor-slayer' by medieval Spain after an entire anti-Muslim myth was constructed around him. The myth centres on a made-up battle called the Battle of Clavijo, in which the Christians – led by Ramiro I, the king of Asturias – find themselves outnumbered against the Muslims, led by the Umayyad Emir of Córdoba. It is at this point, despite being dead for eight hundred years, St James suddenly appears on a white horse to lead the Christian army to victory, slaying five thousand Muslims along the way. The myth, invented long after the date of the fictional battle, became central to the Spanish national identity and was often repeated during the medieval period, when numerous famous painters and sculptures depicted the made-up scenes of the saint slaying Muslims. Statues of Santiago Matamoros (St James the Moor-slayer) on a horse slaying turbaned Muslims can be found in almost every major church in Spain today, including the former Umayyad Mosque in Córdoba. The legend even made its way to the Americas where he was depicted as a conquistador, and many places in Latin America were named Matamoros in his honour. There is no evidence the real St James ever set foot in Spain, despite claims that his remains are in the Santiago de Compostela Cathedral in Galicia.

'Ya Allah!' Kasim was now laughing out loud. 'They take one of Isa's *sahaba,* make up a whole story about him killing Muslims in a battle that didn't even happen, eight hundred years after he died, and then make him the country's national saint, even though he never even stepped foot in Spain. *Subhanallah!*'

Kasim asked me where else we had been on our trip through the Balkans. I told them how we started in Bosnia with Sarajevo, Mostar and Blagaj before passing through Višegrad to enter Serbia. I explained my astonishment at just how Muslim the southwest was, and how strange the idea of Muslims in Serbia is to the outside world.

'People think it is just a Christian country.'

'This is what the Serbians want… They want everyone to think there is no such thing as a Serbian Muslim,' Edlir said.

I then told them about our time in North Macedonia and my disappointment with the drive to adopt a cultural heritage that seemed to ignore the country's rich Muslim one, especially in Skopje.

'Skopje has that much Ottoman history?' Edlir asked.

'Yes, I was blown away by it. I couldn't believe just how many monuments there were.'

'I know there are many Albanians there, but I didn't know there was so much Muslim history.'

We then spoke for a while about the square in Skopje that was at the forefront of the drive to reimagine the nation's cultural heritage and link it to the ancient Macedons. They knew the square well as it had made the news many times. For both of them, it was yet another example of how the Balkan history was being rewritten to marginalise any positive impact of Muslim culture in the area.

When it was time for us to say goodbye, Kasim handed me the white prayer cap he wore to lead us for *Isha* as a parting gift. I was deeply touched by this and thanked him before we all hugged and shook hands, promising to stay in touch. Edlir and I saw off Kasim near the former bazaar area and watched as he disappeared into the darkness of one of the many narrow medieval alleyways. Edlir then walked me to the foot of the hill where my apartment was and looked up.

'Do you think you will remember where your house is?' he laughed.

'*Inshallah*, brother,' I said, before giving him a big hug and heading up one of the cobbled paths near the Hotel Belgrad Mangalem.

Capitals Old and New

DURRËS, TIRANA AND KRUJË

I was sad to leave Berat. I could have spent many more days wandering its medieval alleyways in conversation with Kasim and Edlir. Along with Gjirokastër, it had been the highlight of our time in Albania. The two towns had offered a wonderful glimpse of what Evliya's Muslim Albania would've looked like, a glimpse we had not expected to find. Next on our itinerary was the country's capital, Tirana.

We set off early in the morning and made not for the city but its beach in the nearby town of Durrës which, although thirty-five kilometres west, feels like an extension of Tirana. The corridor linking the two is heavily built up along the busy SH2. Lined with malls and large retail outlets, driving through it feels like you are just going from one end of a large city to the other.

Durrës was a picture of what the rest of the Albanian Riviera wants to be. Bronze expats lounged around on sunbeds, cocktails by their side, enjoying their well-deserved break back home, and local city slickers, down from Tirana for the day, sat in little beach huts lining the shore, admiring the view. The sea was filled with children on their school summer holiday playing with large inflatables, their parents occasionally joining them. Some were working on sandcastles beneath colourful parasols.

We had come to Durrës not just to enjoy a day by the sea, but also to meet the woman whose flat in Tirana we would be staying in for the next couple of days. Iryana met us for a coffee in one of the cafés that spilled out on to the beach. She had curly strawberry-blonde hair, large sunglasses and enjoyed a smoke. As she talked me through finding the apartment, where to park the car and, most importantly, how to use the lift, the girls tucked into plates of fresh pasta and Tamara enjoyed a bit of shut-eye on her sunlounger.

The rest of the afternoon went exactly as we had planned it; the girls drifted in the blue waters, clinging to their floats like two wilted plants that hadn't been watered for weeks. Occasionally, Tamara and I joined them, but mostly we watched from the shore as we caught up on our reading and I mapped out the remainder of our journey. Tamara had not been able to get the time off work to stay for as long as we had originally hoped and she was due to fly out from Montenegro's capital in five days. However, before then we ambitiously planned to see Tirana and pop into Krujë on our way to Shkodër before hitting the spectacular Montenegrin coastline and finally the capital, Podgorica. After that, the girls and I would have ten days left to recover, and slowly see Bosnia again.

The sun was already beginning to dip as we entered the busy centre of Tirana. Our apartment was on Zogu I Boulevard, named after Zog I, who served the nation as prime minister, then president and finally king during an oppressive monarchy in the interwar years of the early 20th century.

Ahmet Muhtar Zogolli was descended from a powerful Muslim family of Ottoman beys and held several government positions when the country was the Principality of Albania, before being exiled. He returned with Yugoslav support to become the country's prime minister and then dictatorial president in 1925. During his reign, Zog suppressed civil liberties and formed an alliance with fascist Italian leader Mussolini that led to Albania becoming an Italian protectorate. Having declared the country a monarchy and himself king, Zog then fled into exile. He was not allowed to return to Albania under Hoxha and died in France in 1961.

Zog's only son was welcomed back after the millennium as King Leka I and, when he died, his son, Leka Zogu II, the Crown Prince of Albania, became head of the House of Zog.

Our road was one of the main ones leading to Skanderbeg Square, in the middle of which was Albania's most iconic statue of Skanderbeg, mounted on a stallion. This was the heart of modern Tirana. The central location of the apartment, next to the University of Tirana's Faculty of Natural Sciences, made it easy to find, even without a satellite-navigation system. I parked the car in front of the faculty's yellow block and stepped out to find a burly-looking man stood by a small doorway squeezed in between several shopfronts, just as Iryana had described it to me. We loaded ourselves up with rucksacks and suitcases and headed for the door. The security guy didn't move, looking us up and down. It was only when I produced the key to the door he was guarding that he came to life. Now smiling, he held open the door and even offered to help take the bags into the dark hallway where there was a tiny lift entrance and a set of concrete stairs. I was instantly transported back to the high-rise blocks of my east London upbringing.

The lift arrived with a large clunk that made the four of us look at each other nervously. Not that we had a choice – the apartment was on the eighth floor. We all literally squeezed in; Anaiya, who struggles with confined spaces and is petrified of lifts, looked a little white so I gave her a cuddle, which probably suffocated her even more.

We all listened for the passing floors in silence, counting each one in our heads. It seemed like an age before the clunk that announced the lift had come to a halt. When the ancient metallic doors creaked ajar, we fell out of the square tin can in relief. Our apartment was wonderfully modern and spacious, with a nice open-plan kitchen, diner and living area, and a small balcony at the back. I went over to it and opened the door, letting in a blast of warm air and the noise of the busy city outside. Tirana's high-rise towers sprawled out in front of me, their lights twinkling in the dark night sky. I looked out to see if I could spot minarets over the tops of the houses, but I couldn't see any. Up above in the clear, cloudless night, the near-full moon was visible.

Tirana dates back to the Middle Ages and, although mentioned during the struggles of Skanderbeg with the Ottomans in the 16th century, it was not really considered a town until around 1614. This was when a feudal lord called Sulejman Pasha Bargjini built a mosque, hammam and *imaret* in Tirana, promoting it to the status of a *kasaba* or township, which is probably why Evliya paid it very little attention when he passed through. He wrote that it sat on a broad plain with fully tiled and splendid public buildings as well as mosques, *hans*, bathhouses, bazaars, vineyards and gardens, but notes there was nothing remarkable about the town.

Tirana only began to gain significance once Skanderbeg's old fortress capital of Krujë collapsed in the 18th century and the powerful feudal family, the Toptanis, ancestors of Zog, transferred their seat from Krujë to Tirana. After this, Tirana became a relatively prosperous centre of trade and crafts with around forty mosques in the city. Many of these were beautifully painted, as Austrian diplomat Johann Gorg von Hahn discovered in the middle of the 19th century – he was charmed by the 'gaily-painted' mosques in their green surrounds and the city's tall poplars. Tirana's population just before it was made the capital in 1920 following independence was split almost fifty-fifty between Sunni Muslims who followed the Rifa'i Sufi order and Bektashis.

Sadly, almost all of the historic mosques and many religious buildings, including tekkes and *türbes*, were destroyed during the liberation struggle and later, when Hoxha's plans for an atheist state were enforced – this included Tirana's first recorded mosque, built by Sulejman Pasha Bargjini. The only historic mosque still standing in Tirana just happened to be around the corner from our apartment, and it was there I was headed for the *Isha* prayer on my first night.

There is something very cathedral-like about Tirana's Hadji Et'hem Bey Mosque. It sits in the centre of town, close to the statue of Skanderbeg, and is a pretty single-domed Ottoman mosque with an elegant slimline minaret. The most striking feature though is the stunning multi-arched portico covered in fresco-style paintings and floral patterns. I was immediately reminded of the Ali Pasha Mosque in Tetovo, North Macedonia. This was one of the 'gaily-painted' mosques von Hahn had seen. Once open to the elements, the portico is now protected on all sides by toughened glass.

I walked inside to find a room with the top half covered in elaborately painted floral patterns of reddish-browns and greens in the now ubiquitous baroque-roccoco style of the Tulip era. Many of them framed miniatures of historic Ottoman landscapes. I scanned them for Sinan's Sulaymaniye Mosque and found several multi-domed paintings that might have qualified. One sat close to the arches holding up the patterned dome, and another was high above the *mihrab*. The mosque's wooden *mimbar* was much taller than the ones

I had seen elsewhere and, unusually, had a three-pronged chandelier hanging inside the section at the top of the stairwell, suggesting it was not actually used by the imam. The room also had a small decorated *mahvil* at the back, though I saw nobody using it.

The mosque was started around 1793 by Molla Bey, a local feudal landlord from Petrelë, a small town south of Tirana. Molla, who was the great-grandson of Sulejman Pasha Bargjini, only managed to get the dome built before passing away. The rest of the mosque, including the minaret and the portico, were completed by his son Et'hem Beg around 1821, a 'Hadji' who had performed the Muslim pilgrimage to Makkah. It is Et'hem Beg the mosque is named after. To add the final, artistic touch to his father's project, Et'hem Beg hired renowned painters of mosques and churches all the way from the villages of the Pindus mountains in modern-day Greece, and it is these artists who were responsible for the mosque's beautiful frescos.

I sat down and waited for the call to prayer. Slowly, the room began to fill up, mainly with clean-shaven men wearing regular Western attire: shirts and T-shirts with trousers or jeans. After a little while, one of these men, dressed in a short-sleeved check shirt and beige chinos, walked over to the corner of the room and grabbed a microphone. He then placed his right hand over his right ear, in a half *Takbir*, before making one of the most beautiful *adhans* I had heard so far. His voice was a strong, melodious one that held the elongated sections much longer than I had heard anywhere else in the Balkans, with no wavering whatsoever. The man looked middle-aged and had a small moustache. If I passed him on the street, I would never imagine for a second that he was such an accomplished *muezzin*. The call sounded all the more beautiful as it bounced off the high ceilings of the Et'hem Beg, reverberating like the interior of a cathedral. When he finished, I stood up and shook his hand to thank him. He looked a little surprised but smiled.

On my way out of the mosque after the prayer, I noticed a stone tablet above the entrance. It confirmed the original builder was Molla Bey, describing him as the 'Great Chief, Lord of Good Deeds' and a 'noble commander' and claiming the mosque's construction revived Tirana - no doubt in the same way his great-grandfather had initially put it on the map with his now-destroyed mosque. The inscription also mentions a 'Suzi', which may be a reference to the 19th-century Ottoman poet Suzi Ahmed Efendi, before making the slightly trumpeted claim that the completion of the mosque made Tirana as beautiful as the Haghia Sophia made Istanbul.

Tirana is bordered to the east by Dajti National Park. It is from here you get some of the most stunning views of the capital city, and nowhere are the views more impressive than aboard the Dajti Ekspres, the park's excellent cable cars.

The Dajti Ekspres sits at the eastern edge of Tirana, tucked away at the back of a dirty old road in a residential part of the city. The mountains had been popular hiding grounds during the Cold War, and as we got closer to the Ekspres, I could see signs to a place called 'Bunkart': an old nuclear bunker now converted into a museum and art gallery, complete with its own theatre-like hall where live events and concerts are held.

We pulled up in an empty car park and excitedly headed over to board the cable cars. The climb up to the lush, green mountains was a dramatically steep one. For fifteen glorious minutes, as the urban sprawl of Tirana began to shrink behind us, we passed over small lakes and tiny rural farms with neatly ploughed fields. I spotted a white minaret peering out from amongst a thicket of trees.

'That mosque isn't as small as I thought,' I said as we got closer to the minaret.

'Wow, look at how high the cable cars go,' Anaiya said, spying our final destination up ahead and tactfully ignoring my comment. She was clearly tired of spotting minarets.

'It's going to the top of the mountain. Look, it says it here,' Tamara said, reading the small brochure she had picked up at the Dajti's boarding station.

As we neared the last leg of the steep incline it soon became apparent just how high we really were.

'Ooh, my ears are popping,' exclaimed Tamara.

'Ow, so are mine.' Amani was cupping hers.

The cars stopped at the Dajti Tower Belvedere Hotel, a building that looked more control tower than luxury accommodation. We paused to grab some refreshments at a small café near the exit of the cable cars. As I waited for our coffees, I noticed that most of the cars coming up the mountain were empty; this wasn't a busy attraction. One of the few that did have passengers had a married couple inside. The woman was covered from head to toe in a burka and niqab – it was the first time we had seen this in Albania – and the man was dressed in cargo trousers and a long-sleeve top. If this were Bosnia, it would have been easy to assume the couple were tourists from the Gulf, but this was Albania, a place not noted for Arab travellers. As our experience in Berat had revealed, Albanians were also adopting conservative Islam and in all likelihood they were locals.

The path leading into Dajti National Park was lined by young boys holding sports guns offering passers-by the opportunity to shoot various wooden targets. The boys looked scruffy and bored. There were also a few men offering pony and horse rides. They looked like they could be the fathers of the boys and seemed equally bored. Most people simply walked straight past them and headed into the woods. One family was busy putting up bunting in preparation for what looked like a young girl's birthday picnic.

As we headed into the woodland, we passed two abandoned hotels in various stages of decay. Squeezed in between them was a restaurant, outside which, turning slowly on a thick iron skewer above a barbecue, was an unappetising-looking lamb. Blackened by the charcoal, the lamb still had its head, complete with eyeballs that looked at you every time they came around; the girls flinched when they noticed it. Above us the sky was now overcast.

We walked along the concrete footpath past a series of ancient oak trees with thick, knotted, exposed roots before coming across the first of several partially submerged concrete bunkers. Mentioned in every guide to the country, we had seen them scattered all over the Albanian countryside, but this was the first time we had been up close with one. Anaiya quickly spotted another.

'What are they?' she asked, peering inside.

'They're bunkers, built to be used if there was the outbreak of war,' I explained.

'They look creepy,' Amani said.

She was right; the round concrete domes looked like eerie relics from a bygone era.

'How do you get inside them?' Anaiya asked, circling hers. 'There's no door or entrance.'

The bunkers were made out of reinforced concrete. The front had a narrow slit so weapons could be fired out of them. These were also wide enough for the soldiers to crawl in through. Paranoid dictator Enver Hoxha built over 173,000 of these bunkers all over Albania; that's nearly six bunkers for every square kilometre!

The bunkers were built over a twenty-year period from the mid 1960s, draining the national coffers and causing much resentment amongst the people. Hoxha built them so that every Albanian, if necessary, could hole themselves up in one and defend the country. They never served that purpose but some were used in the 1997 Albanian insurrection and then two years later in the Kosovo War. These days, most lie abandoned, like the ones we were staring at. However, some of the larger ones have been reappropriated into things like small homes, cafés and storehouses.

'I think they had to crawl in through the front...' I bent down to assess the size of the openings.

'Look, Dad, there's something written inside,' Anaiya said.

Somebody had graffitied the interior of the bunker she was looking at. I tried to read it but it was too dark. Amani and Tamara were photographing the other bunker and so Anaiya decided to step forward and take a closer look.

'Be careful, you don't know who might be inside,' I joked.

Anaiya gave me a stern look. She edged forward, a little slower now. The bunker was in the shade of a large oak, and no light could get inside. 'HELLLLOOOO?' she shouted into the mouth of the bunker. No sooner had she done this, a small bat came flying out, making her retreat quickly. 'Wooah! Amani! Mum! Did you see that? There was a bat living inside my one!' she squealed.

'Where?' Amani asked. But it was too late. The bat had fluttered away.

'It's gone now. Let's see if there's a bat inside your one!'

The two of them walked over to the one Amani and Tamara had been photographing and stood in front of the entrance before proceeding to shout 'Hello!' several times, but neither was willing to get too close, just in case a bat was asleep inside. After a while they gave up, looking disappointed.

I glanced at my phone. It was nearly 3pm, and we still wanted to visit one more place before heading to our final destination for the night, the town of Shkodër. It was time to get back aboard the Dajti Ekspres.

From the Dajti Ekspres we took the SH1 out of Tirana. We had barely left the city when we began seeing signs for Albania's very first capital, Krujë. Less than an hour's drive from Tirana, the town pronounced 'Kruja' is two thousand feet above sea level at the foot of Mount Krujë, close to the Ishëm river. When the Principality of Arbanon (or Albanon), the very first Albanian state, was founded in 1190, it was Krujë the medieval ruling family of Progoni chose to be their capital.

Krujë later became the first capital of the Kingdom of Albania, and, after the Ottomans took it early in the 15th century, it was the city that Skanderbeg recaptured for the Albanians.

The road up to the town was steep and offered us the first glimpses of modern Krujë. Most of the town was one- and two-storey houses with terracotta-tiled roofs surrounded by olive trees, giving the place a Mediterranean look. One side of the hill was far more built up and had a number of new tower blocks, some yet to be finished. They rose up the mountain in terraced fashion, making it impossible to tell which ones were the tallest.

As we got closer to the top, the houses began to age. In the distance the iconic bastion of Krujë's historic castle came into view. We left the car and walked towards it. The path led us down an old, cobbled street that looked as if it belonged in Skopje's old town. Narrow and lined by shops inside renovated Ottoman houses with wooden shutters, there was even a slimline minaret looming overhead. With the peaks of Mount Krujë in the background, the setting was really rather spectacular. It was a bright, sunny day and the narrow lane offered us shade as we passed shops selling traditional Albanian clothes, red-and-black national flags, metalwear engraved with Arabic, and copper frames of Skanderbeg.

Skanderbeg was the city's Ottoman governor before he deserted and returned to take control of the town for his League of Lezhë, a confederation of Albanian chieftains that had united under his leadership against the Ottomans. Over the next two decades or so, Skanderbeg successfully defended Krujë until his death, helping to secure his legend as a national hero.

Remnants from that historic period include ruins of the wall of the original castle that Skanderbeg defended and the ruins of the town's first mosque, built by Krujë's Ottoman conqueror, Mehmed I. We passed the latter in front of the newly built Skanderbeg Museum, where most people were headed. We decided to make our way to the southeastern corner of the fortress, where there was a cluster of old houses. I wanted to see if we could find one of the two historic tekkes said to be within the fort. We made our way along narrow cobblestoned paths overgrown with moss, squeezed in between tiny Ottoman houses. I wondered if either of the tekkes could be another Sarı Saltık tomb; devotees of the maverick saint have been coming on pilgrimage to Krujë since at least the 17th century.

As we got near the back of the houses, the mountains beyond came into view. Soon we were passing raised graves with stone hats:

the graves of Bektashi babas. These were in the shade of a magnificent ancient olive tree, behind which, perched at the very edge of the mountain like an eagle's nest, was the tekke and *türbe* of Hajji Mustafa Baba: the Dollma Tekke.

The tombs were housed inside a beautiful octagonal *türbe* with stained-glass windows, wooden doors that had their lower parts painted an iridescent green, and an interior of stunning floral patterns. The patterns suggested the *türbe* dated from the 18th century, but there was no signage in English to confirm this. Inside, unusually for a *türbe*, there was a *mihrab* at the far end; it was clearly not for prayer, as a small iron cabinet with a chimney had been installed in its centre so devotees could light candles inside. The *mihrab's muqarnas* pattern was blackened from smoke. I counted three tombs, two together and one by itself in front of another, much smaller niche. I wondered if any were the actual tomb of the tekke's founder, Hajji Mustafa Baba.

The tombs were raised and had the Toblerone shape I had seen across the Balkans. They all had a number of patterned small rugs and scarves draped over them, and one had a giant *tasbih* and an Albanian translation of the Qur'an leaning on it. I was completely alone. After the scene in the Murad *türbe* near Pristina, Tamara and the girls were not going near any more tombs. All three of them were outside exploring the rest of the tekke, whose 19th-century leader, Shemin Baba, according to one legend, was responsible for converting Ali Pasha to Bektashism. I scanned the walls for the Sulaymaniye but could find only one painting of a mosque, above the entrance. It wasn't the Sulaymaniye; this one only had two minarets.

After a while, two young men walked in. One had wild, curly hair and wore glasses, and the other had short, mousy hair and also wore glasses. Both men were in shorts that went beyond their knees.

'I'm trying to learn more about the Islam of my country,' said curly-haired Olen Goli after we had introduced ourselves to each other. 'I'm a convert to Islam.'

'You are? And what was it that brought about your conversion?' I asked.

I recognised the smile Olen gave me. 'Well, there are actually two reasons,' he began in excellent English. 'I kept hearing about crazy Muslims and crazy Islam, and wanted to know what was so crazy about these people, so I started to learn about Islam...' Olen was still smiling. We both were. He knew, I knew. 'And the more I learned about it, the more I became drawn to it.'

I nodded. It was the familiar story of the sceptic gone native. I had heard so many conversion stories that began just like that.

'I had come to Islam to find out why I should hate it, and instead fell in love with it!'

We both laughed.

'And the second reason?'

'Now, that is more complicated, and it is something I thought about afterwards. I realised that being Albanian today and historically has always been very closely tied to being Muslim.' Olen paused; he wanted me to understand this properly. 'It is Muslims that have always supported the Albanian people here, in Kosovo, in Macedonia, and whenever there has been any aggression towards the Albanian people it has been by the Christians that surround us, not the Muslims.'

'So, are you saying you converted to Islam also because it made you feel more Albanian?'

'I think so; I think on some unconscious levels, this is definitely true.'

I was amazed. I had been fascinated by the ethno-religious nationalist politics of this region, but always imagined people had chosen their 'sides' a long time ago and the lines drawn were fixed. I never imagined I would actually meet someone making a decision about which religion to follow based on their ethnicity today, and yet here I was talking to a young Albanian who had decided to leave his Christian upbringing for Islam because for many in the Balkans to be Albanian is to *really* be Muslim. There were, of course, many Albanian Christians, almost twenty per cent actually, and Olen used to be one of them, but clearly becoming Muslim made him feel more Albanian, even if he admits this was an unconscious part of his decision. It was something I found truly mind-blowing. Religion wasn't about what was right and wrong around here; it was identity.

'And what do you make of the Islam in Albania?' I asked.

Olen thought for a moment and then answered. 'I think Islam in Albania is re-emerging, because if you look at the history, for so long religion was banned in Albania, and so many people lost their way, they had to do things in secret and hide their religion, this makes things very difficult.'

'And the Bektashis, what do you make of them?'

'This is a part of Albanian heritage and this is their choice. They want to do things in this way, they should be free to do it,' Olen replied, again picking his words carefully.

I left Olen and his friend photographing the tomb, promising to stay in touch, and went in search of Tamara and the girls. They had found the main worship space, which was in one of the fort's repurposed old bastions. I stepped into a circular room painted lime green with framed images of Hasan, Husayn and a number of babas on the walls. There was comfortable low seating going all the way around, where all three of them had found themselves a space to sit and rest.

'Wow.' I stepped down on to the dark wooden flooring.

'Mad, right?' said Tamara. 'It's like that other place you described in Tetovo.'

'Yeah, only the walls on that were absolutely covered with pictures, and it did not have these ridiculous views!'

'Yep, it is pretty stunning out of those windows.'

I stuck my head out of one and the view took my breath away. The vast valley we had driven through on our way up from Tirana lay before us, with mountains disappearing off into the horizon. The Bektashis certainly knew how to pick a spot, like the tekke at the foot of the mountains in Tetovo and the other at the mouth of the river Buna in Blagaj. It was easy to see how worshippers might lose themselves in *dhikr* in a place like this.

PART FIVE

MONTENEGRO

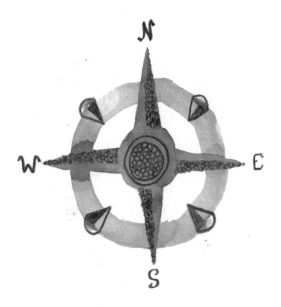

Muslim Montenegro

PODGORICA

From Albania we headed straight to Montenegro's stunning Kotor Bay so that we could savour our final few days with Tamara before she returned to London for work.

We spent two wonderfully relaxed days enjoying the dazzling bay area and its beautiful Venetian fortified town, indulging in simple family holiday larks: eating ice cream, swimming in the sea and dining out. Then, after a spectacular drive to Podgorica along the spine of the 'black mountains' that give the country its name, the girls and I said a sad farewell to Tamara the next morning.

The three of us travelling together was nothing new. Thanks to my teaching job we were always on holiday at the same time. This meant lots of day trips: taking part in a National Trust hunt here, a British Museum activity there, or hanging out with family. As they got older and began to dictate the agenda more, it was shopping together in a vintage market or heading out to an exhibit at a quirky art gallery.

And, of course, occasionally we were lucky enough to spend time together abroad, with Tamara joining us for the periods she had off work. As parents, we really saw the value in these types of experiences alone with our children; they allowed us to nurture our individual relationships with them. This is why Tamara had also been away with just our girls, most recently to Santorini in Greece and New York, and why, shortly after finishing her GCSEs, Amani and I backpacked through Andalusia in Spain. She was keen to explore the region's Muslim history and learn the ropes of solo travel, and we both wanted that exclusive dad-and-daughter time together. When the global pandemic passes, I intend to do something similar with Anaiya when she finishes school.

This is why we already had an itinerary planned for our remaining time in the Balkans, one that balanced all of our interests. Throughout the time Tamara had been with us, it had often been easy for me to go off and explore local Muslim heritage alone if I needed to. Usually this was when Tamara and the girls had planned something less 'dull' than exploring local history, like browsing for gifts in the local market, laying on a beach for hours or taking in an art exhibition.

With Tamara now gone, the girls and I would compromise and humour each other like we always did when it was just the three of us, which is why Amani and Anaiya had spent the past week coming up with a list of things they wanted to do. The list had activities like bowling, more swimming in the sea, going to a cinema, finding a McDonald's, eating a curry, looking for more waterfalls, and visiting an animal sanctuary or zoo. There were also a few teenage requests like being allowed to sleep in late and spend time on their phones.

The three of us then put these into a balanced ten-day itinerary. So whilst this afternoon would be spent in Podgorica's Ottoman Old Town, this evening I would cook their favourite dinner while they had some time online with their phones. It also meant tomorrow was all theirs, when we would go in search of waterfalls on our route back to Bosnia.

Even after the Ottoman conquest in the 15th century, Podgorica was little more than a provincial town – yet, as Evliya discovered, it was important enough for the conquering sultan, Mehmet II, to build a fortress there. Evliya says the sultan did this to protect nearby Shkodër. The inaccessible nature of mountainous Montenegro, plus the support the local tribes got from the Venetians, meant it was only really the south of Montenegro the Ottomans managed to subjugate.

The majority of the country became de facto independent in the 18th century and then fully independent about a hundred years later. After World War I, it slowly drifted into socialist Yugoslavia and was part of a smaller version known as the Federal Republic of Yugoslavia, along with Serbia, before becoming fully independent again in 2006.

The ruins of Mehmet's fortress were near the confluence of two rivers: the larger Morača river and the smaller Ribnica river. That's where the girls and I were now headed. Our route would take us through the Old Town, known locally as Stara Varoš, where I had identified two historic mosques and an Ottoman-era clock tower.

The Osmanagic Mosque was built at the start of the 18th century by Mehmed Pasha Osmanagic, whose *türbe* stood in the small courtyard outside. I pulled up with the girls in the car just before the *Asr* prayer. Like everywhere else in Podgorica, the streets of the Old Town were empty – during the summer months, all the locals head for the coast. I wondered if anyone would be attending the mosque or if it was open at all. Outside, a black-and-white photograph showed a badly damaged minaret and a crumbling mosque beside it. This was what the Osmanagic had looked like before the Ottoman guardians, TIKA, renovated the historic monument.

Small and modest in size, the mosque was built of stone and had a wall around the perimeter topped with the same terracotta tiles as its roof. It was classically Ottoman in design with a slimline white minaret. I asked the girls if they wanted to come inside, but they were busy playing 'Bus Stop' – a new word game they had come across – so after checking they could call me using Amani's phone, I told them to lock the car doors and headed into the mosque to pray *Asr*.

Inside, I was greeted by a recently renovated interior: a beautiful wooden *mahvil* sat over exposed stone archways. The floor was covered in a mustard-and-red carpet. The rest of the walls had been plastered fresh white, and each window framed with pretty, understated flowers; these were complemented by a number of painted plants in blue vases. The *mihrab* and *mimbar* were both intricately carved from dark wood and looked brand new, as did the ceiling.

I placed my shoes in the small wooden racks and sat down. It was very close to *Asr* when Mirza walked into the mosque. I had never met a Montenegrin Muslim and was quite excited by this. Mirza walked straight past me and flicked a switch near the *mimbar*. He then slowly and melodically made the *adhan*. Mirza then performed his four *rakats* of *Sunnah* prayers. After he finished, I approached him as I had the lonely imam in Berat, and offered my *salaams* and a firm handshake. Mirza wasn't the mosque's imam, but I urged him to lead the prayer.

Afterwards, as we headed for the exit, we began talking.

'I was born Muslim, like many Montenegrin Muslims in Podgorica, but when I was young I didn't practise,' he explained, as we stopped near the mosque's iron gates, so I could see the girls in the car. It turned out Mirza had also been waiting to talk to me, intrigued by my presence in his local mosque. He asked about the girls when he saw me wave to them.

'They are my two daughters, we have been travelling around the western Balkans for the past month or so, but my wife had to fly back to London and she took a flight from Podgorica this morning, so we decided to explore the town before heading back to Bosnia.'

Mirza was impressed and thought it was wonderful I was spending time with just my daughters. He was dressed in a black T-shirt with faded English words across the front and a pair of three-quarter-length tracksuit bottoms – the Muslim male's preferred alternative to shorts in the summer, as they reach below the knees and can be worn for prayer. Mirza had a dark brown beard and the beginnings of a moustache. I asked him what the congregations were like when Podgorica wasn't so empty.

'The five daily prayers are small, but *Jumua'ah* is full in both mosques.'

'It's the same in London,' I said.

This seemed to surprise Mirza; he had heard that the Muslims in London were extremely observant and religious.

'To be honest, when you think about the number of Muslims here and the numbers in London, relatively speaking it is probably the same percentage of the Muslim population attending the mosques,' I said.

Mirza spoke excellent English, this was down to the fact all school children in Montenegro learn English from an early age. I asked him what he did, and whether he was still in education. He had a young face, but his beard suggested he was older, and this made it difficult to tell just how old he really was.

'I studied graphic design in Skopje, which is a much more Muslim city,' he explained.

'Yes, isn't it just? I was really amazed when I was there. It could be a city somewhere in Turkey, right?'

'You have been?' Mirza's face lit up. I nodded. 'Exactly. There are lots of Muslims in Macedonia.'

'More than here?'

'Yes, there are not that many here any more,' he said, his voice becoming flatter.

'What about when you were younger, what do you remember of life around here? That picture of the broken minaret. Do you remember that?' I said, pointing to the black-and-white photo on the sign.

'Of course, this mosque was broken and just a pile of bricks from World War II. It was very dangerous and we were not allowed to go near it. Nobody could use it.'

'So, was it TIKA that fixed it?'

'No. Way before TIKA, the elders in the area decided to fix it. All the locals helped clear more than a hundred tractor loads of garbage in and around the building. Then they all put their money together and began to repair the building.'

'Was this only Muslims who did this?'

Mirza thought for a while, as if trying to remember. 'This was before I was born, so I do not know for sure, but I am certain *everyone* in the area, Muslim or not, wanted to fix it, because it is a part of their city and their history.'

'So, you remember this mosque being used when you were young?'

'Yes, I remember both the mosques being used, mainly for Friday *Jumua'ah*, but the group was always small. Now the Friday groups are very big.'

'I see, so when did TIKA come to help?'

'That was in 2011. TIKA came along and offered to help to renovate it after the mosque suffered an arson attack.'

'Somebody tried to burn the mosque down?'

'Yes, I think some people hear bad things in the media about Muslims and they get a bit silly, but we don't actually have this kind of problem in Podgorica. People have known these mosques have always been here. They know Muslims have always been in Montenegro. It's just some people, maybe stupid young ones who do not know their history, that sometimes decide to do this.'

I could see Mirza glancing at his watch and remembered I wanted to ask him one last thing before he left. Pulling out my phone, I showed him a picture of the small doughy treats our hosts at the apartment we had rented in Podgorica had presented to us on arrival.

'What are these called?'

Mirza thought briefly and then his eyes lit up. 'Priganice!' he exclaimed. 'You eat them savoury or sweet, and they are a long-standing tradition with the Montenegrins, and I am sure they are a legacy of the Ottoman period too.'

I laughed at this, telling him that was what I had suspected when we received them and how the girls had made fun of the fact that I thought everything was Ottoman around here. This made Mirza laugh too. We then shook hands and embraced, before I watched him walk down a narrow street beneath a mock-Ottoman house painted an off-yellow colour.

Islam is the second largest religion in Montenegro after Orthodox Christianity, with Muslims making up almost twenty per cent of the population. As with their neighbouring countries, those that identify as Muslims in Montenegro are mostly ethnic Bosniaks or Albanians. The number of Muslims like Mirza that see themselves as ethnically Montenegrin are a mere two per cent of the country's population.

The girls and I decided to leave the car parked near the Osmanagic as the ruins of the fort were within walking distance. The narrow roads surrounding the mosque were medieval in size, and the properties were an eclectic mix of colourfully rendered little houses and older ones with exposed stone, like the exterior of the mosque. Some had features that offered a nod to historic Ottoman heritage. Most had gardens with vine leaves growing from them and one or two also had palm trees. We didn't pass a soul on our wander through the neighbourhood. The only noise was the passing of an occasional car and the barking of a small dog in someone's front yard. On one corner of a beaten-up wall, there was a series of graffiti and Anaiya's eyes lit up when she spotted the name 'Tamara'.

'Look Amani!' she shouted, running to the writing.

Beneath Tamara was a '+' sign and a name that had been angrily scribbled over. The heart with an arrow going through it had been left alone. I tried to make out the scribbled-out name as the girls struck cheesy poses in front of their mother's name. It definitely didn't say Tharik.

The first people we came across were two elderly women outside Podgorica's only other mosque, the Starodoganjska, a whitewashed building also with a terracotta-tiled roof and a single minaret, only this minaret was wider. The women were busy scrubbing a large Eastern rug and the small courtyard was awash with water. The mosque was clearly open, and I gestured to the women that I wanted to go in. One of them, dressed in a cream cardigan and with short blonde hair, realised what I was suggesting and broke into a smile, urging me in.

The girls followed me in to the narrow courtyard with the mosque on the right and the offices of the Grand Mufti of Montenegro on the left. Only the mosque doors were open, and again it was clear it had been recently renovated. The layout was identical to the Osmanagic, but the interior less elaborate; the *mihrab* was a simple white niche and all the walls were plain, devoid of any colour or patterns.

The mosque also had a series of round windows, giving it a slightly nautical feel. According to a sign outside, this was the location of Montenegro and Podgorica's oldest surviving mosque, originally built by a Skender Causin in the late 15th century.

I thanked the two women for letting us peek inside and turned to find Anaiya had located the mosque cat, and was now stroking her with a leaf. I smiled as she pointed out that she was still sticking to the rules Tamara and I had agreed with her at the beginning of the trip of not touching any cats with her hands.

The map on my phone said the river could be reached via a path behind some of the houses close to the mosque. Our first effort to do this led us into a small cul-de-sac where a girl of about five or six was happily riding around on her pink bike, singing to herself. Seeing us arrive, she stopped and fell silent, staring at us quizzically. We waved, but she just continued to stare. We then found a small dirt track, which wound its way past some old rocks that looked like they had belonged to a wall once. Walking beside it, we heard rushing water. The path led down to the site of the fort, which was now mostly a series of low-rise ruins and later landscaped features. This was the heart of the Ottoman settlement; when Evliya visited, it had been little more than a military outpost. He counted three hundred houses, a mosque and mostly storehouses inside the fort, which was home to seven hundred garrison troops. Evliya says he found no *madrasas, hans* or bazaars to suggest the place was home to a real community of people.

The most impressive structure left today was the Stari Most na Ribnici, which straddles the smaller river close to where it joins the rushing Morača. Also known as Adži-paša's bridge, after the local Ottoman pasha who commissioned it, the Stari Most is the oldest bridge in Podgorica and sits at the foot of two steep banks, close to the ruins of the fort. Small and perfectly formed, the stone bridge has a large rainbow arch, just like the famous bridge in Mostar, except this one is barely wide enough for two people to walk over it. The bridge also has a unique feature on the southern bank where, next to a smaller arch, is a portal just the right size for maybe a sentry to stand guard inside. The river beneath was almost dry, exposing all the large stones on its bed – each one smoothened by the water during the wet season. The girls took one look at the crystal-clear streams passing through the narrows of the stones and leapt straight in, discarding their flip-flops and squealing as the cold water touched their naked feet. Soon they were busy taking pictures, building small stone structures and playing like two children at a beach.

High above us, the city's busiest road passed over the Morača on the Blažo Jovanović bridge, named after the country's post-World War II president and national hero. It was a large concrete structure with a huge arch that mirrored the design of the tiny Ottoman bridge beside us. I wandered on to Adži-paša's bridge, which offered a good view of the southern bank, where most of the original fort would have been. A rebuilt wall along the outer edge, overlooking the Morača, suggested the original footprint of the fort extended right up and into the neighbourhood we had just come through. Today, all that remained were a series of crumbling walls, scattered up the hillside, with the largest right at the top. The new stairs and walls added to the site by the town's landscapers had been done using similar stone and were virtually indistinguishable from the original ruined walls. The walls were not much to look at, but they had been built by one of the greatest Ottoman sultans ever, Mehmed the Conqueror – a man who changed the course of history because of his battle with walls.

Mehmed's greatest challenge in capturing the coveted Byzantine capital of Constantinople was overcoming its reputedly impenetrable walls, an inner and outer one. The main inner one stretched for about twenty-three kilometres around the mythical city, stood at a height of forty feet and was fifteen feet thick. Up until Mehmed successfully laid siege on Constantinople, it was widely assumed that walls and ramparts were enough to defend a city from invaders. Previously, Constantinople's walls had helped to repel two Muslim attacks by the Umayyads, and earlier sieges by the Sassanids, Slavs, the Rus' and Bulgars. But when Mehmed breached the walls of Constantinople with his huge cannons, it also signalled the end of heavy reliance on fortifications to save a city.

I looked down at the girls still playing on the dry riverbed. Anaiya was damming a section of the stream using some of the large rocks Amani was sourcing as she waded through the shallow waters. On the opposite side of the stream there were two middle-aged men in shorts and T-shirts. One had grey hair and wore glasses whilst the other was balding. They were carrying large, empty paint pots repurposed as buckets. I watched as they bent over inspecting the smooth stones one by one. If they liked the stone, they popped it into the bucket. When their buckets were full, the men climbed up the side we had come down, disappearing into the collection of houses, before returning to fill their buckets again. I had read that one of the reasons the old fort's ruins were so small now was because locals had stripped away some of the raw materials and used them for building their own homes, and wondered if that's why the men were sourcing the stones, for building material, but then I noticed they were actually selecting each one for how smooth and aesthetically pleasing it was. They were not building anything at all; someone's garden was getting a makeover!

We left the bridge by the northern bank and heading up towards the busy St Peter of Cetinje Boulevard. On the way up we spotted 'Tamara' written again on the side of one of the rebuilt walls. This time it was much larger, in black with a red shadow effect. The girls and I couldn't help but laugh. In all the years we had travelled together we had never come across their mother's name written anywhere as graffiti, yet today we had come across it twice. The girls were convinced she had left reminders of herself for us to find.

There was just one more monument I wanted to find, the *Sahat kula* or Clock Tower, which lay up on the high ground behind the bridge, in the same direction as the Osmanagic Mosque, where our car was parked. According to the map, it was in a small square beside a supermarket, where I could also pick up ingredients for our dinner this evening.

The brick tower looked ominous against the darkened sky. At first, I wasn't sure if we were looking at the right thing, because it had no visible clock faces, just a wooden door at the bottom, a series of small holes for viewing outwards from the stairs and an empty archway at the top.

'It reminds me of the tower from *Trapped*, Anaiya,' said Amani, squinting as she looked up at the foreboding structure.

'Oh yeah,' Anaiya agreed.

Trapped was a children's programme they both liked that had lots of medieval iconography. They were right; the tower resembled a kind of medieval prison. It was not at all pretty like the one I had seen in Skopje. Only one side of the square tower had a clock face on it. It was black with white Latin numerals; the hands and the numerals were beginning to rust. The clock tower stood alone in the sad-looking square, where the only other people were a few drunks on benches.

We walked across the road to the VOLI supermarket and picked up the ingredients for our dinner, and the girls grabbed some treats. On the way back, I received a message from Tamara telling us she had arrived home safely but felt sad in a lonely house with just the cats for company. I wrote back promising to video call her after dinner. When she asked where we were headed tomorrow, I didn't mention it to the girls. I just wrote: 'Niagara Falls!', to which Tamara responded with a puzzled emoji.

The route to Montenegro's Niagara Falls took us southeast along the busy E762 past dry agricultural land until we hit the Cemi river at a junction overlooked by large warehouse-style barns. The dusty path we entered followed the river southwest, past rural residences where old women sat under porches looking out to the fields as their husbands took an axe to firewood. The houses were much larger than in Podgorica and appeared to have been built in stages as time passed and families grew. Most were timber framed and had a small plot of land. Many backed on to the river we could hear but couldn't yet see. This was probably the flattest part of Montenegro we had driven through, though the silhouettes of the ever-present mountains could still be made out in the distance.

I had told the girls to wear their swimming costumes before we headed out and then given them the task of looking out for a sign that read 'Restoran Niagara'. What we were visiting was not a formal tourist site, but an accessible part of a shallow ravine by the River Cemi, where a combination of soft and hard rock had created a series of stunning pools, crevices and sheer drops for the aqua-blue waters. A small dam had been built to keep the water from overflowing and flooding the surrounding areas, and this had created a crystal-clear pool of shallow water where local families came to let the children paddle and swim, surrounded by waterfowl.

The directions I had said we could either follow the sign to the restaurant and use that as an access point or, just two hundred metres further along, park at a small iron bridge where steps led down to the falls. We soon spotted a rustic wooden sign for the restaurant and decided to continue on to the bridge.

'Look, Dad, that must be it!' Anaiya shouted, pointing to two rusty crossbars. I could see no bridge; clearly something had been lost in the translation I had made of the directions online.

'That's not an iron bridge!' Amani scoffed, reading my mind.

We got out and peered over the edge of the 'iron bridge' to be greeted by quite the sight: aqua-blue water sat in a large shallow pool halted by the sheer drop of the small dam. The restaurant overlooked the pool and a number of families and couples were stationed around it, either sunbathing or enjoying a dip. Beyond the drop was a narrow ravine that resembled a mini canyon. This slowly opened up to a wide riverbed, where large chunks had been cut away and huge boulders helped to create a wild waterscape. The dry season meant there were no big waterfalls, only shallow waters at the foot of the ravine, but it was nevertheless spectacular and safe enough for the girls to enjoy. Amani and Anaiya took one look and began climbing down the iron steps.

By the time I came down, all I could see were two heads of black hair bobbing around in the crystal-clear waters. I sat myself at the edge of the pool; two geese waded past, followed closely by some ducks and their chicks. On one side of the lake, a grandmother sat on a large boulder dangling her legs in the water. Beside her, in a pair of blue shorts, knee deep in the shallows, was her husband; he was playfully spraying their granddaughter with water. To avoid the spray, the little girl disappeared underwater and swam away. But the waters were too clear and every time she came up for air, granddad was waiting.

Ambitious name aside, Montenegro's Niagara Falls had been a great choice. The girls had ticked off one of their things to do and added 'swimming in a river with ducks' to the list.

PART SIX

RETURN TO BOSNIA AND HERZEGOVINA

The Effendi's Library

FOČA AND ZENICA

The road to Foča was littered with memorials to the dead. I wanted to stop and examine each one, but I couldn't. We just didn't have the time, as we were on the last long stretch of our trip, a four-hour drive from the south of Bosnia to Zenica, right in the middle of the country. We had left later than planned after a slow, lazy breakfast and were now playing catch up for our midway stopover.

The past few days had allowed us to tick off more things from our list by sneaking in a little trip to Dubrovnik from our southern base of Trebinje, near the Croatian border. We got to swim in the blue Adriatic off the coast of Dubrovnik's green and rocky outcrop, Lokrum; and the girls added 'visit a film set' to their list as we wandered through the spectacular walled city while Amani and Anaiya educated me on which sections had featured in *Game of Thrones*.

In Trebinje we ate dinner in the shade of the quaint Osman-paša Resulbegović Mosque and the girls got to wake up late every day, including this morning, which was why there was to be no stops until we came to the halfway town of Foča. This was a shame as the landscape outside was spectacular: craggy rock faces dotted with greenery rose like sheer cliffs on either side of the road, trees clinging to them like bonsais on the steppes of a Japanese rock garden. These gave way to more gentle grassy slopes as we climbed up through the peaks of the Sutjeska National Park, where we heard the bells of grazing mountain cows swaying in the gentle wind. The brilliant midday sun was painting the landscape a golden yellow. Farmers leant on rickety old fences, and we passed through villages where women in patterned headscarves sat beside tables of local honey and home-brewed *rakija*. The road climbed higher and higher up the spine of the national park towards Foča, the home of Bosnia's first-ever mosque.

'Woah! Look at those,' Anaiya exclaimed, noticing the sudden appearance of skull-and-crossbones signs.

'Are there landmines here, Dad?' Amani asked.

'Yes, I think I remember reading that many parts of the Balkans remain off limits because of the sheer amount of landmines that were planted during the war and are yet to be cleared.'

'So, you mean, if we accidentally walked into that area there, we could actually get blown up?' Anaiya's voice was one of genuine concern.

'Yeah, don't you remember the story I told you about Idar's childhood friend who died after finding a live grenade? It can happen, but don't worry, we won't go trekking into any uncharted parts.'

'Do you think they have labelled all the areas that it could happen, or do people still accidentally get blown up?' asked Amani.

'I think they have identified most of the danger zones now. You don't really hear of people dying from landmines in these areas any more, and I'm sure the government is making an effort to rid the land of the mines.'

During the Bosnian War, it is believed around two million mines were planted by all three ethnic military factions. Despite huge efforts to demine the country, there are still around eighty thousand live mines scattered across Bosnia and Herzegovina, making it one of the deadliest countries in Europe to go wandering off-track, with nearly 2,500 people injured or killed by them since the war. The problem was so worrying that, just before our trip, a local NGO warned players of Pokémon Go, like little Hamza and Amre in Novi Pazar, to avoid areas littered with unexploded mines.

The reason Anaiya had spotted so many signs on the road to Foča is because the town was heavily targeted by Bosnian-Serb soldiers during the war. Like Višegrad, Foča became the site of genocide, with nearly three thousand of the town's Muslims killed and, also like Višegrad, many of the women and girls were held in rape camps.

Locals claim one of the reasons was because the area of Foča is seen as the 'home' of Bosnian Islam, as it is believed Muslims lived here even before the Ottoman occupation. The mosque of Turhan Emin-Beg, ten kilometres to the north in the town of Ustikolina, is widely thought to be the country's first mosque. It is named after one of the generals of Sultan Murad II, and said to have been first built around 1448. The current building was finished a decade ago after the original was completely destroyed in the war, along with every one of Foča's fourteen mosques. The effort to systematically remove Islam and Muslims from Foča was so successful that towards the end of the war local Bosnian-Serbs changed the town's name to Srbinje: 'Serb's Town'. It has since been changed back.

Today, at least three of Foča's destroyed mosques have been rebuilt by the town's returning Muslims – less than a quarter of the original community. This includes the Careva Džamija, which sits in the same neighbourhood as the ruins of what was once one of Bosnia's most famous Islamic schools, the Mehmed Pasha Madrasa. Close to this is the Mehmed Pasha clock tower. Both are believed to have been named after the Bosnian-Serb grand vizier, Sokollu Mehmed Pasha.

After grabbing lunch at a delightful riverside restaurant overlooking the Drina tributary, the Ćehotina, we went for a drive looking for the Careva, which sat high above the town centre in one of its oldest districts, overlooking a small market square. The road up to the mosque was a winding cobbled street lined with traditional shops that had tall, old-fashioned wooden shutters and small benches outside where locals sat chatting in the sun. The whole area looked very Ottoman and was in stark contrast to central Foča with its tall, modern buildings.

We arrived to find the mosque closed, but that didn't matter too much. I just wanted to see it being built. Almost finished, the Careva's wooden features were so fresh they hadn't even been weatherproofed yet. The new wood pillars of the portico were probably the most powerful symbol of its resurrection. These stood on the old Corinthian-style stone bases, and had been chiselled and carved to be the same width and height as the originals. The contrast of the surviving stone morphing into the new light wood was a poignant metaphor of the mosque's rebirth.

The Careva was perched on the edge of a hill that offered nice views over Foča and the lush green hills of the national park. The girls and I stood on the edge for a while admiring the views, before jumping back into the car to continue our journey to Zenica.

We awoke to a miserable, wet Thursday in Zenica. It seems that, during Balkan summers, central Bosnia is the only place it constantly rains.

'My friend from London loves Bosnia in the summer for that reason. He says the weather is just like London,' grinned Mevludin Sahinovic.

He was right about the weather: the sky was grey, there was a chill we hadn't felt since being in Sarajevo, and I could even see London's famous fog as we walked through the misty town centre.

Mevludin had lived through the Bosnian War, where his brother died fighting for the 'resistance' Army of the Republic of Bosnia and

Herzegovina (ARBiH). He now lived in London and we met when he gave a talk at an event to commemorate the Srebrenica genocide, where I was exhibiting some of my photography exploring the Muslim heritage of Europe. Mevludin spent his summers here at home in Zenica, and when I told him about our plans to travel around the Balkans, he insisted I come and see him in his home town.

Knowing the purpose of my trip, he had arranged a visit to a beautiful local Ottoman Islamic school dating from 1720, called the Sultan Ahmed Madrasa. We entered through a set of dark wooden doors into a small, square courtyard, in the centre of which stood an ornate fountain with bronze taps.

'Come with me, I want you to meet someone,' Mevludin said, leading all three of us towards one of the larger rooms overlooking the courtyard. Entering through an open doorway, we were suddenly transported several centuries back in time. Row upon row of ornate wooden bookshelves lay before us, overflowing with books written in a host of languages, from Bosnian through to Persian. Many sat in messy piles, sometimes on the stools and stepladders used for reaching the higher ones. They were waiting to be organised and squeezed in somewhere. Larger books poked out as they lay flat due to a lack of space. Some shelves had 'Allah' and 'Muhammad' written in gold on large black plaques at the ends, others had black-and-white photos of previous teachers at the school. The air was filled with the stench of stale tobacco and old books. It was as if I had walked into a huge secondhand bookshop from another century. Mevludin's frame filled the aisle as he wandered through it. He was a typically large Bosnian but, untypically, he had a large beard and a shaved head. When he got to the end of the aisle and stepped aside, a huge, old-fashioned librarian's desk emerged, behind which, cigarette in hand, sat an elderly man wearing a black skullcap, a short-sleeved, stripy shirt and a grey Eastern waistcoat.

'*Salamaleikum*, Effendi,' Mevludin said, greeting the man, who had a short, neatly trimmed white beard. The man returned his greetings and then they began conversing briefly in Bosnian. Mevludin then turned to me, Amani and Anaiya.

'This is Ibrahim Babic Effendi, the librarian at the Sultan Ahmed Madrasa,' he said.

I *salaamed* the man, and so did the girls, before I asked why he was called Effendi. A throwback to the Ottoman days, it was apparently an honorific Turkic title given to Ibrahim because he was one of the lead imams at Zenica's main mosque. During the Ottoman era, Effendi was often used to refer to 'educated gentleman' and was the second most-widely used title after *Agha*.

'This is the oldest book in the library,' translated Mevludin as the Effendi held open an ancient book with yellowing pages and Arabic writing covering every inch. The most legible Arabic was the main words of the book in the centre of each page; emanating from this, in what would have been the margins, were several other paragraphs written in smaller script.

'These are commentary notes,' explained Mevludin, who was fluent in Arabic himself, having studied Islam for many years.

The script was in the widely used *naskh* style of calligraphy, and was apparently a book of religious jurisprudence.

'It's a book of *fiqh*. That's why there is so much commentary added to the main text.' Mevludin began examining the text, reading segments of it.

'It is a combination of Hanafi and Shafi'i *fiqh*,' he concluded.

These were amongst the two most popular schools of traditional Islamic theology, the Hanafi being the most popular in Ottoman territories and the one my parents brought me up with. It was developed by the 8th-century Islamic theologian Imam Abu Hanifa.

'How old is it?' I asked.

Mevludin turned to Ibrahim Effendi and the two of them had a brief but animated exchange that made Mevludin's eyes widen behind his thick-rimmed spectacles.

'Apparently, it is more than six hundred years old according to some recent experts from Turkey who came and visited the library.'

'Wow! That's older than the *madrasa*. In fact, that's older than Sarajevo and the Ottomans.'

Mevludin nodded. I could see he was also genuinely astonished.

The Effendi put the book away, before disappearing to grab another.

'This one is my favourite,' he said, opening a slightly smaller book with pages that were cleaner than the previous one.

'This is a *Seerah* of the Prophet Muhammad *sallallahu alayhi wa sallam*. It is more than three hundred years old,' he said, smiling to reveal his nicotine-stained teeth.

A *Seerah* was a biography of the Prophet. The style of the calligraphy in this book was a more modern *naskh* font, and it didn't have a commentary around the main text, which sat two inches in from the edges of the page, all neat and justified. The scribe of this book was not as skilled as the one who had written the *fiqh* book, as the script was not as artistic. There were markings in red highlighting certain words and, as the Effendi flicked through the pages, we noticed one or two had small annotations on them.

'I am working on a book that I hope will warn young people,' he said sitting back down at his desk, which was piled high with papers.

I had asked him about Islam in Bosnia and if he had concerns about young Muslims beginning to lean towards more radical interpretations. He lit a white cigarette and inhaled deeply. His old eyes went from the window into the courtyard where I could see Anaiya posing in front of the fountain. I noted the deep wrinkles under his eyes and around his mouth. He stroked his small, neatly trimmed white beard, as Mevludin and I waited for him to continue.

'People think Wahhabism arrived here during the war with the mujahideen that came to fight for us. But it was here long before that, when the humanitarian efforts from the east first arrived.'

He flicked his cigarette into a small wooden ashtray, overflowing with used butts.

'They have taken out the name of Muhammad and the oneness of God from the faith!' he said, raising his voice and waving his hand angrily. This sent bits of ash all over his desk, which he then carefully swept up.

'The worst thing is that Saudi theology fails to accommodate or appropriate the Muslim's heart for *taqwa* [piety].'

The Effendi stopped abruptly. Mevludin, who was being brilliantly tactful with his whispered translations, fell silent too. We both waited, but he now seemed reluctant to continue, so I tried to cajole him.

'So why do young people find this attractive?' I asked. The question snapped him back into life.

'It offers them a purpose. They are young and this harsh way is attractive to them. This is the fault of the ideologists. Did you know that someone tried to renounce this by writing refutations about the creed and he was not allowed to publish in Saudi so he had to publish his book in Egypt?'

Mevludin and I both shook our heads.

'We need to go back; we need to go back to Abu Hanifa, and also the great *ulema* of the past. Young Bosnians need only look at their own heritage to figures like Hasan Kafi Pruščak, who made it clear that "actions" and *iman* [faith] are not the same thing. "Deeds" are the fruits of *iman*.'

I had no idea who Pruščak was and couldn't ask the Effendi either. He was in full flow and becoming more and more animated, jumping from one chain of thought to another.

In the end, the call to prayer from the school's mosque brought the conversation to a halt. The Effendi explained he needed to lock up to go and perform his *salah*.

As we headed for the door, I asked him what he made of the rise in Gulf tourism to Bosnia. Was he happy about this?

'No, I'm not happy about this at all. It is just money chasing,' he said, locking the library door behind him. I wanted him to elaborate but it was too late, he was already shaking our hands, and so we thanked him for his time as he hurried off in the direction of the old mosque.

Coffee with Bosnian Kings

VRANDUK AND TRAVNIK

Vranduk had been one of the many seats of the medieval Bosnian kings and therefore an important place for Bosnian identity. This is because Vranduk links Bosnians back to the pre-Ottoman Kingdom of Bosnia, proving there was a historic 'Bosnian' identity before the Muslim occupation of the country.

This, explained Mevludin as we drove towards the fort in a familiar drizzle, was something that became very important to counter the Serb war propaganda.

'One of the things they claimed was that Muslims in Bosnia were just Islamised Serbs, and we just needed to "remember" our true identities again,' he said, as I noted that our route closely followed the River Bosna.

As befitting a medieval monarch's seat, Vranduk sits high up on a sheer rock overlooking the green waters of the Bosna. Flanked on all sides by the thick, forested green hills that rise up around the river's canyon, the fort is surrounded by a handful of surprisingly modern two-storey houses with terracotta-tiled roofs, resembling Swiss alpine lodges.

Not much is actually known about Vranduk, but it is believed to have been used by several of the medieval Bosnian kings as a place to receive guests and sign important documents. These kings ruled over the brief medieval Kingdom of Bosnia that existed for about a hundred years between the 14th and 15th centuries, having evolved out of a Hungarian state dating back to the 12th century. Vranduk was almost certainly used by the last Bosnian king, Stephen Tomašević or Stephen II, who was captured and beheaded by the Ottomans.

The steep, cobblestoned pathway to the entrance leads up and past the small Džamija Sultan Mehmeda II El Fatiha. A sign outside said the Ottoman guardians, TIKA, had also refurbished this mosque recently. Resembling a small white house, the mosque had a light wooden minaret, the first I had seen in Bosnia. The minaret had the green flag of the Balkan Muslims flying from it, and outside the mosque sat three middle-aged women in hijabs.

'They are local women,' Mevludin explained as we *salaamed* them. 'They look after the mosque.'

Another woman with a bright pink hijab had a stall selling traditional knitwear. We headed up towards the small citadel, passing a stone trough above which, inscribed on two tablets, were the names of local martyrs from the Bosnian War. A group of blackbirds suddenly took flight from the surrounding woodland and, up above, the sky remained overcast, giving the fort a truly medieval look. Mercifully, the drizzle had now stopped.

We entered the main turret to find medieval displays across two floors. On the ground floor was a dinner table set out, complete with glass goblets, plastic food and a bright red tablecloth. This was overlooked by two glass cabinets displaying the regal velvet cloaks Bosnian royals wore. The male piece was in the royal colour of purple and had six gold fleurs-de-lis. Although commonly associated with French royalty, Mevludin explained that six of these stylised lilies were in fact on the coat of arms of the medieval Kingdom of Bosnia. He also explained that they were used briefly after the Bosnian War on the actual flag of Bosnia and Herzegovina. The upper floor was empty except for a quaint wood writing desk with an inkpot and a feather quill on it.

Leaving the small museum, we walked along the edges of the fort's wall, which looked up towards the surrounding green hills where mist could be seen rising up near the summits like smoke from a fire. The Bosnian kings had certainly picked a dramatic setting. At one end of the wall was a small iron cannon loaded on a wood frame, but otherwise there was not much else to see. Anaiya pointed out we were the only ones in the fort, as we headed down to the grassy inner court. In the middle was an archer's target, and Mevludin spotted a wooden bow and its accompanying blunt arrow. I assumed these were for display purposes, but Mevludin insisted we should have a go. This excited Anaiya more than anything else we had seen today and, after being told the dos and don'ts, Mevludin and I left the girls to carry out some target practice and headed for the fort's small café.

'I think it is time for you to learn how to drink Bosnian coffee, Bosnian style!' Mevludin said, as a small platter arrived with two medieval-looking bronze ladles, containing thick Turkish coffee masquerading as Bosnian, and two small, ceramic, thimble-shaped cups to drink it from. In the middle was a bowl of sugar lumps.

'How to drink coffee?' I asked, looking puzzled, but Mevludin had already begun his demonstration by popping a large lump of white sugar in between his teeth. Realising he could no longer talk, he popped it back out.

'So, you begin by putting the sugar, not in your coffee, but between your teeth like this,' he said, before showing me again and then removing it once more.

'Then, you have to suck the coffee through the lump of sugar, like this.' He popped the sugar back between his teeth and this time brought up the small thimble of coffee to his mouth. He then began sucking the brown liquid through the sugar, making a low, slurping noise. I watched, intrigued by this bizarre method. Somehow, Mevludin managed to finish half of the cup using the one lump, before it fell away in his mouth.

'The sugar has to be this old-fashioned hard, lumpy stuff,' he said, holding a piece up.

'I see, and why is that?' I asked, looking closely at the lumps, which resembled little chunks of crystal.

'Because they haven't been processed in the same way as modern sugar lumps, they don't disintegrate as quickly,' he explained. 'OK, now your turn.'

I rummaged through the sugar bowl for a nice big lump.

'Yes, that's a good one,' Mevludin said, approving of the huge white chunk I had picked up. I popped it in between my teeth and, bringing the thick brown coffee to my lips, began sucking. The warm coffee tasted extremely sweet as it passed through the sugar lump, slowly washing tiny granules through with it. After a few seconds, I could feel the lump begin to disintegrate, until suddenly my mouth was awash with sickly, sweet, sugary coffee.

'Not bad for a first time!' Mevludin laughed, watching my anguished reaction as the lump disintegrated.

'A very novel experience,' I said, washing the remaining sugar in my mouth down with more coffee, 'but I think I prefer to put the sugar in the cup where it spreads more evenly.'

'Yes, I know what you mean. To be honest, nobody really drinks the coffee like this any more, except maybe some of our elders.

In fact, not many people even drink this type of coffee any more; all the trendy lattes and cappuccinos have taken over.'

'And you?' I asked.

'Yes, I still like to drink Bosnian coffee. I like the thick, grainy taste and the bitterness, but maybe this is because it reminds me of Bosnia.'

'I must admit, I've had this coffee in many places – mostly, former Ottoman lands – and I'm not the biggest fan, although it's nice every now and then. It's just too bitter for me,' I said, pulling out a bottle of water from my rucksack. 'But thanks for showing me the proper way to drink it. I don't think you could have picked a more appropriate place to teach me how to drink coffee the Bosnian way than sat in the castle of Bosnian kings!' I laughed and Mevludin joined in, before pointing out that it was very unlikely the Bosnian kings would've ever tasted coffee, as it arrived much later with the Ottomans. This made us both laugh even more.

The traffic from Vranduk to Travnik was awful as we hit the late-afternoon rush. What should've been an hour's journey took nearly two.

'This is probably the busiest stretch of road in all of Bosnia,' Mevludin said as we edged closer to Travnik.

We sat in a lengthy line of single-file traffic surrounded by businesses mainly owned by wealthy Croats. There were large car showrooms, supermarkets and retail outlets. None were owned by the local Muslims, explained Mevludin.

'During the war, nothing could reach Bosnian Muslims without being heavily taxed by the Croats in Croatia and the Bosnian-Croats in Bosnia. Basically, the embargo on weapons was effective only on Bosnian Muslims. Bosnian Catholics [Croats] had everything they needed through Croatia. Therefore, their businesses boomed during the war.'

I noticed some soldiers walking past wearing what appeared to be Croatian flags on their sleeves. I pointed them out to Mevludin.

'The flags are on there because many municipalities in Bosnia have kept the Croatian white-and-red chequers as part of their municipal emblem,' he explained.

The car crawled forward a few more inches. We hadn't had lunch yet, so I asked Mevludin if he knew anywhere we could stop to get something to eat.

'Actually, there's a good restaurant just up here called Bajra, it does excellent *ćevap*.'

'That's fine with me,' I said before turning to Amani and Anaiya. 'Girls, what do you fancy?'

'Erm, I would like some chicken, please,' Amani replied.

'Yes, same,' Anaiya nodded.

'Do you think they will have chicken?' I asked Mevludin.

'Yeah, I'm sure they will,' he answered. Here it is, just on the left there.' Mevludin pointed to a Scandinavian-looking restaurant with a series of thick wooden posts under the small porch. The entire front of the building was glass, framed in wood. It was obvious other people had the same idea as it looked busy.

'So, you and me are OK with *ćevap*, right?' said Mevludin. I nodded; I couldn't wait to eat the Bosnian version of *kofte*. These were succulent, slightly salted, chipolata-shaped mincemeat kebabs, served with freshly baked *somun* – Bosnian bread – and chopped onions. Simple and delicious. I had eaten a version of them in Bosniak Serbia, but this would be my first time eating *ćevap* in Bosnia.

'And chicken for the girls?'

'Yes, please,' said Amani and Anaiya.

It was mainly families sat in the restaurant's rattan chairs and tables, and almost everyone had ordered the house speciality of *ćevap*.

'I'm afraid they don't have chicken, what I thought was chicken in the display is actually veal, we can go somewhere else if you want?' Mevludin had returned looking disappointed.

'What do you want to do, girls, do you want to try *ćevap* or go somewhere else?' I asked.

Amani and Anaiya looked at each other. I knew they were hungry.

'We'll try the *ćevap*,' Anaiya decided.

'Are you sure? We really don't mind driving on to somewhere else.'

'No, it's fine, we'll have what you guys are having,' Amani said.

'*Ćevap* all round it is!'

What arrived was the largest portion of *ćevap* I had ever seen. A mountain of small, grilled sausage-shaped pieces of mincemeat sat on a large silver tray, dressed with finely diced, raw white onion at each end. As the girls and I exchanged glances – I think they were having flashbacks of the amount of meat Idar had ordered – the waiter arrived with some silver dishes containing thick, freshly baked *somun*, each split into two, with steam rising from their spongy, soft centres.

'Mmm, you're gonna love this bread, girls,' I said, passing a piece to each of them.

'This is a lot of meat, Dad,' Anaiya said.

'Don't worry,' I laughed. 'As you can see, Mevludin is Bosnian and they tend to be very big, so I am sure he is capable of eating most of it!'

'Yes, don't worry,' Mevludin reassured us. 'Eating this much *ćevap* is no problem for me! Just eat what you can.'

A father of two girls himself, Mevludin spoke to Amani and Anaiya with the warmth of a dad.

The girls ate about four pieces each and lots of bread, which just kept coming, whilst Mevludin and I comfortably polished off the rest of the *ćevap*. The meat was much more succulent than that which I had tried in Serbia, and more importantly, it wasn't too salty. The reason the quality of meat was so good, explained Mevludin, was because the restaurant was part of an excellent butcher's.

Travnik is a pretty little town nestled in the Lašva Valley, overlooked by Vlašić mountain, one of the country's tallest peaks and a popular spot for skiing. Although there is evidence of Bronze Age and Roman settlements in the area, the town was part of the medieval Kingdom of Bosnia until the Ottomans came along. After this, much of the population converted to Islam and Travnik became an important settlement, home to several consulates and the residence of a number of important Bosnian viziers. Travnik was even briefly the capital of the Eyalet of Bosnia, which is why it has quite a few stunning Ottoman monuments. It was also where Ivo Andrić was born.

Mevludin had been desperate to squeeze Travnik into the day as it was where he had spent four years at a boarding-school *madrasa*, from the age of fourteen to eighteen, and he had fond memories of the place.

'When we were kids, we used to love climbing that minaret and sitting right on the edge up there,' he said, pointing to a locked-up minaret inside the grounds of Travnik Fort.

'What, on the top where there are no barriers or anything?' Amani asked, her eyes growing wide with disbelief.

'Cool,' chipped in Anaiya.

'Yeah, we used to love just sitting there with our legs dangling off the edge. We'd usually do this after sneaking out of the *madrasa*.

We knew all the streets like the back of our hands and could return in time without anyone noticing,' he laughed, appreciating the irony, now that he was a schoolteacher himself.

We could see Mevludin's old school from where we stood inside one of the Ottoman-built watchtowers. Elči Ibrahim-pašina Medresa was a large, impressive complex built in a pseudo-Moorish style. The highway beside the *madrasa* disappeared into the forested green slopes of the mountains as they cascaded down the valley and off into the distance. Backing on to it, on the gentle slopes of Vlašić mountain, were a number of the ubiquitous white graves seen all over the Bosnian landscape.

Mevludin's large frame meant he had to lower his head to walk through the tower's archway, and now stood, rucksack slung over one shoulder, staring out at the familiar vista of his youth, framed by the medieval arch.

'My friends and I would scamper up the side of those grassy hills down there,' he smiled, pointing to the pine-covered slopes far below us. It was easy to see why they came here. The views over Travnik were stunning.

As Amani and Anaiya ran around exploring the different watchtowers, making their way along narrow ramparts where Ottoman soldiers once stood guard, Mevludin and I watched the mist gently rolling off the mountains as the skies began to darken, a reminder that evening would soon be upon us. We counted the town's minarets together: five in total, though Mevludin said there were more we couldn't see.

'The reason we can see so many is because Travnik was defended well during the war, so the mosques here were not destroyed like elsewhere,' Mevludin said, looking at his watch as we made our way down the grassy steps of the fort. 'I think we can still make it to the castle's small museum.'

I called out to the girls, who were standing near one of the outer walls. Amani had her Polaroid ready and Anaiya was acting as creative advisor for the Travnik shot. I could hear them discussing the importance of ensuring a minaret was part of the composition, and waited for the photo to be taken before I shouted over to them to follow us.

As we headed towards the roundhouse in the centre of the fort's grounds, I asked Mevludin how he had ended up in London.

'I first went to the UK because I got a scholarship to study in Wales. That's where I met my wife. She had converted as a child after her mother embraced Islam through her aunt who became a Muslim whilst working out in Nigeria. *She* was the reason I decided to stay in the UK.' Mevludin laughed as he said this. 'We both lived in Luton after we were married and now we live in London with our two daughters and teach at Islamic schools.'

Like the museum in Vranduk, the Travnik Fort museum was also set across two floors. The upper floor was mainly displays on the walls detailing the various finds in and around the fort, some of which were displayed in a small cabinet, but the most interesting floor was the lower one. Here a huge wooden loom took centre stage. Some of the woven clothes were displayed in cabinets on the walls. Positioned around the edges were other small domestic pieces of furniture and a display dedicated entirely to the local passion for drinking coffee.

'Look.' Mevludin grabbed one of the items: a small metal barrel with a long, thin handle. I noticed Amani and Anaiya exchange glances; we were not used to museums where you could touch the displays.

'This is what we use to roast the coffee beans in,' he said, turning it around to reveal a small window with a sliding door on it. Pushing it open, he explained it was where the beans went in. Then he began to rotate the entire can-like object using the long handle. The three of us watched, like students on a field trip.

'It is slowly turned over a fire in the home so the beans begin to cook,' he said, before showing us the contraption used to grind the beans, and another to make the coffee in. The entire experience sounded wonderfully fulfilling, but also very time-consuming.

'Wow,' Amani said, 'all that work for a cup of coffee!'

Mevludin and I laughed.

'Coffee is a very serious matter in Bosnia,' he said.

The fog and mist that had been swirling around on the mountain slopes were making their way into the town as the four of us walked across the stone link bridge leading out of Travnik Fort. Mevludin pointed out a few more places he used to visit with his school friends, including one of his favourite mosques, the Ornamented Mosque, where we were now headed. At the bottom of the bridge, we were greeted by the words 'Never Forget Srebrenica' painted on to a low wall in a beautiful font, a reference to the town in the west of the country where the worst genocide of the war took place and more than eight thousand Muslims were massacred by the Bosnian-Serb army.

'The place hasn't changed much at all,' Mevludin told us.

Our walk took us past beautiful historic houses dating from the Austro-Hungarian period. Travnik was built on hills and the pathways sometimes led up, then down. Passing a small pink bakery on the corner of two streets, we turned to be greeted by a square mosque surrounded by a tiny canal. In front was a small stone fountain under a wooden shelter. I looked up at the mosque; an array of faintly painted plants decorated the gaps between the latticed windows along the top. Once-colourful borders decorated with stunning floral patterns ran around its midriff. It was easy to see why it was called the Ornamented Mosque, but it was in desperate need of renovation.

Mevludin and I walked up the steps leading to the large, patterned oak doors at the entrance; the left one had a crack that went from the top all the way down to the bottom. Inside, the wood ceiling had a series of geometric patterns coloured green, blue and yellow. A large, circular gold chandelier hung from its centre. The wooden *mimbar* was also painted green, as too was the *mihrab*; both were surrounded by intricate floral patterns that matched those on the Persian-style rugs covering the mosque floor. A late-middle-aged man stood praying before the minaret. He wore a sleeveless jacket that said 'Bosnia' on the back, and a white skullcap. The mosque's green *mahvil* went around three sides of the hall.

Once the *Maghrib salah* was over, Mevludin took me to meet the imam.

'This was one of my first teachers at the *madrasa*,' he said, introducing me to the man who had led us in prayer. I reached out my hand, which the imam took in both of his. He then smiled and asked in Arabic how I was. I replied, before apologising about my poor Arabic. I then stepped to one side and watched as Mevludin exchanged pleasantries with him, someone he was clearly fond of. The imam was a short, stout man dressed in the Turkic robe and turban I had seen imams all over the Balkans wear. As they spoke, I could see the mutual love and respect they had for each other and it was genuinely warming.

'He has been leading the five prayers in this mosque for almost twenty years now,' Mevludin said as we made our way out. 'We used to pray here a lot when I was a student in Travnik. He was a really nice man and I miss him a lot.'

Dumped for De Niro

SARAJEVO

Our second apartment in Sarajevo sat high up on a steep hill in the residential district of Višnjik, overlooking the Old Town. Most of the houses here date from after World War II, when the area was developed for residents. Prior to that, Višnjik – which means 'cherry orchard' – was full of cherry trees. It was a nice location, home to lots of local families and surrounded by green spaces. Višnjik was squeezed in between Sarajevo University Clinical Center to the north and the city's smart diplomatic zone to the south.

Yesterday, when we arrived by car from Zenica, the hill hadn't seemed so steep, but now as the three of us walked down towards central Sarajevo, zigzagging through neighbourhoods where bombed-out houses rubbed shoulders with apartment blocks peppered by bullet holes from the war, the incline felt painful on our calves.

Anaiya was helping all of us better understand Sarajevo by describing bits from *Zlata's Diary*, which she had almost finished.

'Basically, that friend died too because a slate from the roof fell and shattered her head,' she said, very matter of fact.

Amani and I looked at each other – it was a painful window into the Bosnian War through the eyes of a child.

'Then her uncle died when someone threw a grenade into their house.'

'That's so sad,' Amani said.

Anaiya looked at her feet as she walked. I didn't know if this was to avoid tripping on the steep hill or because *Zlata's Diary* made her feel sad.

'What a brave girl though, right?' I said.

'Yeah, she's like the Bosnian Anne Frank because of the way she wrote everything down in a diary and gave the diary a name,' explained Anaiya.

'What was her diary's name?' Amani asked.

'Mimmy.'

'Did you enjoy reading it?'

'I wouldn't say enjoy, but it did make me realise how bad things were for Bosnian people,' she said, still focusing on the ground.

Whenever we travelled, Tamara and I always tried to encourage our girls to read books or watch films and documentaries that connected them to the countries in a meaningful way. Sometimes we would recommend things for them, but Anaiya had picked *Zlata's Diary* all by herself. Maybe it was because Zlata was a similar age to her when she wrote the diaries, I'm not sure, but I do remember being very proud of her when she told us she would be reading it on our trip through the western Balkans.

At the town's famous Sebilj in the Baščaršija, we were met by Lejla from the Bosnia tourism board and a young student called Haris Kusturica. I got to know Lejla when I interviewed her for an article, so when I began planning this trip I reached out to her asking if she could help me get to know Sarajevo better. Lejla made a few suggestions, including a tour of the Old Town.

'Hi Tharik, wonderful to finally meet you.' She smiled as I shook her hand and introduced Amani and Anaiya. 'Hello girls, I have a small gift for you.' Lejla handed them both a little I-'heart'-Sarajevo key ring. They both thanked her.

'So as you know, Tharik, because of the Sarajevo Film Festival, Ms Razija was dragged away...' she began.

'I know, at first I was a bit put out thinking that's very late to cancel, and then I saw her profile picture on WhatsApp.'

'Yes, I'm really sorry, the festival organisers made the request at the last minute and we said we couldn't send Ms Razija because she was already booked, but then they told us who it was that needed taking around and, well... How could we say no?' She laughed.

'Don't worry, when I saw her photo with Robert De Niro I thought, "OK, that's a good enough reason to dump us at the last minute!"' Everyone was now laughing, except for Haris, who was smiling a little awkwardly beside Lejla.

'Again, let me apologise, but I assure you, as I explained in the email, I have a very capable replacement and someone you might even find a little more interesting, given the journey you are on.' She now turned to Haris. 'Please allow me to introduce Mr Haris Kusturica, who is a local student and is working with us for the summer.'

Haris shuffled forward and I shook his hand.

Ms Razija was one of the board's more experienced tour guides and I had been looking forward to being taken around by someone who really knew Sarajevo, which is why I had been initially very disappointed by the last-minute change of plan. However, knowing she was dumping us for Hollywood A-lister De Niro did soften the blow. Lejla had then suggested young Haris and been extremely apologetic about the last-minute change, explaining she would understand if I wanted to rearrange the tour, but I couldn't really do that. The girls and I had planned lots of other stuff either side, like bowling and heading to the city's zoo, so I agreed to go with Haris.

After committing, I began thinking about the positives: Haris was only working for the board over the summer and less likely to trot out all the rehearsed tourism-board lines. Plus he was a local, born after the Bosnian War, and this meant we would get the perspective of a Sarajevan who had *not* experienced the horrors of the war. Haris, I realised, might turn out to be just as interesting as the city.

'Mr Haris is very knowledgeable about our city, so I think he will be a great guide for you,' Lejla said, still trying to sell the young student to me.

'Yes, I'm sure he will,' I said, smiling at Haris.

'OK then, I am now going to have to leave you guys, as I must get back to the office, there are so many things I still have to do for the festival…'

Lejla waved to us all as she headed off.

We had arrived at the start of the most important arts event in Sarajevo's calendar, the annual Sarajevo Film Festival – the largest in the Balkans. This was a really big deal for the city and I knew the tourism board would be busy, so despite being bumped for ol' Bob De Niro, I was still very grateful for Lejla's support.

'So, Haris, what do you study?' I asked as he finished explaining the history behind the Sebilj to us.

'I'm studying fine art and sculpture,' he replied.

In truth, I might have guessed this. Long haired and fresh faced, Haris wore Converse trainers beneath a pair of stonewashed black jeans and a checked flannel shirt, looking every bit the art student. I asked him what made him do *this* job over the summer.

'I wanted to do a job that meant learning more about my own culture and the city I love'.

I was impressed. Haris had not only got a summer job but one that involved taking pride in his own heritage. He was my kind of young person, and he had also clearly been doing his homework

'Did you know, in 1989 we gave a Sebilj to Belgrade and one to Louisiana in America?' he asked.

I shook my head. 'I knew two had been given as gifts to Novi Pazar and Sjenica, but I had no idea they had also been sent to the Serbian capital, and certainly didn't know about the one in the US!'

Haris smiled. His confidence was growing.

As we headed into the heart of the Old Town, through the narrow alleys of the Old Bazaar, I asked Haris more about his own life.

'I was born in the Old Town and have been learning English since I was a child through things like Cartoon Network on the TV, pop music and films. The films are subtitled here so it is easier to learn what the English words are. As well as the Balkan languages, I can speak two others.'

'Wow, so let me get this right, you are nineteen years old, multilingual and working your way through the summer.'

Haris nodded.

'If you are the future of Bosnia, I think this country is going to be just fine!'

Haris laughed, a little embarrassed. The girls were off looking for gifts in the Old Town shops. I told Haris not to worry too much about the history of the market as I had already visited it the first time around.

'When I finish my studies, I want to go to Germany, where there is a strong Bosnian community. Lots of people my age want to go there. There is no work here and what there is pays badly.'

Haris wasn't the future of Bosnia after all. His aspirations lay abroad. It was a classic problem across the Balkans: the brain drain. As soon as the smartest and brightest young people are educated enough to leave, they do just that. Haris explained why.

'The price of houses and the cost of rent just keep going up, but salaries don't. It's not a very positive future to stay here in Bosnia for young people.'

We left the market district and headed towards the banks of the Miljacka and the city's town hall, or Vijećnica. The striking red-ochre and yellow building was originally designed by the Austro-Hungarians in the same neo-Moorish style as Mevludin's *madrasa*. It opened to much fanfare in the late 19th century as the European superpower's largest building in Bosnia and Herzegovina, explained Haris. Inspired by the art and architecture of Muslim Spain and Morocco, the loud horizontal stripes and rows of horseshoe arches were taken from the design of the Muslim Umayyad dynasty's most famous mosques in Damascus, Syria and Córdoba, Spain.

The city hall was pretty and eye-catching, but stylistically it felt out of place. The architectural heritage of Vijećnica was not Balkan, which was all the more bizarre given Sarajevo had an ancient and distinct Islamic style.

Haris felt this was because it had been built by a non-Muslim coloniser who didn't understand or respect the local heritage. I wasn't so sure.

Whilst the Austro-Hungarians might have got the style of local Islamic architecture wrong, they certainly were not against Islam being practised in Bosnia and Herzegovina after inheriting the territory from the Ottomans. In fact, whilst leaders in neighbouring regions tried to homogenise their population through powerful nationalist ideologies, the Habsburgs granted Muslims in Bosnia more religious freedom and allowed them to continue nurturing their relationship with the Ottoman caliphs, as heads of the global Muslim *ummah*.

This was not to say the Germanic world was any less Islamophobic than the rest of western Europe though. German intellectuals were often very demeaning about the Ottomans and their Balkan 'offspring', as a series of letters by Karl and Eleanor Marx proves. In these, they describe the Balkans as a place the Turks had failed to civilise because of the 'fanaticism of Islam' and blamed the Eastern Question on the presence of the Ottoman 'alien substance' in Europe's 'living flesh'.

The Vijećnica was also where the Archduke Franz Ferdinand, whose assassination sparked World War I, enjoyed his last reception. In fact, the spot where Gavrilo Princip gunned him down shortly after was only a few hundred metres down the road, marked by a plaque.

The building became the National and University Library of Bosnia and Herzegovina after World War II, explained Haris, housing rare books and manuscripts important to the cultural heritage of Bosnia. This was why the Vijećnica was one of the main targets of the Bosnia-Serb army during the Siege of Sarajevo. Its constant bombing reduced the beautiful monument to a pile of rubble, upon which the 'Cellist of Sarajevo' – Vedran Smailović – was famously photographed playing his cello.

'I wasn't even born, but I know the picture so well. Everyone does,' Haris said, when I asked him about Smailović. 'You will see it being used in the work of some of the artists when we visit the gallery in my university later.'

The university was not part of the official tour, but this was already becoming a tour of Haris's Sarajevo, and the girls and I were keen to see some local art, which is why he had suggested visiting his faculty building.

Haris had not lived the experience of the Bosnian War and yet, like every Bosnian I had spoken to, he was very familiar with it. This was not really a surprise. When Haris walks the streets of Sarajevo, he can still point to holes on the walls of buildings made by bullets from the war. When he looks out towards the surrounding hills, he sees the slim white tombstones of the martyrs looking down on him; a constant reminder of those that died, so he could live. And on the second day of Eid-al-Fitr every year, Haris joins the rest of Bosnia in praying for the fallen. It doesn't matter that he was not born when it happened; the genocide of his people is also a part of who he is.

We sat on the river wall opposite the Vijećnica. The sun had broken through the earlier clouds and the red and yellow walls of the building gleamed in its light. We had been walking for quite some time now and I could see the girls were tiring.

'Maybe we can stop somewhere for some coffee?' I said. Haris looked around before breaking into a smile.

'I know the perfect spot and it has a great story too.'

We didn't have to go far. The Inat kuća is a pretty whitewashed Ottoman house with a beautiful green wooden turret, sitting across the Miljacka river from the Vijećnica.

'There is a very funny story why this is called Inat kuća… which means "spice house",' Haris began as we walked across the bridge. 'It used to sit on the spot where the city hall is and was owned by a very stubborn man called Benderija who was asked by the Austro-Hungarians to sell the land, but he refused. However, the new rulers really wanted to put their city hall there, next to the historic centre and kept asking Benderija. Eventually he agreed, but only for a huge amount of gold, and on the condition that his house was taken brick by brick and rebuilt on the other side of the river!' He laughed as he told the story.

It was amusing and I liked the thought of a local Bosnian sticking it to the imperial powers.

'Legend has it the old man sat on this very bridge every day and watched the house being built brick by brick. And that is why it is called Inat kuća!'

'So, he was a spice dealer?' I asked, wondering if I'd missed something.

'Spice?' asked Haris, looking momentarily confused, before he realised what had happened. 'Oh no, no! Not spice, *spite*, with a "t"! Because he was a spiteful man.'

I now joined in with Haris as we both laughed at what had been lost in translation.

'Sorry, my English…' he apologised.

Haris had translated wrong; the word *Inat* actually means 'stubborn', which of course better describes Benderija's behaviour. Sadly, we were turned away from the Inat as they were due for their lunch rush and were only taking diners, so Haris suggested we hold on for a little longer and go to Rahatlook in the town centre. We had popped in there before leaving for Mostar at the start of the trip and the girls remembered how good the cakes were, so we agreed to wait.

From the Inat, we headed along the riverbank on a road named after the founder of Sarajevo and Novi Pazar, Obla Isa-Beg Ishaković. We passed the Emperor's Mosque, the site of Sarajevo's first mosque, built in the middle of the 15th century and dedicated to Sultan Mehmed II. When that one was destroyed, said Haris, another was built on the site dedicated to Suleiman the Magnificent, which is the reason the mosque is called the Emperor's Mosque.

A little further along, we passed the city's impressive Ashkenazi synagogue, built in 1902, when members of the Ashkenazi Jewish community came to the city during Austro-Hungarian rule. Haris explained that inside the main hall there was a splendid painted Moorish wood ceiling with geometric patterns similar to those seen in Spanish Islamic art.

When we finally arrived at Haris's university, the Abrahamic set of religious buildings was complete. The University of Sarajevo's Academy of Fine Arts was housed in a beautiful evangelical church dating from the end of the 19th century. The church had been built to serve the then-large evangelical community that had also arrived with the Austro-Hungarians. However, when the Habsburgs left following the outbreak of World War I, the evangelical community went with them. The building was eventually inherited by the city of Sarajevo and turned into the Arts Faculty.

Had I encountered the mosque, synagogue and church in such close proximity at the beginning of the trip, I might have made clichéd comparisons of Sarajevo with Jerusalem, and waxed lyrical about the historic tolerance and coexistence of this great city. But not any more. Wandering through the western Balkans with Evliya, I had seen that this *komšiluk* had not been exceptional in Muslim Europe. Evliya had shown me it had been the norm. The Habsburgs merely continued that legacy when they came to town.

'It wasn't until I came to study here that I realised what this building used to be. I had always assumed because of the dome it was a mosque at some point,' Haris said, as we entered through a set of modern glass doors integrated with the faculty's neoclassical features.

'Isn't that funny? I would've probably thought the same, because in England, churches have spires, not domes,' I said.

Inside the faculty, Haris found the piece of art he had told us about: Vedran Smailović sat in his tux on an invisible chair holding his cello. Beneath him, a mass of masonry and rubble. Smailović had a thick handlebar moustache and a comb-over. His right hand was outstretched holding the bow as he played, framed by the crumbling, roofless arches of the Vijećnica, his face expressionless.

The artist had placed the famous photo next to another showing the outside of the library engulfed in thick smoke. They had then emblazed the words 'festival Sarajevo, Sarajevska zima '93, Sarajevo winter '93' across them both and put a snowflake in the middle. The girls and I stared at it intently as Haris talked us through it.

'That is such a sad picture,' Anaiya said when Haris had finished talking.

'Was he actually playing the cello, or did he just pose for the photo?' Amani asked.

'Yes, he was playing at the time, that's what he did. He would play in the ruins of the places being destroyed or where people had been killed to bring attention to what was happening.'

'Wow, he was brave...' Anaiya said, her voice trailing off.

'Yes, sometimes he played in places where snipers were shooting at him. But it worked; a lot of people heard about his bravery, and his story inspired many of them to put pressure on the international community to stop the war.'

We left the university and crossed the river at the uber-cool Festina Lente bridge. The girls spent time taking photographs inside the central feature, which resembled an extravagant BMX loop the loop, as Haris explained to me that the bridge had been designed by three students from his university.

'The name means "make haste slowly" in Latin. It was designed to make people slow down and enjoy the views from the bridge.'

We both sat down on the small wooden benches inside the loop and decided to do just that as the girls finished their photography.

The view looked west along the river where battered blocks pockmarked with bullet holes sat beside brightly painted period buildings from the Austro-Hungarian era. In the distance, rising towards the clear blue sky, were the glass façades of the twin towers known as 'Momo and Uzeir' by locals. They had been named after two characters from the popular Yugoslav-era radio comedy, *Cik Cak* – one was a Serb and the other a Bosniak. Momo and Uzeir were heavily bombed during the Bosnian War, yet their shattered shells stood firm, refusing to collapse. As a result, they came to symbolise Sarajevo's resilience.

Back in 'Jerusalem'

SARAJEVO

Rahatlook is popular with locals and tourists for one major reason: it overlooks Sarajevo's famous Jewish quarter. The area is home to the country's oldest surviving synagogue, now the Museum of the Jews of Bosnia and Herzegovina. The synagogue was built a century or so before Evliya came to Sarajevo, so this would have been one of the places he counted when doing his tedious tallying up of the city's religious buildings. In those days, it was part of a large residential complex built around a central courtyard, with numerous small lodgings for the city's poorest Jews.

When Evliya was here, Sarajevo's Jews were mostly the Sephardic ones rescued from Spain. The protection of the Ottomans allowed Sephardic Jews to continue living and flourishing in Europe. Before World War II, the community of Jews in Bosnia and Herzegovina numbered around twenty-two thousand. Most of them lived in Sarajevo alongside Christians and Muslims, helping the capital earn its famous moniker of 'Europe's Jerusalem'. Sadly, those numbers were decimated by the Nazis – almost half of all Bosnian Jews were murdered in World War II. With many of the survivors resettled in other countries, today there are only around a thousand Jews left in Bosnia and Herzegovina.

The Rahatlook café was airy and welcoming. It had simple wood furnishings and curved floor-to-ceiling windows that flooded the interior with light. This was set off nicely by a collection of quirky works of art.

After seating Haris and the girls in the sunshine, looking out on to the Jewish quarter, I walked up to the counter-cum-coffee-bar where a row of light bulbs hung from the ceiling. I squeezed in between Sarajevo's hipsters as they sat sipping lattes on wooden stools, and ordered two slices of Rahatlook's finest chocolate cake for the girls, a can of Coca-Cola for Haris and a flat white for myself.

As we sat sipping our drinks beneath the warm afternoon sun, Haris told me how his family were linked to the story of the Jews of Sarajevo.

'On my mother's side, we are part of the Korkut family,' he began, opening the ring pull of his can with a loud hiss.

'I'm sorry, who are the Korkuts?' I asked.

'My grandmother's great-uncle was Besim Korkut, the author of Bosnia's most famous translation of the Qur'an.'

'Wow, really?'

'Yes, and through him I am related to Derviš Korkut. Do you know who that is?' he asked, taking a sip of Coke, as I stirred the sugar in my coffee.

Amani and Anaiya were both gleefully digging into their chocolate cakes.

'It's soooo good, Dad,' Anaiya said, making the OK sign with her left hand. I gave her a smile and a thumbs up.

'I'm sorry, no I don't,' I said, turning back to Haris.

'Derviš Korkut was Besim's brother and the man who saved the Sarajevo Haggadah from being stolen by the Nazis.'

I nearly spilt my coffee down the front of my top. So this was why Lejla thought Haris would be of interest to me. 'What? You are related to the man who saved the Sarajevo Haggadah… Seriously?'

'Yes, it is such a shame the National Museum is closed for renovation work, otherwise we could have visited it and seen the Haggadah for ourselves.'

I had been gutted to learn that the National Museum of Bosnia and Herzegovina would be closed during our time in Sarajevo, as I knew it meant missing out on the stunning 14th-century relic. Now, sitting with an actual descendant of the Muslim who saved it from the Nazis felt like more than just a wonderful consolation.

The Sarajevo Haggadah is one of the world's oldest Sephardic Haggadahs: a stunning bound manuscript illuminated with gold and silver leaf that tells the story of the Jewish exodus from Egypt. Traditionally, this is read at the feast of Passover Seder to mark the start of the festival of Passover. The Sarajevo Haggadah is believed to have been made in Barcelona around 1350 and is one of the only medieval Jewish manuscripts to contain figurative paintings. One of the scenes of a Spanish Seder is particularly fascinating as it depicts a black woman taking part in the feast. She is dressed in the clothes of a wealthy Jewess and is probably the earliest depiction of a black Jew.

The Haggadah was taken out of Spain by Jews following the issuing of the Alhambra Decree and, although never officially valued, it was reportedly insured for US$7 million ahead of a trip to Spain in 1992.

The Haggadah was bought by the National Museum at the end of the 19th century and remained safely there until Sarajevo was absorbed into the Nazi puppet state, the Independent State of Croatia, during World War II. At the time, the museum's chief librarian was Haris's late relative, Derviš Korkut, an Islamic scholar from a family of scholars and *kadis*. It turns out Korkut did more than just save the Haggadah, as Haris so modestly put it.

As far back as 1940, when Yugoslavia wanted to pass anti-Jewish laws to appease the Nazis on their doorstep, Korkut wrote a paper called *Anti-Semitism is Foreign to the Muslims of Bosnia and Herzegovina*, to remind his country about their long tradition of religious coexistence. And when the fascist founder and head of the Ustaše, Ante Pavelić, said he wanted to 'cleanse' his state of Jews, Korkut wrote another article defending Sarajevo's Jews.

So when he learned that Nazi commander General Johann Fortner had asked to meet with the museum's director, Jozo Petrović, Korkut knew he was coming for the Haggadah.

Rumours had been circulating that the Nazis were plundering Europe's synagogues and cultural institutes for perverse projects, including the apparent creation of 'Jew Towns' and a 'Museum of an Extinct Race' for Aryan tourists to visit after the Jews were exterminated.

Korkut was asked to translate at the meeting as Petrović did not speak German and it was one of the ten languages Korkut was fluent in. Ahead of the meeting, he begged the museum's director to let him take the Haggadah away so the Nazis couldn't get hold of it. After much pleading, Petrović agreed, and together they went down to the basement where the Haggadah was kept in a safe. Korkut put the small codex – measuring six by nine inches – into the waistband of his trousers and covered it with his coat. The two men then went up to meet the Nazi.

'They say he stood in that meeting and lied about the whereabouts of the Haggadah to the Nazi's face, all the time while hiding it in his trousers,' Haris said with a smile.

'What a legend!' I said. 'To simply refuse to bow to the Nazis like that.'

It is not clear exactly what happened in the meeting but, according to one report, when Fortner asked for the Haggadah, the director and Korkut told him it had already been taken by a previous Nazi officer.

Korkut then took the precious manuscript home, telling only his wife, Servet, before heading out of town that afternoon to 'visit his sister'. Korkut actually went to a village in the Treskavica mountain range, where his friend was the local imam. He showed the Haggadah to his friend and asked him to hide it somewhere safe. The imam hid it amongst the mosque's Qur'ans, where it stayed until the war was over. Once the Nazis had left Sarajevo, the imam brought the Haggadah back to Korkut, who returned it to the museum.

'What a great story, Haris; a Muslim takes the country's most important Jewish manuscript and puts it inside a village mosque, where it is kept safe next to Qur'ans. Brilliant, absolutely brilliant!' I was beside myself with excitement. 'How do you feel when you hear this story about your family and your city?'

'It makes me really proud and also very sad, because although Korkut saved the Haggadah, nobody could save the Jews.'

He was right, but Korkut did manage to save one of them, nineteen-year-old Donkica Papo, whom Korkut hid in his home, pretending she was a Muslim servant girl from Servet's village. Donkica eventually settled in Israel where she told the story of her rescue by the Korkuts; as a result, Yad Vashem – Israel's official memorial to the Holocaust victims – recognised the Muslim couple as Righteous Among the Nations (RAN).

The Korkuts are not the only Sarajevans recognised by Yad Vashem: Ahmed Sadik, Zekira Besrević and the Hardaga family have all been honoured for risking their lives to help Jews survive the Holocaust.

'We used to have such a huge Jewish community, and our city was known as "Jerusalem", but I never got to see that.'

'Do you know any Jews left in the city?'

'Actually, I do. One of my best friends is Jewish and I even attended his bar mitzvah, where I met a few more of the very small community that still lives here.'

'What was that like?'

'It was fun, but also sad, as you hear about how many are leaving for places like Israel because they are such a small community here now. Soon there will be none.'

After Korkut, the Haggadah was saved again by a Muslim. This time during the Bosnian War, when the museum was broken into and the Haggadah was found on the floor by librarian Enver Imamović, who put it inside an underground vault until the war was over.

These stories of Muslims rescuing the Jews of Sarajevo and their treasured Haggadah were heart-warming, but it was Korkut's that affected me the most. Described as a handsome man of great intellect and integrity, Korkut had the kind of principles I admired. He had resisted the Nazi fascists and fought against the encroachment of anti-Semitism. A Muslim proud of his religious and cultural heritage, he later resisted the extreme communism of Tito, speaking out against the state's anti-religious stance and again when plans were unveiled to tear down Sarajevo's historic Muslim centre and replace it with communist blocks. For his troubles he ended up serving many years in prison on fabricated charges of colluding with the Nazis. Korkut was part of a group of European Muslims that recognised anti-Semitism went against everything they stood for and were willing to risk their own lives to save the victims of this heinous prejudice. The more I learned about Korkut, the more I wished I could have met him, just to be able to honour him in person. Although Korkut has been honoured by Yad Vashem, his story is barely known outside of Bosnia. The Haggadah he saved has now been placed on UNESCO's Memory of the World register.

The girls had finished their chocolate cakes and were now playing cards. Our time with Haris would soon be up, so I decided to ask him one of the questions that had been playing on my mind since we first met – how did the memory of the Bosnian War affect him?

'Is that difficult for you? I mean, you were not alive when it happened yet so much of your identity as a Bosnian and a Sarajevan seems to be tied up with it.'

'Yes, it is difficult to move on. That is obvious. Whether economically or culturally…' Haris paused, unable to find the words. I said nothing. 'What is difficult for my generation is that we want to respect and never forget what has happened but we also want to write a new and brighter future and not feel like we have to keep looking back in anger and sadness. Sometimes it weighs very heavy around our necks and this makes it difficult to balance the past with where we want to go as young Bosnians.' I could see Haris was being careful to get his words in the right order. He didn't want to make a mistake about something so sensitive and still so raw.

We left Rahatlook and began heading back towards the Baščaršija where we had started the tour. As we walked, I threw a few more questions at Haris that had nothing to do with the tour.

'Tell me, what does your religion mean to you?'

Haris looked a little surprised by the question. 'You mean, being Muslim, Islam?'

'Yes, as an artist, do you feel it is restrictive in any way?'

315

'No... but I don't really like the strict, rigid interpretations, I think they are dangerous.' Haris was hesitant, maybe worried I would judge him.

In many conservative Islamic cultures, art is suppressed because of austere interpretations of Islam. I had always struggled with that, especially given how beautiful the historic Islamic artistic traditions are. From the Umayyads through to the Ottomans right up to the present day, Muslims have continued to develop beautiful and distinct artistic styles. I had even come across a uniquely indigenous European Muslim one in the Tulip style left behind by the Ottomans. I was therefore glad to meet someone like Haris who did not see his faith as a hindrance to his art.

'Do you worry about people in Bosnia becoming followers of *that* type of Islam?' I asked.

'Hmm... I dunno... I prefer Sufism. That's a more traditional form of Islam here in Bosnia and I like the way it promotes love of Allah and focuses on warmth and inclusiveness.'

At the Baščaršija, we said our farewells and thanked Haris for the tour. I made a point of telling him that the most interesting parts were about his life and family. I then told him that I really respected how hard he was working, adding that I hoped he didn't leave Bosnia to go to Germany. Haris looked confused, so I reminded him of what he had said earlier.

'It would be a shame,' I explained. 'Bosnia needs people like you.'

This made Haris smile.

Remembrance in Sarajevo

SARAJEVO

It was our last day in Sarajevo. We had spent the past week treating the city like a second home. With no more driving – the car had been returned as soon as we arrived – we had been getting about on the local trams and buses, eating halal McDonald's for lunch, popping into the city zoo, and even finding a place to go bowling. I had a local mosque I prayed in right near the apartment, and a local *pakeri* where I no longer had to tell them my order in the mornings: fresh croissants for the girls, meat *bureks* for me and Anaiya, and pizza bread for Amani. Despite being a large city, central Sarajevo had the feel of a small town, safe and familiar. It was going to be a shame when the time came to say goodbye to it.

Symbolically, I had saved my return to the Gazi Husrev-beg complex for my last day too. I wanted the first Bosnian mosque I had prayed in to also be one of the last I visited on this trip. Lejla had helped to arrange a chat with the mosque's curator first thing in the morning. It was too early for the girls, who had asked to lie in ahead of our afternoon at the Sarajevo Film Festival watching a series of short films aimed at teenagers called TeenArena Shorts. So having dropped off their usual order from the *pakeri*, I was now making my way down past the 19th-century Sacred Heart Cathedral into the narrow backstreets of the Old Town.

Aldin, like Mevludin, was very tall but not as wide. I walked into his small office in the corner of the mosque courtyard to find him speaking fluently in Arabic on the phone. After he put it down, I introduced myself and shook his hand. Aldin was younger than I had expected.

'We just have to wait for my colleague to come and take over, and then we can go and have a tour,' he explained in perfect English. I wondered how many more languages he was capable of speaking.

As we waited, I asked Aldin about Robert De Niro's recent visit to the complex. He excitedly told me that he had personally given him the mosque tour, but had to admit ol' Bobby was a bit of a disappointment.

'Probably jet-lagged,' he said, before turning to two Arab tourists who had walked in and begun trying to speak English. Aldin responded in his perfect Arabic – much to their relief. The two young men had arrived in shorts and wanted to know if they could still pop inside the mosque to have a look; they knew wearing shorts was a no-no, but thought it might be OK as it was early in the day and no congregational prayers were due.

Aldin could easily have said no, as per the rules, maybe even told them they should know better, but instead he made a sympathetic face and said they could pop in quickly as long as they did not go near anyone in prayer.

Outside, the courtyard was filled with tourists from all over the world; many of them dressed equally inappropriately. For the women, Aldin had a small basket of colourful scarves to put on their heads and around their bare shoulders. There were clear rules about entering the mosque, but these were not rigidly enforced, unless someone was dressed really inappropriately, which happened more often than you might think, Aldin explained.

When the Arab tourists had left, I asked if he had taken any other A-listers around the mosque.

'In 2010, we had Morgan Freeman come along and in 2014 both Brad Pitt and Angelina Jolie were here.'

'Wow, that is quite the list,'

I went to ask Aldin more about the visits, but before I could a Portuguese man also in shorts came to enquire about entering the mosque. Aldin told him the same thing, this time in English, before greeting a short, young Bosnian man making his way across the courtyard. It was the colleague we had been waiting for.

'OK, let's go before more people come with questions!' Aldin said as we made a hasty exit out of the complex and went in search of a café.

Aldin had been a curator at the Gazi Husrev-beg complex for nearly six years after finishing his studies in Islamic theology.

'Wow, if someone in my community had studied that, they would not be working in tourism, they would probably be the imam of a mosque or in a senior position at a *madrasa*,' I said.

But Aldin was not as short-sighted as I was. After picking up his coffee and sipping it very deliberately, he began to speak with a measured tone.

'Now more than ever we need people with knowledge of Islam talking to people without knowledge of Islam,' he said, before continuing. 'This is why we believe it is important people with good knowledge of Islam work in positions where people will be brave enough to ask the questions about the faith they might not normally ask.'

I looked up at Aldin's clean-shaven, young face, as he pushed up his black-rimmed glasses and reached for his coffee again. He was younger than me, yet I felt I was talking to someone several years my senior. I realised he was absolutely right.

One of the biggest issues in the Muslim community was that people who didn't understand the faith were the ones speaking about it to the average man, and as a result, misconceptions and falsehoods were being reinforced. The average non-Muslim on the street had no way of speaking to a Muslim with knowledge because most of the time they were beyond their reach, behind the 'wall' of a mosque, *madrasa* or university. Meanwhile Aldin, a graduate of Islamic theology, sat in the tourism office of the city's most visited tourist site daily and was available to every shorts-wearing Portuguese guy and bikini-clad Brit that came to Sarajevo. The kind of people who had questions, even the bizarre ones that needed answering by someone who knew what the hell they were talking about.

'Is it true your women are oppressed?'

'Do they have to listen to what their husbands tell them?'

'How many wives can you have?'

'Why do you make women wear those things around their faces?'

'Are you ordered to kill non-Muslims?'

'What do you think about what ISIS is doing?'

'Why do you pray five times a day?'

'What is Ramadan?'

'Some questions are more stupid than others,' Aldin said. The people who asked them were the ones he smiled at the most – before answering with the same attention to detail as he gave everyone else. 'I am very careful not to mislead them or confuse them.'

Aldin explained that his methods came from his studies and training in theology. He used logical and practical contexts to explain the reasons certain things are apparent in Islam or have been associated with it. Aldin is in a unique position, in that he has the academic know-how to address these questions, like an imam or a *mufti* might; only he stands there doing this in jeans, a check shirt, and with a disarming smile.

That is why he is *so* important.

Even the guy with the most stupid question doesn't fear asking a tour guide, because that's what they assume Aldin is. Aldin explained that many of his daily interrogators are people who do not live in a community of Muslims, and often the Gazi Husrev-beg is their first exposure to real Muslim culture. Therefore, talking to someone who looks like them makes it easier for them to be open about their misconceptions.

This all sounded great, but I wondered how many more people would do a degree like his, and then take on this kind of job?

'There are no jobs in Bosnia,' he said, 'and that was the reason I originally took this job. But, you know, sometimes a job picks you. At first, I thought it would be a good job because I enjoyed talking to people and learning about different cultures.'

'So when did you realise the job had chosen you?'

'It was when I began to get questions about Islam instead of the complex. I mean, the story of the complex is in books, Wikipedia, etc, so people can easily find this out. I soon realised that what they *really* seemed interested in was understanding Islam. That's why they were visiting a mosque. The questions can also be very tough sometimes, even offensive, and the more I got them, the more I realised the reason I was doing this job.'

I was glad Aldin felt this way, but I wondered for how long. Someone like him surely needed greater intellectual stimulation.

'That is the challenge, the repetitive side of the role, like telling the story of Gazi Huzrev-beg or answering the same basic questions on Islam every day'.

Aldin took another sip of his coffee and decided it was time to tell *me* the story of Gazi Husrev-beg.

'Gazi Husrev-beg's father had been the governor of southern Rumelia and he originated from southern Bosnia. His mother was actually the sister of the great Ottoman sultan, Suleiman the Magnificent.'

'Wow,' I said, realising I had found another link to the great sultan, before asking, 'I understand he was a very pious man, is that true?'

'Yes, he followed the Helveti Sufi order and during his life he had a very pious reputation, because of how much of his own wealth he invested into the building of religious institutes. Gazi Huzrev-beg left all his wealth to the complex and wanted it to be used to build the *madrasa*, the soup kitchen that fed the poor, and buy the books to build the library, all of which remains to this day.'

The sun was now almost directly in our line of sight, getting warmer as it made its way towards the midday zenith. The street we looked out on was quite central and busy, with tourists out in numbers now. I watched as a father bent down to hold his toddler's hand. The toddler was wearing a navy sunhat with a red anchor on it, and had only just learned to walk, getting tired after every few steps. Mum stood smiling proudly from a few yards away.

I heard my phone go off. It was Amani sending me a list of the treats and snacks I was expected to bring back with me. I replied, asking if they had checked the film timings for this afternoon's TeenArena Shorts. They had: '4pm the first one starts,' wrote Amani.

I asked Aldin about the departure from religion under communism – how was Bosnia trying to recover from that as a Muslim nation?

'More than six hundred mosques were destroyed, but now we are rebuilding them as it is our heritage. Our *madrasas* are open again, and we have university degrees in Islam, in imam studies and so on,' Aldin said.

'So who oversees all of these things?'

'We have like a presidency of the Islamic Community of Bosnia and Herzegovina, and they oversee the Gazi Huzrev-beg complex now. We have a special institute connected to this that preserves our cultural heritage. We also have support from TIKA, who have helped to restore some of the monuments.'

'Yes, I have seen they are restoring Ottoman Muslim heritage all over the Balkans on this trip,' I said, adding I was glad this was happening as it was the Muslim heritage of all of Europe and not just the Balkans.

Aldin asked me to explain what I meant by this.

'As a Muslim of Europe, I feel all this ancient Muslim heritage across the Balkans is also my heritage. It is the heritage of every European Muslim and non-Muslim, and there is much we can learn from it.'

Aldin was now nodding in agreement. 'Yes, for Europe this heritage and history is crucial. It has been here for centuries.' He paused before a wry smile fell across his face. 'It makes me laugh when I hear people asking, "What does it mean to be European and Muslim?" There is no need to learn how to be a "European Muslim" or a "Western Muslim". *We* have been living as Muslims in Europe for centuries.'

It was my turn to nod.

'They should come here and look at us; this is what a European Muslim looks like. This is what Muslims living in Europe have always looked like. There is no conflict in us, we are not confused or have any problem with these two identities, we have been happily Muslim and European for nearly six centuries. Come, come and see us.'

Aldin was absolutely right. There are indigenous European Muslims all across this region entirely comfortable in their identities; I had met many of them on this journey. However, the journey had also shown that they have consistently been 'Othered' by the dominant half of Europe. The western Balkans, along with all the areas once part of Evliya's Muslim Europe, has long been alienated by western Europe. The continued insistence to define the area as 'Eastern Europe' is how this Othering and alienation is kept up. This label is often said to be the result of the recent Iron Curtain of communism, and yet the pre-communist literature on the region by Western travellers suggests otherwise. Whether it is those denying the Muslim origins of stunning bridges or writers convinced being white and Western puts them further up the evolutionary 'ladder' than being brown and Albanian-Muslim, one thing is clear: a curtain was drawn long before the iron one fell. That was the curtain to keep out the scary, barbaric 'Muhammedan', 'Saracen' and 'Turk'.

Like the iron one, it is not a real curtain, and yet it has had a powerfully divisive effect. In alienating eastern Europe, western Europe has successfully and maybe even conveniently disassociated itself from the continent's living indigenous Muslim heritage, thereby ridding itself of any suggestion Europe might have an indigenous Muslim identity. This is a falsehood pounced upon by Islamophobes across the continent today.

Aldin and I both took a long, slow final sip of our coffees before he nudged me and said it was time for us to go for a walk.

He wanted me to meet someone.

Jakov's tiny workshop-cum-store was in one of the narrow alleyways of Sarajevo's old bazaar, close to the Gazi Huzrev-beg complex.

Aldin and Jakov knew each other because, whenever a tourist came to Jakov wanting something engraved in Arabic, he often got Aldin to check the script for accuracy before beginning the work. Jakov was born under secular communism when religion and religious studies were banned and he didn't have the privilege of learning Arabic, whereas Aldin was part of the new wave of Bosnians, rediscovering their Islamic roots and Muslim identity. Aldin lives in a country that actively encourages him to study Islam and learn Arabic, but he can only do this because of the sacrifices made by people like Jakov, who remember a very different world.

'There was this friend of mine who was an imam,' Jakov said as Aldin translated, for Jakov didn't speak English either. 'He had a sister in Albania, and whenever he used to go and visit her and sit around the table talking, he would have bottles of alcohol on it. They had to have it, otherwise maybe somebody would tell the secret police. You never knew who it might be, and if they knew that her brother was an imam, well, that would be it.'

I looked around Jakov's little workshop. There was a large copper tray behind his chair, engraved with the word 'Sarajevo' and an image of the Gazi Husrev-beg Mosque. It was the biggest piece in the shop. His worktop was covered with a patterned rug. Different types of traditional coffee holders huddled around a white ceramic ashtray with two cigarette butts in it. Above the worktop was a black extendable lamp, next to which a corkboard had a number of stock geometric pattern sheets pinned to it, and beside Jakov was the large wooden clamp he had made himself to hold the pot or plate as he engraved it.

It was a messy, raw space that had the feel of a traditional metal workshop. Apart from the electric lamp, everything else could have been used by someone like Jakov in the Sarajevo of Evliya's day.

Jakov pulled out a Marlboro cigarette pack and offered one to me. I politely refused. He took off his glasses and placed them on a silver tray, rubbing the bridge of his nose. On our way over, Aldin had told me we were about to meet someone who fought in the Siege of Sarajevo, but not to get my hopes up. I hadn't directly asked Jakov anything yet, leaving him to talk. Now I wondered out loud why a retired policeman owned a metal workshop. Aldin smiled as he translated the question; he knew it would make Jakov chuckle.

Jakov did chuckle, then leaving his cigarette in his mouth, he slowly rolled up his sleeve to reveal a huge scar that went from his armpit down to the middle of his forearm.

'It was 1993, and we were near the Hotel Bristol, right on the frontline. We had no army. We were the army. The military police. And we were under heavy fire from the Serbs.'

He paused.

'The bullet ripped through me, going into a main artery. There was blood spurting out at a ridiculous rate. I became unconscious very quickly and my friends knew they had to get me to a hospital otherwise I would die, but there was no chance of an ambulance coming to get me in the middle of a war.'

Jakov flicked the ash from the cigarette in his hand, slowing the pace of his story.

'Have you seen the pictures of our streets during the war?' he asked.

I nodded.

'They nearly strangled me as they dragged me by my neck.' He wrapped his own arm around his neck to make the point. 'They dragged me into a nearby Volkswagen and then, with bullets raining down on us, they drove me through the streets to a hospital.'

He lit another cigarette and took an extra long drag as the memories began to flood back.

'We left one war zone to enter another in the hospital. It was chaos. There were no drugs, no electricity. Nothing. They operated on me for three hours using a generator and drugging me with morphine.' Again he stopped to flick the ash from his cigarette very deliberately into the ashtray, which had doubled its number of butts in the short time we had been sat with him.

'Even then, they were not sure if the arm would survive and for the next forty-eight hours they kept wondering if it would be better to amputate it. It was horrible.' Jakov told the story not talking to me or Aldin.

Now he fell completely silent.

'I don't watch the news any more and I try not to talk about what happened. None of our friends are allowed to. When we meet up, if anyone does, they are immediately expelled…' Aldin stopped translating and got up to put his arms around Jakov.

He was crying.

I had walked into the workshop of a man who looked as hard as nails. Now, after returning to the horrors of the siege in his mind's eye, he resembled a scared little boy. It made me extremely sad.

When Aldin sat back down, I quietly asked him if we should leave.

'No, it is fine; he wants you to hear this.'

Jakov lit another cigarette. As he slowly smoked it, regaining his composure, he even allowed himself a little smile. He was now ready to answer my original question.

'I do this work for two reasons,' he began. 'Firstly, I find it very therapeutic. I was thirty years old when I fought in the war, I lost a lot of colleagues and saw horrific things, and this work helps me not to think about those things. Practical work is good like that. Having something to do stops me sitting around all day thinking about what happened.'

'Has the state ever helped you to try and come to terms with what happened?' I asked.

'For six months after the war, they helped us, they provided therapy and so on… I remember being with the therapist one day and talking about the war, when I heard the therapist say, "You don't have to yell." But I wasn't yelling. At least *I* thought I wasn't.' Jakov inhaled deeply.

'Do you feel like your country appreciates what you did?'

'No!' snapped Jakov. Aldin didn't need to translate this. 'They have given out more medals to those not in the war than the fighters.' His voice began to pick up pace. 'What they give us as a pension is insulting. At the last convention, I told them this. I said: "You might as well cut it, it is an insult."'

Jakov picked up his glasses and put them back on.

'That's the other reason I do this work. It helps to pay my bills.'

The total combined pension and invalidity payments Jakov got for his injury amount to 540 Bosnian marks a month. The average rent for a small apartment in Sarajevo was 800 marks a month, explained Aldin.

'I have now been doing this for six years, after learning the trade from a neighbour. I first became interested in it when my son had a project from school to complete a large plate and I ended up finishing it for him, that's when I began to really enjoy it. Slowly I realised it also helps me psychologically, because it has a therapeutic effect on me.'

An Arab woman in a niqab was knocking on Jakov's door. She asked in broken English about a traditional coffee set in the window. Jakov told her the price and she thanked him and left. It was nearing the time for me to return to my girls, so I thanked Jakov for sharing his memories with me, and promised to pray for his well-being.

I shook his firm, leathery hand and headed back out with Aldin into the narrow streets of the Old Town.

The Siege of Sarajevo saw at least three hundred shells go off in the city every day, leaving no building untouched; hospitals and media complexes were amongst those completely destroyed, along with libraries and cultural assets. Several streets became too dangerous to walk down because of snipers taking potshots from the hills and the indiscriminate killing claimed nearly fourteen thousand lives and injured over fifty thousand people. One of the opening statements by the International Criminal Tribunal for the Former Yugoslavia in 2003 claimed the siege reduced the inhabitants of Sarajevo to 'medieval deprivation' where they were in 'constant fear of death'.

The sun had already set on our final day in Sarajevo when I headed out to pray one last time in my 'local' mosque. It had a classic chalk-white Ottoman minaret and sat a little way up the hill from our apartment. As I walked towards it, I noticed an old man shuffling in the same direction. This made me smile as it reminded me of the 'uncles' we would see shuffling towards the mosque as teenagers – in those days it was a signal for us to walk in the other direction, just in case he tried to drag us into the mosque with him.

Young girls chased each other into doorways on the cobblestoned road outside the mosque. They looked the same age as Amani and Anaiya except some had blonde hair and blue eyes. I watched as one of their mothers came out and scolded them for being too noisy, and they ran off giggling. The mother spotted me and smiled before walking back in. Overhead, the mosque tannoy started crackling, and the *muezzin* began the *adhan* for *Isha*. The girls heard this five times a day, and on Sundays it was the bells of the nearby Catholic church.

Theirs was a culture not too different from our own in Britain, except Islam didn't feel alien or foreign here.

I caught up with the uncle just as he got to the mosque's large wooden doors. Holding them open for him, I gave him my *salaams*. His eyes lit up and he replied with *walaikum as salaam*, showing me a gappy smile.

The mosque had a light-coloured wood ceiling but no dome. There were no elaborate patterns on the walls. Even the *mihrab* was simple in design: plain white, with a few lines of calligraphy along the top, and a small oriental lamp hanging inside. The old uncle walked past me and sat next to another elderly man praying on a chair at the front. They were both dressed almost identically: loose trousers, a short-sleeved shirt and a waistcoat with lots of pockets, like the ones fishing enthusiasts wear.

The congregation was still small. Besides the two uncles, there was just a young, scruffy-looking fellow sat leaning against a wall. He wore jeans and a blue puffa jacket, and reminded me of the kind of guys you see setting up the stalls at London's markets in the early hours, hardy and a little rough around the edges.

After a while, one of the uncles pointed to the *mimbar* where the imam's outfit was kept and I wondered if he was gesturing to his friend to lead the prayer. But when the other uncle got up, he reached behind the *mimbar*, not for the imam's cloak, but to flick a switch, before walking over to a microphone. The room was filling up now, with around fifteen men and boys, and just a lone middle-aged woman in a coloured headscarf at the back under the mosque's *mahvil*. Most of the men were young. I recognised a few and one of them recognised me; we silently nodded a greeting to each other. The uncle began reciting *surah al-Ikhlas* three times before making a short *dua* with the *fātiḥah*. I now knew that meant the *Iqama* was imminent, and we all began lining up. I still couldn't see who was going to be tonight's imam. I wondered if the other uncle would take up the role, but he just stayed seated. I turned towards the back to see if an imam might be striding in, but there was no-one, just the hurried steps of late congregational worshippers. The locals had turned to the scruffy young man in the puffa jacket. He stood up, removed his coat and nonchalantly made his way to the front where he picked up a small skullcap and placed it on his head.

Checking his feet, he made the *Takbir*.

The young man's recitation was eloquent and steady; it had the air of someone who did this frequently. After reciting the *fātiḥah*, he picked a long *surah* that told me he knew the Qur'an well and was probably a *hafez*.

When the congregational prayer ended, the uncles led a small *dhikr* and the room was filled with the sing-songy praise of God and his Messenger. I joined in for a while and then simply sat and listened. When it finished, I pulled out my now-battered little notebook, one last time.

'Muslim Europe is alive and well,' I wrote, before adding: 'Just.'

Glossary

Adhan	*Muslim call to prayer*
Allah	*Arabic word meaning God*
Asr	*Third of the five daily Muslim prayers; performed at mid-afternoon*
Bayram	*Turkish word for the Eid festivals*
Beg/Bey	*Military title or governor of a sanjak*
Bismillah	*To mean 'In the name of God', often said by Muslims before performing an act in which they seek God's help*
Dervish	*Student or follower of a Sufi order*
Dhikr	*Remembrance of God, performed in various ways by different Muslims*
Dhuhr	*Second of the five daily Muslim prayers; performed in the middle of the day*
Dua	*Invocation; a prayer of supplication or request*
Eid-al-Adha	*Festival to mark the end of the pilgrimage in Makkah (Hajj)*
Eid-al-Fitr	*Festival to mark the end of the month of fasting (Ramadan)*
Eyalet	*Early Ottoman term for a large province*
Fajr	*First of the five daily Muslim prayers; performed at the break of dawn*
Fātiḥah	*The first chapter in the Qur'an, read at the start of each rakat of prayer*
Gazi	*Ottoman term for a soldier of Islam*
Hadith	*Saying or doing of the Prophet recorded in scripture*

Hafez	*Someone who has memorised the entire Qur'an*
Hammam	*Public bathing facilities*
Han	*A caravanserai or traveller's lodge*
Hoca	*Title of a religious teacher*
Imam	*Person that leads the prayer (in Shia Islam this is also the title for the spiritual leader of the entire community)*
Imaret	*Charitable hospice, normally attached to a mosque; offers food and lodging to travellers and the poor*
Iqama	*Call to announce the start of the congregational prayer after the adhan has already been made*
Isha	*Fifth of the five daily Muslim prayers; performed late in the evening*
Jama'at	*Prayer performed in congregation*
Jihad	*A struggle in the way of God*
Jumu'a	*Weekly midday Friday prayer performed only in congregation*
Kadi	*Legal judge of Islamic theology and sometimes governor of a district*
Kafir	*Non-Muslim or non-believer*
Komšiluk	*Bosnian tradition of 'good neighbourliness', associated with coexistence*
La Convivencia	*Spanish term to describe coexistence during Muslim rule in Spain*
Madrasa	*Educational institute; elementary, secondary or higher education*
Maghrib	*Fourth of the five daily Muslim prayers; performed at sunset*

Mahvil	Wooden balcony in most Ottoman mosques at the back of the central hall, usually reserved for female worshippers
Maktab	Elementary school like a modern primary school but where boys are instructed in Qur'anic recitation
Masjid	A mosque
Mihrab	The niche at the front of a mosque where the imam stands to lead prayer
Mimbar	Pulpit inside a mosque used by the imam to give sermons
Mufti	Someone who can issue fatwas or legal judgements in Islam and is a member of the Islamic clergy
Muqarnas	Style of pattern common in classical Ottoman architecture; ornamental stalactite-shaped features that form small point niches
Murīd	Literally means 'seeker' but usually refers to a novice in a Sufi order
Musafir	Arabic word for traveller
Musafirhan	Traveller's lodge
Nargileh	Traditional smoking pipe
Pasha	Title given to high Ottoman officers
Pashalik	Like Eyalet, a large province
Rakats	Segments of Muslim formal prayer; usually in twos, threes or fours.
Salaam	Literally 'peace' but usually the Muslim greeting. In full: 'Assala mualaikum' (peace be with you)
Salah	Formal prayer performed by Muslims
Sanjak	Administrative division within an Ottoman province

Seerah	*The Prophet's biography*
Shia	*One of the two main branches of Islam*
Sufi	*Term used to describe a follower of a mystical branch of Islam: Sufism*
Sunni	*Larger of the two main branches of Islam*
Surah	*Chapter in the Qur'an*
Takbir	*The phrase 'Allahu Akbar' (God is great); made at the start of prayer*
Tambour	*Architectural feature on Ottoman mosques holding up the dome*
Taqwa	*God consciousness*
Tasbih	*Collection of thirty-three or ninety-nine (coloured) beads on a thread to aid with dhikr*
Tekke	*Place where a Sufi order gathers for worship*
Thobe	*Long garment traditionally worn in Arab-speaking countries, especially in the Gulf*
Tughra	*Signature of an Ottoman Sultan, usually in artistic calligraphy*
Türbe	*Turkish word for tomb*
Ulema	*Muslim scholars*
Ummah	*Term used to describe the global Muslim community*
Waqf	*Donation of an asset as endowment for religious or charitable purposes*
Wudu	*Ritual ablutions performed by Muslims before praying*

Acknowledgements

In writing this book, no-one has been more important than the three people that came on the journey with me. First, to my wonderful wife, Tamara: thank you for your unconditional love, support, patience and encouragement; for believing in me, even when I didn't; and for being the most amazing, fun and interesting life and travel companion. And to my two daughters Amani and Anaiya: you have both grown up to be brave and fascinating young women who continue to educate and inspire me; you make me laugh and are a pleasure and delight to be with, which is why raising you is amongst my greatest joys and achievements. I thank all three of you for allowing me to tell my version of our fascinating adventure and hope we continue to have many more together. I must also thank the bright little star that entered our lives, just when we needed her most, during the darkness of the global pandemic that raged as I wrote the final chapters. To my third daughter, Maya: one day when you read this, I want you to know that this story is yours too.

I owe thanks to so many people – indeed there are too many to name individually – but I need to single out a few who have supported, encouraged or humoured me throughout this literary journey: my cousin Nurul Uddin and my good friends Tahsin Pak, Nizam Malji, Matthew Teller and Simon 'Ismail' Dale, for listening to sketchy early drafts, never letting me lose belief and offering the kind of honest feedback a writer needs to hear. I am grateful too for the amazing love and support of the community I grew up with, in London's East

End, who answered every one of my calls for assistance and continue to have my back.

My dear friend Mevludin Sahinovic deserves a special mention for his constant and honest support, his feedback and his expertise on all things Bosnian and Balkan Islam. And Elmedin Musić in Sarajevo and Egon Loli in Vlorë for providing the kind of local knowledge that's just not in books.

I also thank Professors Abigail Green and Llewelyn Morgan at the University of Oxford for their invaluable support and advice.

Huge thanks must go to my agent and mentor, Jennifer Barclay, who was able to pick up a disillusioned writer devoid of confidence and breathe new life into him and his manuscript. And to the entire team at Bradt Guides for being so sensitive to and accommodating of my needs, requests and various, no doubt irritating, tendencies. Thanks also to my amazing editor, Ross Dickinson, for really getting it and helping me shape the text into exactly the kind of narrative I wanted to write. And to Ollie Davis whose art for the cover and map perfectly captured the atmosphere and energy of our journey.

I am deeply grateful to the people of the western Balkans, from the unnamed many who let us into their lives and helped us on the road to all the martyrs who died trying to bring peace to this beautiful region. I ask for their understanding and, if necessary, forgiveness for anything I have written that is different to how they recall it.

Finally, it is to my parents that I owe the most: my mother, Rina Khanam, for giving me her spirit of adventure and my father, Mozir Uddin Ahmad, for his studious and bookish nature.

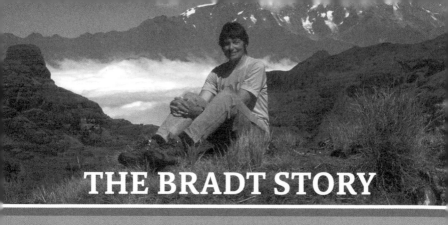

THE BRADT STORY

In the beginning

It all began in 1974 on an Amazon river barge. During an 18-month trip through South America, two adventurous young backpackers – Hilary Bradt and her then husband, George – decided to write about the hiking trails they had discovered through the Andes. *Backpacking Along Ancient Ways in Peru and Bolivia* included the very first descriptions of the Inca Trail. It was the start of a colourful journey to becoming one of the best-loved travel publishers in the world; you can read the full story on our website (www.bradtguides.com/ourstory).

Getting there first

Hilary quickly gained a reputation for being a true travel pioneer, and in the 1980s she started to focus on guides to places overlooked by other publishers. The Bradt Guides list became a roll call of guidebook 'firsts'. We published the first guide to Madagascar, followed by Mauritius, Czechoslovakia and Vietnam. The 1990s saw the beginning of our extensive coverage of Africa: Tanzania, Uganda, South Africa, and Eritrea. Later, post-conflict guides became a feature: Rwanda, Mozambique, Angola, Sierra Leone, Bosnia and Kosovo.

Comprehensive – and with a conscience

Today, we are the world's largest independently owned travel publisher, with more than 200 titles, from full-country and wildlife guides to Slow Travel guides like this one. However, our ethos remains unchanged. Hilary is still keenly involved, and we still get there first: two-thirds of Bradt guides have no direct competition.

But we don't just get there first. Our guides are also known for being more comprehensive than any other series. We avoid templates and tick-lists. Each guide is a one-of-a-kind expression of an expert author's interests, knowledge and enthusiasm for telling it how it really is.

And a commitment to wildlife, conservation and respect for local communities has always been at the heart of our books. Bradt Guides was championing sustainable travel before any other guidebook publisher.

Thank you!

We can only do what we do because of the support of readers like you – people who value less-obvious experiences, less-visited places and a more thoughtful approach to travel. Those who, like us, take travel seriously.

Bradt GUIDES

TRAVEL TAKEN SERIOUSLY